LEGACIES OF THE SILVER STATE

NEVADA GOES TO WAR

STEVEN RANSON
KENNETH BEATON
DAVID C. HENLEY

This book is published by BookBaby Publishing

7905 N. Crescent Blvd.
Pennsauken, New Jersey 08110

Paperback ISBN: 978-1-09832-951-8
ebook ISBN: 978-1-09832-952-5

Printed in the United States of America

To the men and women who grew up
in Nevada or who adopted the Silver State as home
after returning from war

You are truly our heroes

Iwo Jima Memorial, Washington, D.C.

Steven R. Ranson

LEGACIES

We may never see a generation like the one who served during World War II to ensure the world was a safer place—free from the tyranny of leaders and nations.

That point was illustrated to me not too long ago when I received a call telling me that one of our World War II vets from an Honor Flight had died. Slowly, the number of World War II veterans diminishes with each passing day, month and year. Along with co-authors Kenneth Beaton and David C. Henley—all of us seasoned newspapermen—we have interviewed numerous World War II veterans over the years and have learned about them and how they helped the war effort more 75 years ago. Additional writers have also written about our World War II heroes—including Kaleb Roedel's two stories on Native American veterans—and our bylines have been noted at the end of their articles. During the past two decades, our articles have appeared within the pages of newspapers and magazines in Carson City, Fallon, Gardnerville … in addition to other communities.

From lowering the ramps of landing ships at Normandy on June 6, 1944, to crawling on the snow on their bellies and enduring extremely harsh weather during the Battle of the Bulge, to providing medical care on a remote island in the Pacific, our men and women showed intrepidness and bravery when facing the enemy. We interviewed POWs, survivors of the Nazi concentration camps and veterans who, remember in detail, where they were and what they did. On several occasions, I flew on two Honor Flight Nevada trips to Washington, D.C., and most recently to Pearl Harbor in early 2020. It was at that point I felt it was necessary to preserve our past newspaper articles and include them into a book for both our current and future generations so they will know of the heroism of the men and women we interviewed.

Too many times, we discovered, veterans from the World War II era have been very reluctant to tell their stories, but we have also discovered many of them are now more willing to talk about their service to their country or, as with the Holocaust survivors, they never want the world to forget the atrocities committed by their Nazi captors.

I approached Ken, who has contributed his articles for many years to the Appeal, and he sent me numerous articles. David's expertise in writing about the USS Nevada and its role during the bombing of Pearl Harbor and at D-Day show the determination of Americans ready to defeat a formidable enemy.

We thank those men and women who, at one time in their lives, have called this great their home and also the sailors and Marines who served on the USS Nevada and other ships with Nevada-related names. They are all Legacies of the Silver State.

Steven R. Ranson, August 2020

OUR LEGACIES

SURRENDER

On Sept. 2, 1945, aboard the battleship USS Missouri anchored in Tokyo Bay, Japanese officials signed a written agreement formally ending World War II. Gen. Douglas MacArthur, commander in the southwest Pacific and supreme commander for the Allies, signed on behalf of the Allied powers.

Although the surrender occurred thousands of miles from Nevada, the initial training to end the war in the Pacific began in 1942 at the Wendover Air Field, 125 miles west of Salt Lake City. Begun as a remote installation on the western fringes of the Bonneville Salt Flats in 1940, the installation became a sub-post of Fort Douglas (which is located in Salt Lake City) almost one year later. The Wendover Army Air Field, though, was activated in March 1942—three months after the Japanese bombing of Pearl Harbor—for training B-17 and B-24 bomber crews for missions in both Europe and the Pacific.

In late 1944, the federal government activated the 509th Composite Group to train B-29 bomber crews to test ordnance, electronics, high-altitude and long-range flying in preparation to conducting bombing missions over Japan. Eventually, two B-29s designated to drop two bombs over Japan were sent to Tinian, an island in the Pacific, a round trip to Japan of 3,000 miles.

While the United States and its allies pressured the Japanese government to surrender in July 1945, it took the dropping of two 20,000-pound atomic bombs—Aug. 6 over Hiroshima and Aug. 9 over Nagasaki—to force Emperor Hirohito to end the war on Aug. 15.

The last anniversary before the 75th in 2015 elicited remarks on the war's end and also the training conducted at Wendover.

"It was one of the world's best secrets," Kerri Supanich of the Wendover Tourism and Convention Bureau said.

Because of its remoteness on the Utah-Nevada border, the U.S. government kept silent on the Wendover Field training missions and the project that led to the dropping of the atomic bombs. Local veterans who served during the second world war—many of them in Europe—were relieved to see the fighting in the Pacific end. Many of these vets from 2014, though, have passed on but their words will last forever.

Fallon's Cecil Quinley, a B-17 co-pilot who died in 2016, flew on 13 missions over Germany before being shot down in enemy territory in 1943. The Germans took the crewmen who safely parachuted out of the Flying Fortress and kept them as prisoners of war until the Allies liberated Germany during the spring of 1945.

Between V-E Day (Victory Europe) and the time the two atomic bombs were dropped on Japan, Quinley spent some time on leave. Quinley, though, never knew another war-time mission. He said other pilots, though, volunteered to train on other types of bombers.

"The Japanese gave up before my leave ended," said the 100-year-old Quinley, who died in 2016. "I had received a telegram to take more leave."

Because of the atomic bombs dropped on Hiroshima and Nagasaki, Quinley said the American servicemen did not know much about the effects of the raids except they felt the United States would not do anymore bombing over Tokyo. Quinley said the B-29 was a state-of-the-art bomber during the latter stages of the war. He knew of one fellow aviator who served as a flight engineer on one of the planes.

Like Quinley, 92-year-old Ray Gawronski of Carson City served aboard a bomber as a flight engineer and completed 25 missions over Germany. After returning to the U.S., Gawronkski was placed from the B-25 to the B-29 program, but because of the August raids against Japan, he never flew in combat again.

"I never trained at Wendover and never had the opportunity," he said.

Although the war ended in 1945, Gawronski said it's important for students to know about the action in Europe and the Pacific and of the sacrifices the military and civilian communities made for four years.

"The younger generation needs to know the history of World War II, not only for what I did but for the others who sacrificed," he said.

Valerie Bamford, 91, of Fallon said she was very happy to learn of the Japanese surrender. Bamford, who has since died, enlisted in the U.S. Army Air Force in late 1940 and stayed for almost six years, served most of the war at Fairfield-Suisun Army Air Base—now Travis Air Force Base—outside of Fairfield, Calif. She was an administrative clerk who primarily processed awards.

At the time, both Army Air Force and Navy aviators trained there.

"I enjoyed serving, but it was sad to see the planes fall from the sky," she said of the aerial dog fights in the Pacific.

As for the end of the war, she said everybody was relieved. Bamford enlisted in the military at the age of 16 after talking to her father about joining the Army.

"It was the thing to do," she said.

Infantryman John Martin "Marty" Wilson grew up in Scotland, enlisted in the British army and fought in Europe, seeing action in France, Belgium and Germany.

With the fighting over in Europe in May 1945, the 89-year-old Fallon resident said his unit was being trained to fight against Japan until Japan surrendered after the dropping of the second atomic bomb.

"I never heard much about them," Wilson said of the atomic bombs and the devastation they caused.

While Europe had parades after Germany surrendered, he doesn't remember the same amount of fanfare leading up to the formal surrender.

While historians and scholars have questioned the dropping of the two bombs, the late Marine Corps First Sgt. Chuck Harton of Reno said the two B-29 runs saved the lives of more than one million Americans and Japanese—possibly more. Harton, who was 90 years old in 2015, and his fellow Marines were training at Maui, Hawaii, in preparation of invading Japan when the bombs fell.

"I do envision a million dead Americans if we had to invade Japan," the veteran said, adding that as many Japanese may have lost their lives from conventional bombing attacks over their major cities.

For those who landed on Japan after the war to become part of the occupation force, former Marine Harold "Gus" Forbus of Fallon, who died in 2012, explained the eeriness of post-war Japan in a manuscript written by him and his son.

Forbus said after almost four years of war—during which it was kill or be killed—he didn't have to fire a shot to protect himself or anyone else on the Japanese mainland.

"With the reality of the surrender and our victory, it was a different world," he wrote. "All anxiety was gone and the troops could really relax."

Steven R. Ranson

**Names of the killed sailors and Marines are enshrined
at the USS Arizona Memorial Gardens at Salt River in Scottsdale,
Arizona. Richard Walter Weaver of Fallon, Nev.,
was one of three Nevadans who died on Dec. 7, 1941.**

Steven R. Ranson

USS ARIZONA'S
FATEFUL MORNING

The presentation from Navy historian Jim Neuman explained the importance of Dec. 7, 1941, and how a surprise Japanese attack pulled the United States into a global war.

More than 77 years ago, battleships lined up in Pearl Harbor in a way to represent the Navy's own Murderers' Row in late 1941.

Named after the states of Arizona, Oklahoma, West Virginia, California, Nevada, Tennessee, Maryland and Pennsylvania, the battleships' sterling handsome hulls protruded into the glass-faced harbor. On the other side of Ford Island was the moored USS Utah. In less than an hour on Dec. 7, an attack carried out by Japanese pilots from the Imperial Japanese Navy shattered the tranquility of a quiet Sunday morning.

With flames and smoke rising above the horizon, all eight battleships lined up in the harbor suffered damaged, but four sunk. Two torpedoes slammed into the USS Utah, causing the battleship to roll over and sink. The USS Nevada managed to sail out of the harbor under its own power despite being hit by one torpedo and at least six bombs.

Many sailors never knew what happened to them because of the swiftness of the attack. The greatest loss of life came aboard the USS Arizona, and to this day, 1,102 sailors and Marines remained entombed in a cold, steel casket.

Only three Nevadans died aboard the Arizona—Richard Eugene Gill, seaman first class Richard Walter Weaver and Eric Young—and their bodies were never recovered.

Gill attended schools in Wells and Reno and eventually earned his high school diploma from Montello High School. According to the USS Arizona Mall Memorial, Gill's father worked for the railroad and his mother was a homemaker. When Gill enlisted in the Navy in 1940, his family lived in the small Eureka County ranching community of Beowawe where he worked as a grocery clerk.

Neuman specifically revealed the names of the two Nevadans, but he only elaborated about one of the sailors who joined the Navy while a senior in high school.

The 18-year-old Weaver, who was born in in Fallon, joined the Navy on Nov. 27, 1940, and performed the duties of standing watch and serving as a gunner while on the ship. His parents were Ray Rhese and "Marge" Lois (McCuistion) Weaver. Ray Weaver, a veteran of World War I, gave him permission to enlist. Only years later, though, did Weaver's father learn his son had been kicked out of school for arguing with his teacher.

According to information both the Reno Gazette and Nevada State Journal, the young sailor" had been sweet" on Wanda Temple, who also lived in Fallon. After he left Fallon, they traded letters. Wanda's family moved to Honolulu in October 1941 because of her father's employment. The Temple family invited Weaver and his Navy friends to dinner every Sunday evening.

According to newspaper accounts 54 years after Pearl Harbor, Temple called Weaver "a handsome boy-doll in a sailor suit" and "I've never adored anyone as much."

Temple married after World War II ended, and the article said she named here only child Richard. According to Weaver's record, he earned the following awards posthumously: Purple Heart, American Defense Service Medal with Fleet Clasp, Asiatic-Pacific Campaign Medal with star and the WWII Victory Medal.

Three words summed up Young: "Big, jolly and likeable." After Young's death aboard the USS Arizona, the Reno Gazette, described him as a popular young man who graduated from Reno High School in 1934 and then attended the University of Nevada for two years. Anther Reno newspaper, the Nevada State Journal, called him popular and active who pledged the Sigma Nu Fraternity west of the campus and also played on the freshman football team. Young was born in in San Diego, Calif., on Sept. 6, 1916.

Attending the University of Nevada kept him close to his father, James, a psychology professor. His mother, though, died in 1931. Young left Nevada after receiving an appointment to the U.S. Naval Academy and graduated in 1940.

The 1940 yearbook descried Young as a young man of the West: "An unfailing sense of humor coupled with an above-the-average mentality have enabled Eric to remain himself in spite of a rigorous academic training. At heart he is still a lad of the 'Wild West.' He can be recognized from afar (you'll hear him before you see him) by his characteristic laugh, which more than once has sent whole theaters into hysterics. Never too busy to refuse help to anyone, Sandy has pulled many a plebe through the intricacies of steam and math. Though he has had a hand in lacrosse and football, crew is his sport. Who knows, you might have to row a battleship home some day, eh Eric?"

Young was commissioned an ensign at graduation.

According to the Reno newspapers, Young had two cousins who were also at Pearl Harbor. Lt. Eric Allen, also a Naval Academy graduate, was killed by friendly fire as he attempted to land his plane at Ford Field. Ensign Richard Allen survived, but he was killed the next summer when his destroyer, the Jarvis, was sunk at Savo Island. The entire crew of 233 died.

Steven R. Ranson

USS NEVADA MEMORIALIZED

Every December, Americans commemorate the anniversary of the Japanese attack on Pearl Harbor and other Hawaiian military installations that killed 2,388 service members and civilians and plunged the nation into World War II.

Hundreds of thousands of visitors travel here each year to view memorials dedicated to that devastating raid at 7:55 a.m. Sunday, Dec. 7, 1941. Among these monuments are two that honor the warship and crew of the famed battleship USS Nevada that was heavily damaged and nearly sank on that terrible day.

One of these monuments, a large, whitewashed concrete slab emblazoned with the words "USS Nevada," is located in the waters of Battleship Row near Ford Island in Pearl Harbor, where the Nevada was tied up at Quay F-8 immediately east of battleships Arizona, Tennessee, West Virginia, Maryland and Oklahoma before the attack. Close by the Nevada marker is the dramatic USS Arizona Memorial which sits over the underwater wreckage of the Arizona that contains the remains of its 1,177 crew members who lost their lives the morning of Dec. 7.

The second memorial, consisting of another prominent USS Nevada sign-board and a bronze tablet honoring the 50 Nevada crewmen killed and 105 injured during the attack, is located at Hospital Point on the southern end of Ford Island where the 583-foot, 29,000-ton Nevada was purposely run aground after receiving direct hits from Japanese torpedo bombers.

Following the surprise Japanese raid, the Nevada had gotten up steam, left its mooring and was attempting to reach the ocean. But the Japanese bombs proved so deadly that the ship's officers, fearing the blazing and listing Nevada might capsize or sink in the channel, thus closing the waterway to shipping, decided to beach her on the hard sea bottom.

Two hours after the beaching, however, the Nevada floated free as the tide began to rise. By now, the Japanese planes had returned to their six carriers offshore and harbor tugs were able to move the shattered Nevada and beach her a second time on the sandy bottom of Waipio Point adjacent to a cane field.

Fires continued to burn aboard the Nevada until 11 p.m., and during this period the injured and dead were transported ashore by launches from nearby ships and shore stations. Two Nevada crewmen were subsequently awarded the Medal of Honor and 15 received the Navy Cross for heroism during the attacks.

Following temporary repairs in Pearl Harbor, the Nevada, which was commissioned in 1916, was towed to the Puget Sound Navy Shipyard in Washington State to undergo a $23 million refitting and modernization that lasted seven and a half months.

By late 1942, the ship was back in action, joining the fleet and U.S. Army in clearing out 7,600 Japanese troops that had landed in the Aleutians. Then came convoy duty in the Atlantic and participation in the Normandy landings and allied invasion of German-held Europe.

Returning to the Pacific in 1945, the Nevada supported the landings at Iwo Jima and Okinawa and was hit several times by Japanese "kamikaze" or suicide planes that crashed on her decks, killing 14 and injuring 48 crew members.

After occupation duty in Tokyo Bay following Japan's surrender on Aug. 14, 1945, the Nevada, by now nearly 30 years old, was decommissioned and towed to Bikini Atoll in mid-1946 to serve as a target ship for the testing of nuclear bombs.

Miraculously, the Nevada stayed afloat. Two years later, though, she was towed to an area approximately 65 miles southwest of Hawaii to meet her fate. Still radioactive from the Bikini tests and too elderly for any use, the 32-year-old dreadnought rolled over and sank following two days of intense naval gunfire.

Today, after its launching at the Charleston Navy Yard in Boston and the Pearl Harbor attacks, the Nevada is memorialized not only in Hawaii but also in the state of Nevada. The Nevada State Museum in Carson City displays the ship's original sterling silver service, uniforms of its early day crews, portions of its wooden deck, a large made-in-Nevada chest that contained Carson City-minted silver dollars presented to its crew during World War II, a model of the ship and an extensive photo collection.

The ship's bell and wheel that had been part of the Carson City museum display are now in Las Vegas, awaiting installation in the new Southern Nevada Historical.

The Carson City museum also sells brass and silver USS Nevada medallions for $15 and $60, respectively, and a book detailing the history of the ship.

David C. Henley

RETURN VISIT TO PEARL

Two veterans traveling to Oahu can remember the last times they visited Pearl Harbor, one of the Navy's premier bases that came under attack from Japanese pilots more than 77 years ago.

Dayton resident Edward Tremper and his adopted daughter, Lori Schierholt, reflected on the visit to the USS Arizona, one of the battleships destroyed during the surprise attack on Dec. 7, 1941.

The 93-year-old Tremper, who also served during the Korean War at Chosin Reservoir, sailed into Pearl Harbor twice during his military career and both aboard troop ships. His first visit came in December 1944 with 5,000 Marines, and the second on November 1950 with 2,500 Marines headed to the Korean peninsula.

Tremper said the trip to Hawaii has been emotional but none more emotional than the visit to Pearl Harbor.

"Some of the battleships were still there, but the airfield was cleared," Tremper recalled of his first visit.

As Tremper and his fellow Marines stood silently as the troop ship sailed through Battleship Row, they still saw oil oozing to the surface from the Arizona.

"Amazing," Tremper said of the 1,177 sailors who perished on that day. "Those kids never had a chance. It is emotional."

About 900 sailors remained entombed in the mighty battleship.

"I can't imagine how they felt," Schierholt said of the men who were trapped and knew time ticked against them. "It was emotional thinking about all those young men."

Tremper, who grew up in New Jersey, enlisted on July 24, 1944, belonged to the 1st Marine Division. The fight for Okinawa began April 1, 1945 and after the war, many Marines from Tremper's division went to China to disarm Japanese soldiers still on the mainland.

"They didn't know the war was over," he said.

After visiting the memorial, Tremper said it was a devasting time for the United States to be put into that position by that surprise attack.

Navy veteran Bruce Robison of Reno served on the USS St. Louis, a Brooklyn-class light destroyer. Within days of the Pearl Harbor attack, the St. Louis began transporting civilians from Pearl Harbor to the mainland.

"You could throw a rock out there and it wouldn't sink. The oil was this thick," Robison said, using his thumb and forefinger to about 2 inches. "I still remember them resurrecting a lot of corpses out of the harbor."

Robison said the St. Louis was also one of the first ships able to leave Pearl Harbor without suffering damage. Sailing from Pearl Harbor, he said the St. Louis encountered two miniature Japanese submarines, but the sailors fired the ship's big 6-inch guns at one of the subs.

"The ship was known as 'Lucky Lou' because it was the first one out," Robison said, who also served on the USS Grapple.

"It's a definite time for the United States to be put in that position by the surprise attack," said his son Lee Robison. "It was a horrible way to die … there was confusion and fear."

Bruce Robison said he was thankful he wasn't at Pearl Harbor on the fateful day.

"I was fortunate enough to be in school when the war started, so I missed the horrible tragedy by being there. Now, I think I was pretty fortunate," he said.

Robison also recalled a day when Japanese aircraft strafed a harbor in the South Pacific.

"We were working on an LST (landing ship-tank) off the beach," he said. "Enemy planes came over trying to clear the harbor. They came pretty close to us, and I was shooting."

During the short fight, shrapnel struck Robison, but the sailor didn't notice he was hit until a shipmate told him he was bleeding and blood dotted the deck.

"I continued to stay and be strapped in until the planes were gone," he explained.

Once the planes departed the harbor, Robison, who was later awarded a Purple Heart medal, went to sick bay for treatment.

John Waranietz of Sparks said the skyline of Honolulu differed greatly from 1940. Only one major hotel dotted the beaches.

"The hotel was the Royal Hawaiian, the biggest hotel near the beach," he said.

During the early 1940s, Waranietz said the hotel stood out because of the siding's pink hue.

As a World War II veteran, Waranietz returned to Oahu in February 2020 and visited several key sites such as the USS Missouri, the battleship where the Instrument of Surrender was signed, and the USS Arizona Memorial, sunk during the Japanese attack on Dec. 7, 1941.

"They died for our country," Waranietz said, looking at the names of the sailors and Marines killed on that Sunday morning. "It still hurts."

During the war, Waranietz served on a minesweeper near the Marianas, and the ship eventually headed toward the Sea of Japan near the end of the war where it cleared the harbors of hundreds of mines. He ensured the minesweeper carried adequate water and fuel. During the various operations, Waranietz said the minesweeper didn't encounter too many threats, but on one occasion, a sailor fell overboard, but the search team couldn't find the body.

Born in New York state, Waranietz met his future wife in California and remained there, eventually moving to Nevada to be closer with his son and family. Waranietz worked for the U.S. Postal Service.

Steven R. Ranson

WE INTERRUPT
THIS PROGRAM

At 2:31 p.m. Eastern time on CBS radio, newscaster John Daly interrupted programming to announce a catastrophic attack near Oahu … "We interrupt this program to bring you this special announcement. "The Japanese have attacked Pearl Harbor, Hawaii, by air, President Roosevelt has just announced. The attack also was made on all naval and military activities on the principal island of Oahu."

When news broke that planes from a Japanese carrier group had bombed part of the Hawaiian island of Oahu and the U.S. Navy's fleet at Pearl Harbor, Fallon's Nellie Nelson, who formerly lived in Sacramento in the early 1940s with her two toddlers, leaned closer to her radio to listen to the ominous news of the attack.

"I was stunned, you bet," said Nelson, who had her 100th birthday party in 2016.

Then, a 25-year-old mother living in Sacramento, Nelson felt very frightened, especially after learning armor-piercing bombs destroyed many U.S. Navy warships. Then volunteers walked house to house, telling occupants to darken the houses by turning off outside lights and pulling drapes where no light shined through any cracks. Nelson said at the time, concern grew that if the Japanese attacked Pearl Harbor, then a fleet of ships and planes could sail east and bomb along the coastline from Washington State to California and into the inland communities.

"There was a major concert of an attack on the West Coast," she said.

During the next four years, Nelson stayed at her Sacramento house with her two young daughters. Her husband joined the Merchant Marines as an engineer and sailed the Pacific Ocean to deliver goods to the islands and to the military.

She religiously tuned to the radio every day to listen for news from the Pacific and Europe, while she read more details of the fighting from her hometown Sacramento Bee newspaper.

"I remember the entertainment shows, but I remember (newscasters) Lowell, Thomas, Walter Cronkite and Edward R. Murrow," she said. "I always tried to have the radio on."

Nelson remembers the nation coming together and pitch into help wherever possible. The government began selling war bonds to raise money for the fighting in the Pacific and Europe.

"Ronald Coleman was in town to sell war bonds, and I bought one," Nelson said, adding Coleman was a very handsome man. "I bought a bond for $25, which was a lot of money."

Nelson swooned over Coleman, a popular English actor in the 1930s and 40s. Coleman knew the horrors of war. He joined the British Army's London Scottish Regiment in 1909 but was wounded during World War I in 1915. In 1942 Colman and other Hollywood actors and actresses traveled the country to encourage residents to buy war bonds.

Nelson said everyone received ration books for food. According to various sources, "each person was allowed a certain amount of points weekly with expiration dates. 'Blue Stamp' rationing covered canned, bottled, frozen fruits and vegetables, plus juices and dry beans, and such processed foods as soups, baby food and ketchup.

"Ration stamps became a kind of currency with each family being issued a 'War Ration Book.' Each stamp authorized a purchase of rationed goods in the quantity and time designated, and the book guaranteed each family its fair share of goods made scarce, thanks to the war."

One of the first items rationed were silk stockings because Japan produced the majority of silk. Used pairs of silk stocking helped the war cause by making war-related items such as parachutes.

"We never went without anything," Nelson said.

Even after 75 years, Nelson became teary when thinking of her friends who died during the war. Even those who served—including her husband—were reluctant to speak of their exploits years after war ended in Europe in May 1945 and on Sept. 2, 1945, when the treaty was signed between the Japanese and United States aboard the USS Missouri in Tokyo Harbor.

Near the end of the war, Merchant Marine ships hauled two atomic bombs to Tinian Island, one of three islands in the Northern Marianas that served as the launching point for the atomic bomb attacks against Hiroshima and Nagasaki, Japan. The aviation training to work with B-29 bomber crews to drop the atomic bomb was part of the 509th Composite Group, which trained at the Wendover Army Air Base on the Nevada-Utah border west of Salt Lake City.

Nelson said her late husband sailed on one of the Merchant Marine ships that delivered the new type of bomb used over Japan.

"He joined the Merchant Marine and was gone for most of the war, and I raised the little ones myself," she said. "He never talked about (the mission) before the explosions."

Nelson, who died in 2018, said she was relieved the wars ended in 1945. Like in the late 1930s and early 1940s, she learned of the war's end from radio newscasts and her Sacramento Bee.

Steven R. Ranson

SAILING PAST BATTLESHIP ROW

A converted, pale white troop ship that once sailed the seas with civilian passengers slowly passed Pearl Harbor's Battleship Row, a grouping of eight Navy warships that endured armor-piercing bombs from an attack of Japanese torpedo bombers more than two months prior.

As the Marines crowded on the deck and pressed against the railing, they saw the USS California followed by the Maryland and Oklahoma loosely wedged side-by-side and then the Tennessee and West Virginia. Astern to the Tennessee lay the Arizona and then last in line the empty quay for the USS Nevada, which steamed out of the harbor during the attack before suffering major damage that caused the captain to beach the battleship. The USS Pennsylvania, the fleet's flagship, remained in dry-dock at the nearby Navy Yard.

Oil oozed from the twisted wreckage of the damaged battleships into the dirty water, while the stench—however faint—of oil and ship fuel still permeated the air, Ship apparatus remained strewn on the decks or bobbing in the water alongside the ships or hull.

Roland Christiansen, 19 years old at the time, and the other Marines stared at the Arizona, which sunk as a water-sealed tomb with more than 1,100 sailors aboard. A portion of the ship remained above the water line, but most of the former great warship had sunk 45 feet below surface.

"They hadn't done anything to the ship ... not enough time," Christiansen said when he saw the Arizona and the other battleships. "There hadn't been enough time."

According to numerous historical accounts involving the USS Nevada, "the Nevada was moored singly off Ford Island, and had a freedom of maneuver denied the other battleships present during the attack. As her gunners opened fire and her engineers got up steam, she was struck by one torpedo and two, possibly three, bombs from the Japanese attackers, but was able to get underway. While attempting to leave harbor she was struck again. Fearing she might sink in the channel, blocking it, Nevada was beached at Hospital Point."

For Fallon's 94-year-old Roland Christiansen, the sight of heavily damaged battleships—some beyond repair—became etched in his mind not only for the time he was stationed on Oahu but also for the rest of his life. Even in later life, he could distinctly remember seeing a helpless battleship.

Christiansen grew up in Montana and had already enlisted in the Marines in 1941, but he had to wait anxiously for his boot-camp assignment.

"When I enlisted in the Marine Corps during the summer, there were so many recruits and not enough training slots," Christiansen recollected.

The only Marine basic training facility on the West Coast was in San Diego. Orders to attend boot camp came in December for Christiansen and other recruits. Christiansen, who grew up in Montana, took the train from Butte, Mont., to Los Angeles via Salt Lake City and Las Vegas during the week between Christmas and New Year's. Christiansen first hopped on a train in western Montana along with 11 others then traveled to Salt Lake City in one day as more recruits boarded the train, and from there, they rode through eastern Nevada to Las Vegas and finally to Los Angeles, where security police met the recruits and transported them 120 miles south to San Diego.

"The SPs lined us up right there," said Christiansen of their arrival at the train depot before heading to boot camp. "We went down there and immediately went into a platoon and all of the people who came from Butte stayed in the same platoon. We went into boot camp on Jan. 1, 1942."

Because many of the Marines and soldiers who boarded the train between Salt Lake City and Las Vegas were under age, and because the war had started, he said civilian passengers offered to buy the recruit drinks in their honor. Christiansen noted the recruits and civilians "had quite a lot of partying going on."

To say the attack on Pearl Harbor surprised Christiansen was overstated. He and friends knew something was wrong in the months leading up to the Dec. 7 attack. The nation appeared to be on a collision course with Japan, which had already been waging war in certain parts of Asia.

"Everyone knew something was going to happen. I really do," he said. "The Japanese had moved many of its envoys to Japan. Every individual ... except a few powers to be ... didn't believe an armada (of six Japanese aircraft carriers, battleships, heavy and light cruisers and destroyers) was sailing toward Oahu."

The Marines left San Diego and arrived in Honolulu in several days. Christiansen and the others aboard the troop ship saw the destruction that originated from the Japanese Imperial Navy when they first saw the wreckage. An eerie feeling overcame the Marines, a silence sweeping over Pearl Harbor except for small waves splashing on the quays. Because Pearl Harbor had few facilities for the hundreds of Marines and sailors arriving to the Oahu, Christiansen's detachment left Honolulu and trucked to Lualualei after staying aboard the troop ship for a few days before splitting up.

Assigning the troops to duties, however, took little time as Christiansen remembers:

"I was sent out to guard duty. They lined us up alphabetically, and the sergeants went down ABC and that's where you were stationed."

Whatever letter of the alphabet was assigned to a Marine determined his assignment. Christian drew his ammo, combat rifle, gas mask and rucksack and waited for orders to move out. Because other Marine units were smaller than the Army's, Christiansen said it was easier for them to head to the other side of Oahu less than an hour away from Pearl Harbor to establish a defensive position. The Japanese never returned to Oahu with the size of force that bombed the island just months before.

Yet, Christiansen said it became apparent the Marines would ship out to a hot zone, and during the spring of 1942, thousands of servicemen found themselves traveling to a small atoll west of Hawaii called Midway, the first stepping stone military planners knew the United States had to win, and the second being at Wake Island.

"The ship I was on, unbeknown to us, was headed for Midway Island. It was not a pleasant ride because the little ship that we went on from Pearl Harbor to Midway had been a tour ship on the Hudson River in New York State, and we hit a storm," Christiansen remembered of the 1,300-mile trip. "We got to stand bridge watches if we wanted, and if we didn't, we got to eat with the crew, which was much better food than the passengers got ... it was a pretty bad storm, but we made it. "

Christiansen said the Marines were in Midway about a week before the Battle of Midway commenced.

The Battle of Midway became the turning point of the young war between the United States and its allies and the Japanese military complex. Between June 4-7, the U.S. Navy sunk four aircraft carries and a cruiser that had been involved with the Pearl Harbor attack. Along with the Guadalcanal campaign and the Battle of Midway, the Japanese navy retreated and never became the threat it was at Pearl Harbor and Midway.

Before Christiansen saw the battle unfold, he was originally assigned to an anti-aircraft unit that had 3-inch guns. Upon their arrival at Midway, he said all the guns were 90 millimeter.

"The Battle of Midway was a turning point said the historians," Christiansen recalled. "The Navy and Marines destroyed most of the Japanese Navy ships … destroyed enough that Japan had to reconstruct their outfit."

During his four years in the Marines, his unit jumped around the various South Pacific islands. Christiansen also remembers when the command sent Marines to the Marshall Islands to provide anti-aircraft support.

"We knew it was an atoll of its own—we were sent there and made the landing on Roi-Namure Islets which were in the northern most portions of the Marshall Islands," he said. "Kwajalein, in the Ralik Chain of the Marshalls, was to the east of us. It was a pretty big island—had a landing field and everything."

Near the end of the war, the Marines offered Christiansen an opportunity to attend the University of California and to obtain a commission as an officer; however, Christiansen left the service and returned to Montana for less than two months before returning to California. He married his girlfriend Ilene on Feb. 23, 1946. Christiansen received his degree in 1948 and was hired by the Bureau of Land Management until he left the government agency in the 1950s. The Christiansens moved to Fallon in the 1970s where he ranched. His beloved Ilene passed away in 2010 after 54 years of marriage, and Roland died in July 2017.

Steven R. Ranson

DELIVERING CARGO
IN PERILOUS SEAS

A merchant mariner's life aboard a cargo ship during World War II came with price.

No other group suffered a higher rate of casualties in crossing the Atlantic and Pacific oceans in four years of war. The total number of civilian mariners who died during from 1942-1945 topped 11,000 or one of every 26 mariners going down with the ship. Fighting men on the front lines, though, depended on services and goods transported by the U.S Merchant Marine.

William Pinto of Reno and Charles Montanaro of Carson City served on Victory ships, easily sitting targets for enemy submarines, planes or mines especially during the first years of the war. More than 3.1 tons of cargo was lost along with thousands of ships sent to the ocean's floor. On many journeys across the ocean, most cargo ships sailed without escort.

"We were by ourselves," Pinto recalled. "The only ships we saw were in Pearl Harbor where when they were loading."

Pinto joined the Merchant Marine in 1944 at the age of 16. He remembers one important mission. His ship hauled ordnance to Saipan and Tinian Island both located in an archipelago in the western North Pacific Ocean and the scene of major battles during the summer of 1944. After the 4th Marine Division, with help from continuous naval bombardment, captured Tinian, the island became a major staging area for B-29s on their bombing runs to the Philippines and Japan and in August 1945 when two planes dropped atomic bombs on Hiroshima and Nagasaki.

"We took a load of bombs to Saipan and Tinian," Pinto said, figuring at the time the islands were prime locations for the Army Air Force's offensive against the Japanese.

The heavy cruiser USS Indianapolis, though, delivered the atomic bombs to Tinian not a Merchant Marine vessel.

Montanaro found irony in how he became a merchant mariner. As a young man in early World War II, he wanted to fly.

"They wouldn't let me fly because I was color blind," Montanaro said. "After the war I obtained a private pilot license."

No one was drafted into the Merchant Marines although their mission was just as important.

"We were all volunteers," he said, adding by joining the Merchant Marine, he wasn't subject to the draft.

Approximately 215,000 mariners served during the war. Mariners, though, weren't considered veterans, however, until the Department of Defense granted them that status in 1988 after four decades of pressure from military service organizations and veterans' groups. Mariners said their missions were just as dangerous and harrowing as those conducted by the U.S. Navy in both theaters of the war.

Both men were among 20 veterans who traveled Oahu in February 2020 as part of the first Honor Flight Nevada to Hawaii.

Visiting Pearl Harbor and seeing the memorials on Battleship Row, especially for the USS Arizona, also rekindled memories for the 99-year-old Montanaro, the oldest veteran on the trip. He joined the Merchant Marine shortly after the Japanese bombing of Pearl Harbor. During his time in the Pacific, Montanaro could relate to Pinto's experience. Montanaro's ship mostly carried ammunition from island to island, a feeling he called unnerving. Near the end of the war, his ship anchored near Okinawa, the designated staging area for invading mainland Japan.

The call, though, to sail closer to the Japanese coast during the summer of 1945 never came for Montanaro or Pinto and thousands of other merchant mariners.

"We tried to sail again," Pinto said, "but they weren't sending my ship."

Within weeks, though, the United States and its allies signed the formal surrender treaty with Japan aboard the battleship USS Missouri.

After the war, Pinto joined the California Army National Guard, but he said the government drafted him into the Army because of the fighting on the Korean peninsula. He attended officer candidate school at Fort Benning, Ga., and assigned to a training division at Fort Ord, Calif., after graduation.

"I insisted I go with my unit. They went without me to Korea, and my orders sent me to Germany for two years," Pinto said, not understanding the logic.

Pinto said the visit to the USS Arizona memorial affected him because of his time on the ocean with the Merchant Marines.

"It brought back mixed memories, not knowing what happened to them," he said of the sailors who were entombed in the torpedoed battleship. "They have eternal life. I get overwhelmed easily."

Eight years ago, the cemetery added two pavilions, one containing an orientation map of the memorial and the other showing two mosaic battle maps from the Vietnam War. Montanaro said he was impressed.

"History is in the walls at this cemetery," he said.

Steven R. Ranson

NEVADA'S ONLY MEDAL OF HONOR RECIPIENT

Before the outbreak of World War II, the small, agricultural town of Fallon in west-central Nevada began to grow as a result of more water flowing through the valley. During the second world war, though, the U.S. government built a small airfield in the middle of the desert southeast of Fallon as part of a defensive network to repel any Japanese attack along the West Coast.

Navy pilot and Nevada's only Medal of Honor recipient, Bruce Van Voorhis moved to the Lahontan Valley in January 1909 from Tohalah, Wash., along with his mother, Lillie, and grandmother when his father accepted a position as an Indian service representative on the Quinault Reservation in Stillwater, a half-hour drive northeast of Fallon. A younger brother, Wayne, was born in Nevada in December of that same year. The green fields of Fallon and the surrounding area gave a pastoral look to this small county that had a population slightly more than 3,000 residents.

Eventually, the Van Voorhis brothers attended the newly constructed Oats Park Grade School, now a thriving arts center, on the eastern edge of Fallon's largest park. In 1917, though, Walter left his job on the reservation and transferred to the Fort Washakie Reservation in Wyoming. After nine months, he resigned and returned to Fallon, accepting a job at I.H. Kent Company's lumber yard just north of the two-story white courthouse. Two years later, tragedy struck when Walter died of pneumonia in January 1919.

From there, Bruce, known to his friends as Clint, finished his education at Churchill County High School, graduating in 1924, three years ahead of Wayne.

Traveling to and out of Fallon on a poorly maintained two-lane road proved to be difficult for residents heading to Carson City, the state capital, or to Reno, the state's largest city on the banks of the Truckee River. One of the most exciting events that occurred during the boys' childhood boys took place in 1919 when a cross-country military convoy stopped in Fallon for four days. The convoy, whose quartermaster was a young lieutenant by the name of Dwight D. Eisenhower, used the stop for rest before heading west and over the Sierra Nevada mountain range to San Francisco, its final destination. Although no records appear to exist, the boys may have enjoyed the sight of a long U.S. Army motorized convoy with many WWI veterans soldiers staying in Fallon.

After high school, Bruce Van Voorhis received an appointment to the U.S. Naval Academy and graduated in 1929, the same year Lillie, who had remarried in 1921, took her oath as a Nevada assemblywoman where she became chair of the Irrigation Committee.

Wayne, on the other hand, attended the University of Nevada in Reno and became manager of Kent's lumber yard before leaving for service as a second lieutenant in the Army Air Corps in August 1941. He was immediately shipped off to the Philippines.

President Donald Trump delivered the commencement address at the U.S. Naval Academy in May 2018 and noted the accomplishments of Bruce Van Voorhis, who received his wings two years later at Pensacola after serving aboard the battleship USS Mississippi.

"Beneath his picture in the 1929 Lucky Bag (the yearbook), Bruce's classmates wrote that he spent most of his time teaching the city slickers from the east the correct pronunciation of Nevada," Trump said. "And I had to learn that, too, to win the state. Great place."

President Trump said Van Voorhis, also known as "Van," "Chicken" and "Brute," looked at studying as an unnecessary evil and added the decorated Navy war hero was like today's Navy graduates in many ways.

According to the yearbook comments, "Chicken does not fall in love, but in three cruises and four years in a blue serge and brass buttons has left a trail of broken hearts extending the full lengths of both coasts and radiating for miles around Crabtown.

"Vans know what he wants and usually gets it. This should bring him success in the navy or in another line he might enter."

During his four years at the academy, Van Voorhis competed in baseball, wrestling and gymkhana and played in the orchestra.

The war years, though, were tough on Lillie. She learned in 1942 that the Japanese army had captured Wayne and other servicemen on the Philippine island of Bataan and forced them on the infamous Death March where the enemy killed more than 10,000 men of the 70,000 soldiers who had surrendered. Her youngest son survived the march, but died of malaria in a prisoner of war camp on Luzon. The last letter she received from Wayne arrived in August 1942.

The local newspaper, the Fallon Standard, didn't report his death until June 14, 1944, and the Fallon Eagle printed his obituary on Oct. 20, 1945.

"Full consideration has recently be given to all available information bearing on the absence of your son (Wayne), including all records, reports and circumstances," the Adjutant Office in Washington, D.C. informed her. "The finding does not establish an actual or probable date of death; however, it includes a presumptive date of death. In the case of your son, this date has been set as 8 May 1944."

The Eagle, though reported his actual death as July 6, 1942, but he was officially confirmed dead in May 1944: "Accurate record of his passing was revealed to the war department in hidden accounts of happenings in the prison camp, kept by American prisoners, and never found by their Jap captors. Those records were located by prisoners at the time of their liberation and turned over to Army authorities."

Lillie faced tragedy again when she learned of Bruce's death in the South Pacific in 1943. Prior to the beginning of World War II, Bruce Van Voorhis' biography in the Nevada Aerospace Hall of Fame stated, "After receiving his wings in 1931, Van Voorhis was assigned to the USS Maryland, USS Ranger and USS Saratoga. After a two-year stint at the Panama Canal Zone (flying patrols with Squadron 2F from Coco Solo) from October 1935-September 1937), he served on the aircraft carriers USS Enterprise and the USS Yorktown, where he came board on temporary duty. In 1940, he served on the light cruiser Honolulu."

The events of Dec. 7, 1941, though, plunged the nation into bloody war first with Japan and then Germany and Italy.

"Just over a decade after his graduation, Lt. Cmdr. Van Voorhis found himself at war," President Trump said. "Seventy-five years ago this summer, he was in the South Pacific commanding Bombing Squadron 102 during the battle of the Solomon Islands. That was a rough battle. His only brother had been killed and the Bataan Death March. On July 6, Bruce volunteered for a mission to destroy a crucial enemy base."

Van Voorhis, who was piloting PB4Y-1 Liberator 31992 on a volunteer reconnaissance mission, and his crew died at the southernmost of the Eastern Caroline Islands near Hare Island of the Kapingamarangi Atoll. President Trump said Van Voorhis knew he was going to die, yet he also realized his actions in the South Pacific during the summer of 1943 could prevent a surprise attack on American forces.

"So, his plane took off alone on a 700-mile flight. Bruce flew through the darkness to his target, a tiny speck on the vast open sea," President Trump said. "He braved unrelenting anti-aircraft fire, like nobody had ever seen at that time, and a trail of enemy planes to single-handedly destroy this large enemy base, including multiple fortifications, and a critical communications link. And in this final act of valor, Bruce was caught in the blast of one of his own bombs and perished in a remote lagoon very far from here. His life was lost, but his legacy will live forever."

President Trump said Van Voorhis' old room at Bancroft Hall commemorates his Congressional Medal of Honor that was awarded to him posthumously. The president also said future Navy aviators will follow Voorhis' footsteps to flight training at Pensacola, and eventually refine their skills at Fallon's Naval Aviation Warfighting Development Center or better known to the general public as Top Gun.

"You may even make it all the way out to the legendary combat-training school known as Top Gun in Bruce's beloved hometown in Nevada," President Trump said. "There, you will have the honor to take flight from the Voorhis Field and remember a hero who fought for his country and died for his homeland and saved so many lives with his bravery."

Locally, Churchill County Museum arranged a reflective exhibit on Van Voorhis and his contributions to Navy aviation. Naval Air Station Fallon's airfield was dedicated in his name on Nov. 1, 1959. At that time the 14,000-foot runway was one of the longest in the world but still remains the longest in the Navy.

Van Voorhis' headstone rests at Arlington National Cemetery, but he is buried with several crew members in the Jefferson Barracks National Cemetery in St. Louis County, Missouri. The Fallon graduate was also posthumously promoted to commander. His copilot received the Navy Cross, and the crew earned Distinguished Flying Crosses.

The Nevada aviator is also remembered at the Battle Born Memorial in Carson City and the Gold Star Family Memorial in Sparks, both dedicated to the state's men and women who died in service of their country

The legend of Bruce Van Voorhis still etches into the history of the Lahontan Valley and with the current mission of the Naval Aviation Warfighting Development

Center at NAS Fallon. Rear Adm. Richard Brophy, who assumed command of NAWDC in 2019, said Van Voorhis represents the giants of naval aviation and what they endured.

"I talk about that story of Van Voorhis," Brophy pointed out. "It's very inspirational. He was clearly on a one-way mission, and he was critical to our mission to win the Pacific."

Steven R. Ranson

'DOO' A LOT WITH A LITTLE

During the darkest days of World War II, the day of April 18, 1942, may live as the date of the first piece of good news for every American and their allies. Lt. Col. James H. Doolittle flew the first of 16 25B "Mitchell" bombers off the flight deck of the aircraft carrier USS Hornet (CV-8) to bomb the Japanese cities of Tokyo, Yokohama, Yokosuka, Osaka and Kobe.

Doolittle's Raiders caught the Japanese homeland defenders with "their pants around their ankles" as the medium bombers flew at wave top level under the Japanese radar to attack their home islands. Japanese military leaders had convinced the citizens they were invincible and safe from foreign attack.

From an idea to the actual bombing, the planning, plane modifications, training and bombing took four months. On Dec. 21, 1941, President Franklin Roosevelt met with the Joint Chiefs of Staff and told them wanted to bomb Japan as soon as possible to lift the moral of our country. Navy Capt. Francis Low, assistant chief of staff for anti-submarine warfare, reported to Admiral Ernest J. King on Jan. 10, 1942; he saw twin engine bombers practicing take offs from a runway at the Naval Air Station in Norfolk, Va., with a white outline of an aircraft carrier deck painted on the runway.

Four squadrons of the 17th Bomber Group, U.S. Army Air Force, received B-25B bombers in September 1941. With the most flight hours in "Mitchells," 24 flight crews were selected from volunteers and began training on March 1, 1942 at Wagner Field in Pensacola, Fla. The 24 crews practiced simulated carrier takeoffs, low level and night flying, low-altitude bombing and navigation over water.

The Doolittle Raiders flew to McClellan Field northeast of Sacramento, Calif., on March 25, 1942, and then to the Naval Air Station at Alameda, Calif. on March 31. Sixteen Mitchells were lifted by a crane to the deck of the USS Hornet.

The CV–8, the seventh USN ship to be named Hornet, was commissioned on Oct. 20, 1941. In 1775 the first two ships commissioned in the Continental Navy were the Hornet and Wasp, the same names of two butt kicking aircraft carriers in the Pacific during World War II. On April 2, 1942 Capt. Marc A. Mitscher sailed the Hornet and escort ships of Task Force 18 with sealed orders to be opened at sea. They joined CV-6, the Enterprise, and Task Force 16 in the Pacific. The two carriers were escorted by the Navy ships Salt Lake City, Northampton, Vincennes, Nashville, Balch, Fanning, Benham, Ellet, Gwin, Meredith, Grayson, Monssen, Cimarron and Sabine.

THE RAID'S IMPACT

The emperor's military told the Japanese press the Doolittle Raiders indiscriminately bombed women and children. While the raid inflicted little damage compared to the B-29 attacked two years later, there was more psychological damage to Japan.

At least one of Lt. Edgar E. McElroy's four 500-pound bombs damaged the Imperial Japanese Navy's aircraft carrier, Ryuho. Her launch was delayed seven month to November 1942, causing her to miss the Battle of Midway. The raid caused the Imperial Japanese Navy to recall Admiral Nagumo's fighting ships to the defense of the Japanese home islands relieving pressure on the Royal Navy in the Indian Ocean. The Japanese navy's decision makers were confused by the attack of twin engine "Mitchells." Being vulnerable to air attacks, Admiral Yamamoto decided to capture Midway Island.

Cmdr. Edwin T. Layton broke the newest Japanese code and gave Admiral Nimitz vital information to intercept and sink four of Japan's fleet aircraft carriers at the Battle of Midway. Those carriers also had a part in the attack on Pearl Harbor. At Midway the Imperial Japanese Navy lost its offensive ability which lead to the country's unconditional surrender on Aug. 15, 1945.

President Franklin D. Roosevelt awarded Doolittle the Medal of Honor at a White House ceremony. "For Conspicuous leadership above and beyond the call of duty, involving personal valor and intrepidity at an extreme hazard to life. With the apparent certainty of being forced to land in enemy territory or to perish at sea,

Lt. Col. Doolittle led a squadron of Army bombers, manned by volunteer crews, in a highly destructive raid on the Japanese mainland."

Six Doolittle Raiders did not return—two drowned after bailing out, three were executed as war criminals and one died of starvation as a prisoner of war in Japan. The Raiders continued to fly missions during the war, nine crew members were killed in action.

Five remaining Raiders—Lt. Col. Richard E. Cole, Robert L. Hite, Lt. Col. Edward J. Saylor, Maj. Thomas C. Griffin and Master Sgt. David J. Thatcher—attended ceremonies at Wright Patterson AFB in Dayton, Ohio, in April 2012 to commemorate the 70th anniversary.

Kenneth Beaton

DECLARED SECURED

What was William Herman Mills' first mistake? He believed the U.S. Marine Corps recruiter. "Bill, join the Marines, and you'll have easy duty being part of a U.S. Embassy security detail."

Mills joined the Marines in October 1941, a month shy of his 22nd birthday in November. The recruits were at Camp Mathews rifle range on Dec. 7, 1941, when Mills' drill instructor informed them about the sneak attack at Pearl Harbor.

The next six months in 1942 were intense as Mills trained with three other Marines with their M3 37-mm anti-tank gun. The 2nd Marine Regiment boarded the USS President Adams, APA-19 to become part of the 1st Marine Division. On Aug. 7, they stormed the beach at Guadalcanal, Solomon Islands.

The Japanese had begun constructing an airfield on Guadalcanal that would have cut the Allied supply lines to New Zealand and Australia. The Marines' objective was to capture the island and begin their island-hopping campaign. The Navy's construction battalion, the Sea Bees, completed the construction of Henderson Airfield named after Maj. Lofton Henderson, the first Marine aviator to perish in World War II.

The transport ship loaded with trucks to haul the 37mm cannons had evacuated the area before Mills' truck could be unloaded. The antitank guns knocked out the lightly armored Japanese tanks and provided close infantry support, blasting Japanese pill boxes and caves. Guadalcanal was declared secure on Feb. 9, 1943.

The 2nd Marines sailed to New Zealand to rest and train replacements. Mills, though, had contracted malaria on Guadalcanal, and all the malaria patients were ordered to Camp Pendleton in 1943. After recovering, he used his leave to visit his parents in Leon, Iowa.

I asked Bill, "Did you ever pass through North Platte, Nebraska?"

Immediately, a broad smile came across Bill's face. I knew his answer.

"Ken, for 10 minutes, I was home. A woman who reminded me of my mother smiled and poured my coffee. Another woman smiled as she offered me home baked cookies on a tray. North Platt, Neb., was the best 10 minutes of my life."

Mills was reunited with the 1st Marine Division on Pavuvu Island in the Russell Islands near Guadalcanal. The division replaced 6,526 casualties from the month-long Battle of Peleliu and prepared for the invasion of Okinawa on Easter Sunday, April 1, 1945. By April 18, The Old Breed had cleared the northern half of Okinawa.

Mills and his three fellow Marines used their 37mm antitank cannon to blast more pill boxes and caves for the Marine infantry to verify that all the Japanese troops in the caves died for their Emperor. In late April the Old Breed relieved the Army's 27th Division to fight the Japanese 32nd Army at Dakeshi Ridge, Wanna Ridge, Sugarloaf Hill and Shuri Castle. Okinawa was declared secured on June 21.

The Old Breed was ordered to Yontan in the north of Okinawa where they received replacements. The 1st Marines were assigned to Operation Coronet to plan the invasion of Tokyo.

Mills looked at me.

"President Harry Truman made the right decision, using the Atomic bomb on Hiroshima and Nagasaki to end the War," he said. "We were damn happy! I had enough points to return to Camp Pendleton. I was discharged at the Navy's Great Lakes Base in December 1945."

Mills returned to the Los Angeles area and met Elaine Dysynske. After a whirlwind romance, they drove to Las Vegas and were married in a wedding chapel on Thanksgiving Day, Nov. 28, 1946.

Kenneth Beaton

LAUNCHING OF USS CARSON CITY

The date was Nov. 13, 1943, and for nearly two years the United States and its allies had been embroiled in World War II in the Pacific, Europe and North Africa.

About 11 million Americans were in uniform.

The U.S. was at war with Japan, Germany and Italy. In the Pacific, Navy carrier planes had sunk three Japanese warships, damaged 12 others and shot down 24 Japanese aircraft over New Guinea.

American victories at the battles of Midway and Coral Sea had halted Japanese advances, and with Iwo Jima, Saipan, Okinawa and Guam in its hands, the U.S. was steadily moving toward control of the entire Pacific and eventual victory over Japan.

At the Port of Los Angeles, about 450 miles south of Carson City, Nev., another important event was about to take place that November day. More than 200 people, including two dozen Nevadans and high-ranking Navy officers, had gathered at the Consolidated Steep Corp., shipyard to witness the launching of a 303-foot Navy frigate. As the ship was about to slide into the water, Mrs. C.B. Austin, wife of Carson City's mayor, raised a champagne bottle and smashed it against the bow.

"I christen you the USS Carson City," she proclaimed as the frigate slipped into Wilmington Bay.

The nation's newest fighting ship was in the water at last, ready to join the Pacific fleet and take on the enemy. The USS Carson City is the only United States naval vessel to have borne the name of Nevada's capital city. The first U.S. military ship named Nevada was an Army vessel. It was a lightly armed steam transport used by Union commanders to carry Army troops, weapons, supplies and horses into combat on the Mississippi, White and Yazoo rivers.

Meanwhile, months after the ship's launching, Carson Mayor Austin and a group of Nevadans returned to the Port of Los Angeles for its commissioning ceremony, and after three months of shakedown trials, the USS Carson City and its crew of 12 officers and 170 enlisted men set sail for the Eastern Pacific and action against the Japanese.

The Carson City was a patrol frigate and carried the number PF-50, signaling that it was the 50th of the more than 100 ships of its PF class built between 1942 and 1944, which were named for small and mid-size U.S. cities.

The patrol frigates resembled and were slightly smaller than destroyers, were armed with several batteries of 3 1/2-inch guns and a formidable array of anti-aircraft 20 and 40 mm cannons and drew a draft of 13 feet and 8 inches, and their twin-screw engines enabled them reach a speed of 19 knots.

Although they were Navy ships, they were manned by Coast Guard personnel, as the Coast Guard operates under the Navy during wartime. The only Navy man on the ships was their doctor, a lieutenant.

The Carson City's first assignment was to conduct patrol and escort duty off the New Guinea Coast, shepherding allied transports and supply ships.

The frigate then participated in the U.S. landings on Morotai Island, which resulted in the island's capture from the Japanese under heavy fire. The Carson City's crew fired several rounds at attacking Japanese aircraft, but none was hit and the ship and its men suffered no damage or casualties. The Carson City won the first of its two Navy Battle Stars for this combat.

The frigate then joined in the successful landings in Leyte, again sustained no casualties or damage while under fire and won its second Battle Star. Escort duty throughout the Pacific followed, and the Carson City dropped depth charges on a Japanese submarine. It is not known if the sub was damaged or sunk.

At war's end, the ship was assigned Alaskan patrol duties and was subsequently decommissioned and transferred to the Soviet navy under a lend-lease arrangement. Four years later, the Carson City was again put out on loan—this time, ironically, to the new, post-war Japanese navy, which renamed her Sakura or "cherry blossom tree."

In 1971, the ship was returned by Japan to the U.S. because it had become old and obsolete. The U.S. declared the Carson City surplus property and sold it to a Taiwanese shipbreaking company for scrap metal, and the ship's 28-year career came to an inglorious end.

In the mid-1990s, the USS Carson City's 250-pound bell, the only historical item from the ship that had not been lost or stolen by the Soviets and Japanese, was discovered in Yellow Pines (population 110), Idaho, where it had been loaned by the U.S. Navy Historical Office to serve as the community's school and fire bell.

Then-Nevada U.S. Sen. Richard Bryan persuaded the Navy to relinquish it to Carson City, its rightful place, and the Navy shipped a replacement bell to little Yellow Pines. Upon arriving in Carson City, the bell was initially installed in the public library and then later to the lobby of the Carson City Hall where it continues to be displayed today.

David C. Henley

THANK YOU, CHARLES

Charles T. Sehe was a 17 year old, 5-foot, 6-inch 127-pound 1940 high school graduate became a sailor in November 1940 with his parents' permission. His parents had one less mouth to feed. The more I read about his experiences, the more I wanted to learn about his time on the USS Nevada, BB – 36, from January 18, 1941, to July 31, 1945.

Sehe earned his red badge of courage on Dec. 7, 1941, as the battleship USS Nevada earned her first of seven battle stars during World War II. He served with his shipmates when the Nevada earned her second battle star at Attu in the Aleutian Islands May 11-30, 1943. The pride of the Silver State earned her third battle star on June 6, 1944, by destroying Nazi bunkers for the Fourth Infantry Division at Utah Beach on the Normandy coast of France. Her fourth battle star was earned by destroying the German fortifications at the port of Cherbourg, France in June 1944. Again the Nevada's accurate fire control destroyed German gun positions on Aug. 15, 1944 at Cote d'Azur, France. Operation Dragoon was her fifth star.

After returning through the Panama Canal, the USS Nevada earned her sixth and seventh battle stars in the Pacific Ocean destroying Japanese gun emplacements as Marines captured Iwo Jima and Okinawa in 1945.

Originally, Sehe was scheduled to meet former Gov. Brian Sandoval on Oct. 15, 2015, at the monthly Nevada Veteran of the month ceremony at the Governor's mansion. Everything was going smoothly until Sandoval's China trip was announced, departing on Oct. 14. After numerous phone calls, we resolved the situation. Sandoval planned to take time from his busy schedule on Oct. 13 to welcome Sehe as he deplaned.

Sehe's flight, though, was cancelled because of mechanical problems. When his wheelchair finally entered the lounge for gate C10 at the Reno Tahoe International Airport, the surprise on his face showed as he was greeted by at least 50 people in the passenger-waiting area. They waved small American flags while cheering and clapping. Filled with emotion, Sehe placed both hands to the sides of his face. At that moment he became a Nevadan. He attended a memorial service that afternoon on the east side of the Capitol building and rang the bell from the governor's deck for his shipmates who did not return home.

After he returned to his Minnesota home, Sehe wrote a thank you article to the Nevada Appeal.

Believe me, my recent visit to Carson City has been one helluva rich, rewarding, challenging and enlightening experience for this former shipmate of the USS Nevada.

When I first boarded the battleship, Feb. 10, 1941, at the Bremerton Navy Yard in Seattle, Wash., this Depression-era 17-year-old kid would never expect the events that would soon follow.

Here is the ever changing address that I intended to give to the audience who filled the Capitol grounds that emotional moment I was to say thank you. I could not even start it. Thank you, Nevada. (Aboard our ship, we were always thought of as being Nevadans, even though we came from different states).

I do appreciate the courtesy given to me to visit your great state of Nevada. I am obliged especially to thank those individuals, and the Navy League who, with their generous support of financial aid and time, provided me with this opportunity.

Today, this 92-year-old Navy veteran stands among the shadows of a younger generation of civilian warriors. Those of us who have been in one war or another know that terrorism is not a typical warfare, nonetheless, it is a deadly war carried out by groups of individuals possessed by a fervent idea, determined to destroy the American way of life— freedom of thought and expression. Freedom is not an idle phrase. It is close and personal.

Whatever our feelings about war and regardless whether war is just or unjust, necessary or politically contrived, we are obliged to support our present troops and those of us out of uniform, civilian veterans, for freedom of thought and expression is yet one of our most cherished human rights. Freedom is not an idle phrase. It is close and personal.

As American citizens, we are obliged to preserve our nation's heritage, honor, and to protect her sacred rights, for our flag, Old Glory, drenched in blood through 10 major wars and numerous conflicts, remains our most precious possession as a nation. Friends, they are damn worth preserving, no matter what the challenge, even if from within our own government.

In one's lifetime, an individual usually experiences a gradual transitional change from the age of innocence and imagination to the age of experience and reality. Not so with many teenage Depression-era youth who enlisted in the military forces to obtain the offer of full meals, warmer clothing, and bedding and an opportunity to visit exotic places. The transition came swiftly, abruptly, and life threateningly. I was a Second Class Seaman, having no technical skills yet.

On Sunday morning, Dec. 7, 1941, I became a stunned witness to America's last hour of peace and her first hour of war. Already at 0752 hours, Japanese were crossing over battleship row from all points of the compass. From the searchlight platform, my battle station, one can see over the entire harbor. Machine gun bullets coming from a low-flying Japanese war plane shredded the ensign that was flying at the Nevada's stern. The surprise aerial attack lasted 110 minutes. Underway at 0758 hours, the Nevada began its 98 heroic minutes to reach the sea, despite its gaping torpedo wound and slight bomb hits.

Immediately after the attack, an urgent call came from the commandant's office for volunteers from the sunken vessels to transfer to other ships, raising their complement of officers and crew members to full combat readiness. Some of those vessels leaving the harbor were to engage an enemy having a far more superior naval force—sunk with high casualties.

After the infamous Sunday attack, an extremely painful task awaited the Nevada crew—removal of the dead and wounded amid the numerous fires raging throughout the upper decks and compartments. I, being only a Second Class Seaman, having little technical skills, remained as a member of the 450 skeletal crew to be later known as Pearl Harbor survivors.

Fortunately, the sunken ships lay in shallow depths, 35 to 40 feet, not at sea. This allowed the boarding of the ships by many working crews coming from the machine, salvage and electrical shops throughout the harbor. A major tactical error of the otherwise well-planned and executed aerial assault on the U.S. Naval installations was the failure to order a third strike (originally planned) on the machine ship complex and the numerous oil tank bins located near the submarine base.

Actually, there were moments when we could be free from the strained tension of combat engagement and were able to gain several minutes of rest, relaxation and even a short nap at our battle station. Each shipmate or officer aboard the Nevada sought, in his own way, a moment to relax. The more adventurous, spirited guys would be deep down in the bowels of the ship, engaging in a game of chance (cards or dice), far from the haunts of the Master-at-Arms force.

My favorite place was topside, main deck, near the ship's stern. Here, I could watch the foaming sea water being churned up by the twin propellers located more than 45 feet below. As I watched this mesmerizing scene, I would actually verbalize my thoughts as they entered and left my mind, for I needed to distinguish what I desired and actually needed. If I survived this war, as I sought out my life's meaning, I often asked, why me? Why didn't I die?

Kenneth Beaton

Charles Sehe, who served on the USS Nevada during the Japanese attack on the battleship on Dec. 7, 1941, receives a quilt from Marsha Strand, right, and Monda Crandellhook, both from Quilts of Valor on Oct. 14, 2015.

Brad Coman / Nevada Appeal

DOING HIS JOB

Eighteen-year-old Illinois native Del Schwichtenberg joined the Navy on July 2, 1940. He graduated from boot camp in October and reported to New London, Conn., for three months of submarine training where he proved he could live and work in a confined space and escape from a "disabled" submarine. In January 1941 Schwichtenberg reported to USS 06 (SS67), "a rusted bucket of bolts" moored in the Philadelphia Naval Shipyard.

The USS 06 was a World War I submarine brought out of the mothball fleet. By March 1941 the 06 was ready to perform sea trials including a dive with the 09 and 010. After performing various maneuvers, the 06 and 010 surfaced. The 09 never resurfaced, losing the entire crew.

During World War II the Portsmouth Naval Shipyard built over 70 submarines. The keel for the USS Sand Lance (SS-381) was laid on March 12, 1943, she launched on June 25, 1943 and was commissioned on Oct. 9, 1943, with the skipper Cmdr. Malcolm Everett Garrison.

Schwichtenberg was the eighth sailor to report to the Sand Lance. After conducting training exercises from New London, she sailed through the Panama Canal on Dec. 18, 1943, and arrived at Pearl Harbor on Jan. 17, 1944. The Sand Lance arrived at her patrol station, Paramushiro, on Feb. 24, 1944, after passing through two typhoons, fields of slush ice and intermittent drift ice. She sunk a cargo ship, the Kaika Maru despite the fact her number one periscope had been damaged by drift ice.

Garrison came up to periscope depth to discover a convoy in his cross hairs. Between March 2 and 3 he sank the cargo ship Akashisan Maru while damaging other Japanese ships. On March 3 she sunk an unmarked Russian merchant ship, Byelorussia. The Byelorussia's captain should have flown the Soviet "hammer and sickle" flag to clearly identify it in enemy water. The Soviet government vehemently protested, but Admiral Nimitz defended Garrison.

On March 13, 1944 at 2 a.m., the Sand Lance came up to periscope depth to find itself in the middle of a Japanese convoy, five merchant and three heavily armed warship. With six remaining torpedoes, two stern torpedoes sank a cargo ship with 1,000 enemy troops. The other two stern torpedoes severely damaging the light cruiser, Tatsuta. The two bow torpedoes severely damaged a cargo ship.

For the next 16 hours enemy destroyers pounded the Sand Lance with more than 100 depth charges. The Sand Lance, though, slipped through the barrage and arrived at Pearl Harbor on April 23, 1944. Her maiden war patrol was awarded a Presidential Unit Citation signed by President Franklin Roosevelt.

Her second war patrol involved sinking more merchant Japanese shipping. Her third war patrol began July 3, 1944. At a depth of 100 feet, a submarine is easily spotted by an enemy plane. On Aug. 6, 1944, two Japanese bombs exploded near the Sand Lance lifting her stern several feet damaging her port propeller shaft. Enemy escorts were dropping depth charger. complicating matters, she had a torpedo running "hot" in one of her stern tubes. The Sand Lance came up to 100 feet and fired the "hot" torpedo which exploded 8 seconds after launch.

The bad news was more damage to the stern, yet the good news showed the Japanese escorts disengaged. It took almost two months to arrive at Mare Island Shipyard in the Bay area on Nov. 1, 1944. The Sand Lance was similar to a boxer who won a championship fight with cuts above and below both eyes with his right eye only a slit for an opening.

Her fourth and fifth war patrols were less eventful. She was assigned to a "lifeguard station" picking up downed bomber crews off the Japanese home islands. On Aug. 16, 1945, the sub set a course to San Francisco docking on Sept. 7. The Sand Lance was a fighter. She earned five battle stars and a Presidential Unit Citation.

Schwichtenberg, though, earned a Bronze Star.

"His outstanding performance of duty working two days and nights on top of the periscope shears, part of the time in a heavy snow storm, and always under the threat of Japanese air attack, cutting away the upper bearing to allow the lowering of number one periscope which was bent and jammed in the raised position, aided his Commanding Officer materially in delivering aggressive attacks which resulted in the sinking of enemy ships totaling 28,000 tons and the damaging of additional enemy shipping of 6,000 tons. His efficiency and his coolness under the most trying conditions of enemy counter-attacks were a direct contribution to the success of this patrol."

After 20 years, Schwichtenberg retired from the Navy in 1960 as a chief warrant officer 3. Schwichtenberg died on Dec. 12, 2019, a month before his 98th birthday.

Kenneth Beaton

UNDERNEATH THE SEVEN SEAS

Life aboard submarines during World War II tested the resolve of thousands of sailors who spent tireless days disrupting the enemy's navy and maritime shipping. Many sailors who served aboard United States submarines knew the dangers of the grueling duty with inside temperatures soaring above 100 degrees affecting 80 to 90 men onboard; the inside air slowly grew foul with a combination of cooking, sewage, cigarette smoke, diesel and body order due to a shortage of available water for bathing.

Nothing, though, compared to sailing into enemy water—many times alone with an escort—to launch an attack on a ship and then hurry out of the zone into the open seas.

World War II submariners William Parsons of Sparks and Delmar Schwichtenberg of Carson City remember the harsh duty of serving on a submarine during World War II. They were among the guests for the unveiling of a new home at the Nevada State and Archives Building in Carson City for a model of the USS Corvina, the only U.S. Navy submarine sunk by a Japanese submarine during the war.

A plexiglass display glass protects the model, and an adjacent display of photos will keep the memories vivid for the submarine and its crew of 82 who died during an attack near the Truk (Chuuk) Islands, the Japanese's most forward naval base in the Pacific Ocean.

Stephen Salzman, commander of Corvina Base in Reno, gave a short history on the Gato-class USS Corvina and its fate. Commissioned on Aug. 6, 1943, the Corvina under the command of Cmdr. Rodney S. Rooney left New London,

Connecticut, in September and arrived in Pearl Harbor one month later. The Corvina began her maiden patrol on Nov. 4, and according to her service record, topped off with fuel two days later at Johnston Island before entering enemy waters. Her mission was to attack enemy naval forces south of Truk, and on Dec. 14 the submarine was then to proceed to eastern Australia for refit and duty.

Salzman said when three messages notifying the Corvina of its next assignment went unanswered, the command sent out another message directing the submarine to proceed to Tulagi, but it did not arrive. Eventually, Japanese records revealed submarine I-176 launched three torpedoes against the Corvina on Nov. 16, two of which ripped into the submarine causing it to explode. The Navy announced her loss on March 14, 1944, almost four months after the attack.

Salzman said bases or chapters were established in the 1960s for each state to adopt a submarine that was sunk during World War II. Because of their population size, New York state and California each adopted two. While some states selected submarines based on historical or cultural reasons, Nevada had no significant ties with the Corvina.

Terry Sheldon-Brown said her late husband Donald began the Corvina Base in Reno after the submarine veterans held their 1999 convention at the Peppermill. She said Jim Avitt, who died in 2007, and her husband distributed flyers everywhere – libraries, supermarkets, military service organizations and bulletin boards.

"They had enough people to charter in February 2000," she explained.

The Base began with 32 members, but Sheldon-Brown said the number has swelled to between 80 to 90 submariners who live in western Nevada including Fallon and Fernley. Occasionally, a submariner assigned to Naval Air Station Fallon or the Naval Aviation Warfighting Development Center joins the Corvina Base.

According to Salzman, a sailor from Carlin, 22 miles west of Elko in northeastern Nevada, worked on the Corvina at the shipyard before it left for New London, but he never became a plankowner, one who's assigned to a ship or submarine from the time of commissioning.

"I don't believe we had any members lost who were from Nevada," Salzman added.

During World War II, 263 submarines patrolled hundreds of thousands of miles of open oceans and seas, but 41 of them were lost to the enemy, while another 11 disappeared because of accidents or other reasons. According to Salzman, the Navy's submarine force, which consisted of about 2 percent of the U.S. naval fleet, destroyed more than 30 percent of the Japanese Navy and more than 60 percent of the Japanese merchant fleet.

Salzman spent six years in the Navy and served on the USS Seawolf, a nuclear submarine commissioned in 1957, and two other submarines. His duty contrasts to Parsons and Schwichtenberg and the conditions they faced 30 years prior during World War II.

"I was aboard the USS Thresher (SS 200) which was commissioned in December 1940," said Parsons, who was trained in communications and sonar. "I was never worried about dangers, but we had close calls."

The Thresher patrolled the South Pacific, and Parsons said he was with a naval group that was part of the firebombing of Tokyo during the war's waning months. Parsons and his wife, Mercedes, have been married for 75 years, and their son, a pilot in the U.S. Navy, was assigned to Naval Air Station Fallon 15 years ago. Parsons also served on the USS Queenfish and USS Cubera, both submarines.

Schwichtenberg served in both the Pacific and Atlantic theaters on three submarines—the Sea Dog, Sand Lance (SS381) and 0-6 (SS 67), which was recommissioned for World War II—but the duty was just as strenuous on each boat with long days, harsh conditions and the uncertainty of each day.

"We had our challenges … weather-wise in the Atlantic and enemy-wise in the Pacific," said Schwichtenberg, who remembers how aggressive the German U-boats were in sinking ships.

Schwichtenberg, though, remembers one attack in the Pacific where the Japanese destroyers zeroed in on his submarine.

"We had two destroyers holding us down 15 hours," Schwichtenberg recalled." They dropped 105 depth charges … and every time we tipped, we thought we were going to drown."

DUTY, SACRIFICE AND CAMARADERIE

Churchill County Commissioner Bus Scharmann told the story of duty, sacrifice and camaraderie in the military. His uncle, Navy electrician's mate second class Richard Judd Hinkson, served on a Tambor-class submarine, the USS Grenadier (SS-210), during World War II in the South Pacific. On one of their missions between Australia and Indonesia, the Grenadier successfully sunk Japanese merchant and war ships before their luck turned in April 1943. The crew became engaged in a very difficult fight with the enemy, causing the submarine to suffer severe damage.

"Their captain—Capt. (John) Fitzgerald—took the sub down, all the way to the bottom in the Straits of Indonesia, 270 feet down," Scharmann recounted. "Somehow, he was able to bring it back to surface."

After the Grenadier reached the surface, a Japanese pilot spotted the submarine and its crew, but before an enemy ship could reach them, Fitzgerald scuttled the sub and sent it to the bottom of the sea. The crew evacuated the Grenadier by climbing into life boats, but soon afterward, the Japanese took the sailors as prisoners and remained in that status for the rest of the war, which officially ended on Sept. 2, 1945 with the formal signing to end the costly war.

"My uncle was in a prisoner-of-war camp in the Pacific and in Japan," Scharmann said. "He didn't talk very much (after the war), but talked more to my father. He talked about his camaraderie with the people he was with not only on the sub but the men he was with in the POW camp. He talked about how they would work for hours and hours and hours in a train yard in Japan."

During the POW ordeal, Fitzgerald secretly kept a journal detailing the ill treatment sailors endured; consequently, Scharmann said the captain wrote justice was served after the war against their captors who administered the harsh treatment. Remarkably, only four sailors didn't survive the harsh conditions of a POW camp.

Scharmann also described his uncle as a mean, tough, gruff man who was a hard drinker and smoker but who also had a softer side to him.

"He would sit down with my mom—his sister—and my father—and talk about those old times," Scharmann said. "He would cry because he remembered his crewmates. The crew of the Grenadier got together every four to five years in Las Vegas to talk about old times and to be together."

Scharmann said some of the happiest times for his uncle, who died in 1991 and is buried at the Golden Gate National Cemetery 12 miles south of San Francisco, were being with his Navy friends whom he called his brothers.

Steven R. Ranson

A TEEN TRACKING
ENEMY AIRCRAFT

Carson City's Hazel Ryland served with distinction in her country's military during different eras more than 70 years ago. For Ryland, she entered the military in Great Britain during World War II.

Ryland, whose father at the time was a British general, grew up in England and entered the Territorial Service (became Women's Royal Army Corps in 1949) in the early 1940s as a teenager. Ryland participated in an Honor Flight Nevada trip to the nation's capital and considered the trip a wonderful experience for her and the others on the flight. Being a British war veteran, she

An interesting military background followed Ryland during her enlistment in England.

"I went to a base camp where they decided where we would go," she said.

The military assigned Ryland to heavy artillery, a critical specialty considering the number of times Germany flew over the English Channel to bomb parts of southern England.

"I was a spottie beginning to recognize planes," she recalled. "They (instructors) would put up silhouettes of the planes from America and Germany, and we had to look at those silhouettes with binoculars. They were always a long ways away."

Ryland paused for several seconds, thinking of what she had said about the airplane shapes.

"I don't know if we recognized too many," she said, chuckling.

Ryland first served under her father, a brigadier general, in his unit near Liverpool, but later she transferred to another unit in London, the capital of the British Empire. The unit with its "spotties" watched for enemy aircraft entering Britain's airspace from the east or northeast and down the countryside to bomb the suburbs or central London

"That was my war outside of London … to track aircraft," she added.

The Germans mounted an intensive aerial assault against London in 1940 and 1941. Famed war correspondent Ernie Pyle described a night of bombing in London as reprinted in "The London Blitz, 1940," EyeWitness to History, www. eyewitnesstohistory.com (2001).

"About every two minutes a new wave of planes would be over. The motors seemed to grind rather than roar, and to have an angry pulsation, like a bee buzzing in blind fury.

"The guns did not make a constant overwhelming din as in those terrible days of September. They were intermittent - sometimes a few seconds apart, sometimes a minute or more. Their sound was sharp, nearby; and soft and muffled, far away. They were everywhere over London.

"Into the dark shadowed spaces below us, while we watched, whole batches of incendiary bombs fell. We saw two dozen go off in two seconds. They flashed terrifically, then quickly simmered down to pin points of dazzling white, burning ferociously. These white pin points would go out one by one, as the unseen heroes of the moment smothered them with sand. But also, while we watched, other pin points would burn on, and soon a yellow flame would leap up from the white center. They had done their work - another building was on fire."

Ryland also remembered when she and other women traveled to Southampton days before the D-Day invasion in June 1944. While there, they entertained hundreds of troops who were preparing for the invasion across the English Channel to Normandy.

"We were all dating American boys," Ryland said.

She smiled.

By the end of the war in 1945, Ryland said about 190,000 women fought for Britain in the war by doing various jobs. Ryland said she's extremely proud of her duty.

"We had our own uniforms and used to wear a badge knitted on our shoulder," she said.

Years after serving in the British Army, she came to the United States in 1959 and became a naturalized citizen eight years later. Ryland, who was born Aug. 20, 1925 in Biggen Hill, Kent, England died 91 years later in Carson City, Nevada.

Steven R. Ranson

KEEPING HIS COOL

Delivering milk during Lake Tahoe winters as a young man contributed to Clarence Godecke's ability to remain cool under fire as a B-17 Flying Fortress pilot during World War II.

The 95-year-old Minden resident, who was born in Carson Valley and grew up on a farm near Heybourne, died in Minden in May 2016.

Godecke's World War II exploits included being the first person to fly a jet over Carson Valley and helping save Dutch children from starvation as the Nazis began their retreat. Born Jan. 5, 1921, just off Mottsville Lane, to Clarence W. Sr. and Esther Louise (Menzel) Godecke, the family moved to the Heybourne tract when he was a boy.

He said he would walk to school by following the tracks of the Virginia & Truckee Railroad into town. The train was fascinating to him and he remembered how he and brother Howard would ride a railroad car that workers left with the steam up until it wouldn't go anymore.

It was as a teenager that he decided that whatever he ended up doing for a living, it wouldn't be farming. He graduated from Douglas High School in 1938 and worked for the Nevada Highway Department before taking a delivery job with the Minden Butter Manufacturing Co.

"I drove the Tahoe route in a 21/2 -ton truck," he said. "It was an interesting winter. I had to get up at 3 a.m. and put chains on."

He joined the U.S. Army Air Corps service on his 21st birthday, Jan. 5, 1942, less than a month after the start of World War II. His first combat tour consisted of 50 missions with the 12th Air Force in North Africa and the Mediterranean. He returned home and was stationed at McClellan Field as a test pilot.

That was where he had an opportunity to fly one of America's first jet fighters, a P-80 Shooting Star, right over Carson Valley.

"I gave Carson Valley its first look at a jet in aviation," he said. "I shot the full length of the Valley. It took out past Markleeville to turn around. Bruns was the only guy who saw me, but everyone heard me."

When the opportunity came to return to the conflict in Europe, Godecke said he jumped at the chance.

He spent the final year of World War II with the 8th Air Force flying out of England where he served as squadron commander on 18 more missions.

On one of his last missions, instead of delivering bombs, he dropped food to starving residents in Holland. Lin 2015, he sat down with Minden resident Garry Den Heyer, who was one of the recipients of that flight more than 70 years ago. Godecke received two Distinguished Flying Crosses, 13 Air Medals, the Croix De Guerre avec Palm, and several Presidential citations.

Once the war was over, he said he never again piloted an aircraft.

After the war he married his first wife, Sue Helen Stout, of Kentucky and tried his hand at raising tobacco. When she died in 1960, he and his four children moved to Sacramento where he met and married Ramona Reynolds in 1963 and the family returned to Carson Valley the next year.

He served a term on the Minden Town Board, was past president of the Minden Rotary Club and served several terms as president of Trinity Lutheran Church.

Kurt Hildebrand

OVER TROUBLED WATERS

From the remote islands dotting the Pacific Ocean to the rugged shoreline of northern France, sailors aboard LSMs (Landing Ship Medium—transport) during World War II ferried soldiers and Marines to fight the Japanese and Germans.

The Korean War produced one of the largest amphibious landings during the first year of the conflict when joint forces attacked Incheon, and a generation later, sailors aboard LSMs patrolled the Vietnam Coast and the Mekong Delta.

Although many of these events occurred two and three generations ago, those who served aboard LSMs or LSMRs (rocket) vividly remember their experiences aboard these ships as if they occurred just the other day. These sailors protected their country during three different wars aboard a ship that may have not been as glamorous as a destroyer or aircraft carrier, but these heroic men were navigated the seas to ensure the success of the allied forces..

Sharing memories is what serving entails.

Al Pierre of Fallon, Nev., joined the Navy in 1943 when he was 18 and initially spent time aboard three ships including an LSM. Pierre served 20 years on active duty and after his retirement, he spent 26 years with the Navy Exchange.

"I spent time on one ship, then another, then shore duty," Pierre said.

Chuck Kramer, who now lives in Simi Valley, Calif., joined the Navy in his teens and served during World War II on an LSM. Two days after the invasion at Normandy, Kramer and his shipmates arrived with additional support.

The love of being a sailor at seas inspired Kramer and other men each and every day. As the war effort progressed in 1943, the U.S. Navy decided to build modify its fleet with LSMs, and between 1944-45, the Navy built 558 ships to transport troops to different islands in the Pacific. They were small, 203-feet in length, and could travel 13.2 knots (15 miles) per hour.

"At Iwo Jima, the first ship to hit the beach was an LSM," Kramer said, proudly telling of the ordeal.

The first troops stormed onto the Japanese stronghold in mid-February 1945, and for the next month, both sides suffered staggering losses. As the U.S, military gradually pushed the enemy toward Japan, Jake Jacobsen, a sailor on LSMR 409 felt the war was going to become costlier with the loss of sailors, soldiers and marines. Jacobsen joined the Navy at 16 and left the service after the war, serving a total of three years.

"We were headed out of the Hawaiian Islands, headed to Japan, and then the "bomb" was dropped," said Jacobsen.

The U.S. dropped a second atomic bomb on Japan, and within a month, the Japanese surrendered aboard the battleship USS Missouri. Jacobsen said the sailor aboard LSMR 409 were relieved; however, as the LSMR 409 steamed toward Japan during the waning days of the war, he said it wasn't unusual to see one- or two-man suicide submarines follow their ship. Jacobsen, though, said the subs primarily set focus on the larger ships like aircraft carriers and battleships.

Richard Finch of Redmond, Ore., remembered the horror of war in the Philippines.

"When we were in Luzon on a Sunday afternoon, we watched as one plane (Japanese Zero) went into the USS California," Finch recollected.

John Mount of Thermopolis, Wyo., died in 2012, but he served on LSM 204. Mount stayed in Norfolk, Va., training crews, but the time came when the LSM loaded two 85-ton tugs and began its odyssey to Guam.

"When we arrived in Guam, they didn't have any cranes to get them (tugs) off," Mount said.

Once the Navy found a way to unload the tugs and after much delay, LSM 204 sailed to the Philippines to deliver supplies and later chugged across the East China Sea to deliver occupation troops to Japan. Mount said different LSMs took troops and supplies to different area. Although the war caused anxiety among the sailors, Mount said surviving a typhoon was just as stressful.

"We rode out a typhoon in the Philippines ... that was rough," he said.

Jacobsen echoed Mount's assessment.

"Typhoons were rough. Everyone prayed that the swells wouldn't swamp the ship," he said

Mount spent 20 years in the Navy and was drafted as soon as he graduated from high school.

"They were taking everyone in the Navy," Mount said.

All but one of the actual LSMs or LSMRs constructed for the Navy have been scrapped. One, which is now at Camp Lejeune, N.C., continues to rot, a fact that hurts Kramer and others who served aboard these transport ships.

Their memories cannot be erased as related by Rolf Illsley, 99, of San Raphael, Calif.

When one LSM was on display in Omaha, Neb., in 2000, Illsley said 1,500 vets and families boarded LSM 45.

"There were tears in the eyes of these men after they toured the ship," he said.

Yet, for many of the former sailors, those tears quickly give way to their stories of how these men endured some of the harshest conditions to serve their nation.

Thousands of U.S. Navy sailors served without fanfare, delivering goods and equipment to the many far away islands in the western Pacific Ocean during World War II. Scores of LSTs (landing ship tanks) island-hopped across the Pacific in the waning days of the war and afterward, many of the ships battled high seas and strong storms as well as encountering enemy aircraft.

Serving at sea also became a dream of James "Jungle" Dilts, who lived in Randburg, Calif., a desert small town south of the China Lake Naval Weapons Center at Ridgecrest. Like so many teenagers of his time, the 90-year-old Dilts felt an obligation to enlist in 1944 and serve his country. Joining the Navy for Dilts was much easier than avoiding his mother's wrath when she learned his father took him to Los Angeles to enlist.

"I told my dad I wanted to go into the Navy, so I signed up in L.A.," said Dilts, who was 17 years old at the time. "When we got home, my mother wanted to know where we were. So we told her, and she was mad at me and mad at my dad. She about left us."

Dilts said he left high school without graduating, but he earned his GED (General Equivalency Diploma) after returning from sea duty. Although Dilts served 73 years ago, he still retains a sense of humor in retelling his story about enlisting in the military. His father, according to Dilts, had three monosyllabic words of advice before the California teen shipped off. "Be safe, kid." Dilts quickly noted he wrote an occasional letter to his mother, so she wouldn't raise "hell" when he got home.

Like many teenagers from his time, Dilts had an opportunity to enlist in one of the other services such as the Marines, but the idea of marching didn't appeal to him.

"I wanted to ride, so I didn't go into the Marines," he said, chuckling.

The thought of marching and taking cover to avoid enemy fire didn't appeal to Dilts, who has retained a sharp wit about him. On the other hand, the LST crew encountered high seas that caused the ship to roll from one side to another. LSTs were flat-bottom ships with no keel. Every time the crew encountered rough seas, Dilts said he was worried but not scared.

"Tanks and equipment were strapped down, and sometimes one of the straps broke loose," Dilts explained. "The tanks needed to be strapped down (or chained) because if they broke loose, they would ram into the side walls."

Dilts ironically had an interest in amphibious ships as a young boy growing up in the northern fringe of the Mohave Desert, so his first and only vessel was on LST 997, which served the majority of its time in the Pacific Theater. Launched in May 1944, LST 997 first saw action in Europe during the invasion of southern France in August and September. During the last year of the war, the LST served in the Pacific and also became part of the occupational forces after VJ Day, which President Harry S. Truman declared as Sept. 2, 1945.

"I didn't see much action," said Dilts, who spent time on a 20-mm caliber cannon. "We spent some time on a few islands and New Guinea. I can tell you about the mosquitos there."

Dilts and his shipmates, though, persevered in order to do their jobs. He said LST 997 headed to the Philippines where it saw limited action. After the war, he said the LST took equipment and supplies to the northern part of Japan. Being on an LST compared to other ships appealed to Dilts because the ship did not draw as much attention from Japanese planes and suicide bombers.

"They wanted the big prizes like the aircraft carriers, battleships and cruisers," he pointed out.

Dilts left the Navy after serving less than two years and headed home. From Randburg, he decided to see the country and work in the mines as a hard rock miner. He rode the freight trains and hitchhiked around the country – exploits that cause him to get the nickname of "Jungle"—but his travels returned him to the West where he worked at a mine in Butte, Montana, and later at a mine near Gilman Springs north of Austin, Nev.

Steven R. Ranson

'FLYING FORTRESS'
CO-PILOT'S WAR YEARS

World War II memorabilia lays neatly in several stacks near his bed. Newspaper clippings and a magazine cover one pile, photographs adorn another.

Former B-17 co-pilot Cecil W. Quinley looks at a newspaper clipping written of a "Flying Fortress" visiting Chico, Calif., 10 years ago, when he relived his experiences of World War II by co-piloting the bomber as it circled Northern Sacramento Valley. Quinley and his wife of 68 years, Margaret, lived in Chico before moving to Fallon to be closer to family.

"I had stick time for about 15 minutes as the co-pilot," the then 92-year-old Quinley said, his eyes glistening as he talked about his first ride in a B-17 cockpit since World War II. "I looked at those gauges and couldn't remember any of them."

Although he is more frail than what he was 10 years ago, Quinley's mind is still sharp as he recounts dates and events from his European flying days.

Quinley was no stranger to the B-17, one of the most widely used bombers flown over Europe in the 1940s. But when he saw the B-17 again, he was surprised with its dimensions.

"The B-17 looked awfully big outside, but when I got in, there was hardly any room," Quinley recollected.

DANGEROUS MISSIONS

But 64 years has not diminished Quinley's memories of flying 14 missions over Germany in 1943. Sometimes, a mission would last only three hours; other missions would average eight to 10 hours, maybe more. Most bombing runs took place during daylight hours, a fact that perplexed the British.

"The English thought we were nuts," Quinley said, explaining how the Brits carried out their bombing missions at night.

Prior to entering German airspace, Quinley said P-38 Lightning and P-47 Thunderbolt fighters escorted the B-17s from England. Once the "Flying Fortresses" entered German air space, Quinley said the fighters would turn back, leaving the B-17s on their own.

Quinley, who had been married for four years, wanted to fly, but regulations almost nixed his opportunity. Before World War II, married airmen were not allowed to attend flight school, but the declaration of war on Dec. 8, 1941, quickly altered the requirements.

"After Pearl Harbor, that all changed," he said about entering flight school as a married cadet.

Quinley graduated as a single-engine pilot, but the need for bomber pilots beckoned the Sacramento native to Europe.

"I thought I was going into fighters, but they needed co-pilots for the B-17," Quinley said. "But the B-17 flew just as good (as fighters)."

The crew of Quinley's B-17, the "Feather Merchant," trained at Walla Walla, Wash., before their assignment to the 532nd Squadron, 381st Bomb Group at Ridgewell, England. Jack Pry, the plane's 23-year-old pilot, was a former airplane mechanic before he attended flight school.

"His knowledge of planes came in handy," Quinley added.

Life aboard a B-17 was dangerous during World War II. Out of 12,000 B-17s produced for the war effort, a third were shot down, including Quinley's aircraft.

The "Feather Merchant" flew in the famous first Schweinfurt Raid in August 1943, but the 352nd suffered the most losses of any squadron. Quinley's B-17, though, was lucky on this raid. The aircraft returned to Ridgewell without a loss.

During the next four months, the "Feather Merchant" completed more successful raids, knocking out key industrial areas needed for the German war effort. After their 13th mission, luck ran out for the men of the "Feather Merchant."

SHOT DOWN OVER BREMEN

"We were shot down late in 1943 (Oct. 8)," Quinley, who was 26 at the time, said. "On our 14th mission, we were shot down near Bremen. I was hit by flak (fire from anti-aircraft guns). The anti-aircraft fire knocked the No. 2 engine out, and that was right by me."

Quinley and Pry immediately took their B-17 out of formation, prepping the 10-man crew to abandoned the plane.

"Eight of us bailed out, but I don't know what happened to the other two," Quinley lamented. "The ball turret gunner must have been hit ... and another was reluctant to parachute out."

One by one, the crew bailed out of the plane into enemy territory. When Quinley began his descent, a bullet pierced his right leg.

"I didn't know where the ground was," Quinley explained. "I landed near some barbed wire. I missed the fence, but I came down in the middle of a ditch."

As Quinley sat in the ditch, he saw two figures walking toward him in single file.

"This farmer came over with a Russian POW who was working with him," Quinley said, with a slight laugh, looking back on the situation.

But the next two weeks were no laughing matter for Quinley. He spent one week in the hospital because of his injured leg before moving to solitary confinement at an interrogation camp. Then, the Germans transferred him to Stalag Luft 3 for the next 15 months. Although conditions were harsh at the prison camp, Quinley said pilots were treated well.

Located 100 miles southeast of Berlin in what is now Poland, Stalag 3 was one of six used for downed British and American airmen. Because the Luftwaffe ran it, Stalag 3 became a model camp.

Quinley's health deteriorated at the beginning of his confinement when he almost died. Doctors accidentally overdosed the aviator with immunizations, specifically tetanus, but they discovered their mistake and nursed Quinley back to health.

A SPECIAL LOVE

Margaret, who recently celebrated her 90th birthday, moved before the onset of World War II to Sacramento from Ft. Bragg, a small seaside community known more for its logging industry nestled on the Pacific Ocean's Mendocino Coast, 200 miles north of San Francisco.

After relocating to Sacramento to attend junior college, Margaret met Cecil about a year later when they attended the state fair on a blind date. They were married in a church wedding in 1939. The time they had envisioned together was separated by war that broke out two-and-half-years later.

Their lives changed when Cecil attended flight school beginning in August 1942 for nine months. He had to complete more flight training after that on the B-17, and he left for Europe in June. Cecil wrote to Margaret every day he was in Europe until he was shot down.

News of her husband's fate reached her in an Oct. 18 telegram. One month later, she heard Cecil was a prisoner of war, and Margaret received her first letter from Cecil in January.

"Those three weeks were rough, but I took it one day at a time," Margaret said of the wait. "I prayed a lot and took a beautiful gift of fate. Friends and relatives were really good."

She kept busy when Cecil was in Europe. She worked as a volunteer Red Cross nurse assigned to Sacramento-area hospitals. Long hours took her mind off personal anxieties.

"My joy in life was working in a maternity hospital and watching a birth overnight," she said. "I also worked in a doctor's office and sometimes spent the night as a nurse's aide."

Margaret, though, was one of the lucky spouses.

"I couldn't forget about others who were in the same boat, but I also had friends who had lost their fathers and sons," she said, further explaining how she hated war but knew it was necessary.

Communication was intermittent. Cecil could send only four postcards and a letter each month. Margaret, though, wrote to Cecil every day.

LIBERATION

Cecil Quinley's days were numbered at Stalag 3. Before Gen. George Patton's troops liberated the camp, Quinley learned of the "Great Escape," a venture involving almost 250 POWs, mostly British airmen, who dug three tunnels to escape from Stalag 3. Only 76 POWs successfully escaped from the prison.

Because Russian troops were advancing toward Berlin, the Germans marched the POWs in 10-degree below zero weather in late January and then crammed them on to railroad box cars for a journey to another camp near Munich, a trek that took three days.

Patton's Third U.S. Army's 14th Armored Division rolled into Stalag 7A and liberated the POWs on April 29, 1945. Quinley said he met Patton and received two Purple Heart medals and several campaign and flying medals.

When Margaret and Cecil were finally reunited with each other in California, he was given 60 days leave. During that time they vacationed for 10 days at Carmel and later for two weeks at Del Mar, near San Diego.

After the war, Quinley remained in the inactive reserves and was discharged as a captain in 1962.

Cecil Quinley said he thinks often of his war experiences and of the men with whom he served. But Quinley recently another thrill to go along with his World War II days.

"One of my greatest thrills was seeing (Barry) Bonds break (Hank) Aaron's home run record," Quinley said, referring to the slugger's feat on Aug. 7

"It wasn't as thrilling as flying, but it came close."

Both Cecil and Margaret died in 2016. Their son Dan has written a book about their love and the letters they wrote to each other during the war: "Forever: A True Story of Love and War" available on Amazon.

Steven R. Ranson

HONORED NAVAJO 'CODE TALKER'

The exemplary reputation of U.S. Marine Corps' Navajo "code talkers" during World War II is well documented, and I was saddened to learn about the death of one of those legendary American Indians who served their country with valor and distinction in the Pacific.

David Patterson Sr., who was one of the few remaining code talkers, died in 2017 at his home in Rio Rancho, N.M, from complications of pneumonia and a fall.

"He was brave until the very end, but he just was not strong enough to overcome the battle," according to his son, Pat Patterson, one of his seven children. "This nation is indebted to David Patterson for his service," said U.S. Sen. John McCain (R-Arizona) upon learning of his death.

David Patterson, a USMC enlistee who served in combat on the Marshall Islands and Iwo Jima from 1943 until his honorable discharge at war's end, was one of the 250-plus code talkers who used their native language to confuse and bewilder the Japanese enemy which was unable to translate the Indians' language during combat operations against the U.S. and its allies on the Pacific islands. Although Patterson and the others were generally referred to as "Navajo code talkers" because most of them were Navajos, some were members of other tribes, such as the Comanche, Choctaw, Cheyenne and Lakota, who also used their tribal languages to confound Japanese intelligence agencies which had managed to tap into the Marines' communication networks.

Patterson's responsibility as a code talker, like that of his fellow code talkers, was to translate secret tactical messages from English into their respective native languages and then transmit them from the field to higher echelons. Upon receiving the messages, code talkers at the other end would re-translate them into English.

Adam Fortunate Eagle, a nationally known American Indian historian, author, artist and activist who lives with his family on the Paiute-Shoshone Reservation at Stillwater east of Fallon, has met several of the code talkers, and "they must be praised by all of us as true American heroes."

"They were prohibited from speaking about their wartime role until government secrecy about the code talkers was ended in 1968, 23 years after the end of World War II, he said.

Patterson and the others were finally acknowledged by the government in 2001, when they were presented with special Congressional medals. Patterson also was one of several code talkers who were honored during a half-time ceremony at the Major League baseball All-Star Game in New York City in 2013, he added.

"More than 39,000 Native Americans served in uniform during World War II. Four of them were my older brothers," noted Fortunate Eagle, who was born in Minnesota and is a member of the Red Lake Band of American Indians.

Ironically, just a month after Patterson's death, President Donald Trump presided over a Nov. 28 White House ceremony that honored three of the 13 still-living code talkers along with their families and several officers of American Indian groups. President Trump praised the code talkers as "very special people" who "were here before any of us were here."

David C. Henley

REAR BOMBER'S WATCHFUL EYE

Shortly before his arrival in Guadalcanal as a 17-year-old poised for war, the battle for a small jungle-entangled Pacific island endured some of the fiercest fighting during the first year of World War II. Both Marines and soldiers repelled a six-month Japanese assault on the small 90-mile long island in the Solomon chain, while aviation assets and naval resources aided in the battle.

That was fine with Gerald Edson.

"I had a draft number of 32," Edson explained. "I decided to enlist so I didn't have to sleep on the ground."

The newly qualified naval aviator, who has lived in Sacramento for most of his life, arrived on the island after completing boot camp and flight training, a teenager determined to fight for his country against the Japanese. Upon his arrival on Guadalcanal, Edson became the newest member of a submarine patrol squadron that kept a watchful eye on enemy activity in the southwestern Pacific.

"We had nine airplanes and 11 pilots," the 98-year-old Edson recalled. "We would fly over the ocean looking for convoys and submarines."

Edson, who served in the Navy from 1942 to 1944, said he doesn't remember seeing any enemy ships during reconnaissance flights from his perilous perch, that of a rear gunner on a Douglas SBD Dauntless dive bomber. Each mission tested the crew's skill to avoid enemy fire from the rear, which had inadequate protection for the rear gunner. Edson felt the chances of surviving, though, were better than having boots on the ground when he first enlisted.

Edson, though, never thought he would see up close a two-seat Dauntless. On a recent visit to the Pearl Harbor Aviation Museum, Edson closely viewed each plane and a description for each. There, as he rounded a corner and in front of him, the plane jutted out onto the floor. Edson froze—perhaps only for a few seconds but that may have seemed like eternity to the World War II veteran..

"It made all these years close again," said Edson, wiping away tears.

Crews faced adversity flying the Dauntless over the Pacific Ocean. Some came back, the sea claimed others. Flying over open water didn't bother Edson although he knew of the perils each pilot and gunner faced.

"We had a job, and we did it," he said. "I was one of the lucky ones."

Lucky, said Edson, because the Pacific Ocean didn't swallow him. The memories kept returning.

"It was wonderful. It brought back a lot of memories," Edson said, after viewing the dive bomber. "It was quite an experience and how beautiful it is in the museum."

Within one year, Edson has been on two Honor Flight Nevada trips, the first coming in June when a number of World War II, Korean and Vietnam vets visited Washington, D.C. for four days. Edson 45 years in the air conditioning business in Sacramento. Edson travelled on the first Honor Flight Nevada trip in February 2020 to Oahu—and specifically Pearl Harbor.

Edson marveled at the exhibits at the Washington Navy Museum in June and was in awe of the memorials at Pearl Harbor including those of the USS Arizona and USS Missouri.

"It's been delightful," he said. "This has been a wonderful trip. I am very grateful."

Steven R. Ranson

THE TELEGRAM:
A 'BLUE CHRISTMAS'

Before Dec. 7, 1941, when a teenage boy in his Western Union uniform and cap stopped his bicycle at your house, you were going to receive good news. After Dec. 7, if you were a parent with one or more adult children or married with a spouse serving their country, your worst nightmare was to see a teen in a Western Union uniform walking toward your front door with a clipboard and a telegram.

During World War II when an adult child or a spouse was KIA (killed in action), DOW, (died of wounds) or MIA (missing in action), the immediate relative received a hand-delivered telegram from the Department of War. If nobody was home, Western Union returned to that address when there was someone home to sign and receive the telegram.

On Dec. 22, 1943, my grandparents' home was festively decorated for Christmas. There was the scent of pine and anticipation in their home. My grandparents, Pop and Martha, were working. Phyllis, my mother's 16-year-old sister, was playing girls' basketball in PE class. Nobody was home at 71 Fays Avenue that bitter cold December day in eastern Massachusetts which had a couple of inches of snow blanketing the lawn.

Pop was the first person to arrive home. He removed his key from his right front pocket to unlock and open the door. Today, something prompted him to look at the floor. There was an envelope face down that had been slid underneath the door. Pop picked up the envelope and read the name of the sender, "Noooooooooo!"

He tore the envelope.

"WASHN DC DEC 22 1943 MRS MARTHA DAIGLE, THE SECRETARY OF WAR DESIRES ME TO EXPRESS HIS DEEP REGRET THAT YOUR SON PRIVATE RICHARD E. DAIGLE WAS KILLED IN ACTION IN DEFENSE OF HIS COUNTRY ON THREE DECEMBER IN ITALY LETTER FOLLOWS= UL 10 THE ADJUTANT GENERAL ="

"I came home after Pop," Aunt Phil told me. "The telegram was crumbled into a ball on the entryway floor near the shredded envelope. The laundry room exited into the backyard from the kitchen. Pop had locked himself in the laundry room. All I could hear was his nonstop wailing. It was the first and only time I knew he cried."

During World War II, parents and spouses displayed a Blue Star in a front window for each person serving in our armed services. My grandparents had two sons in the Navy and one in the Army. On Christmas Day, they replaced the middle blue star with a Gold Star, which was for a family member who had made the ultimate sacrifice for his country.

Later on Christmas Day, mom's older sister, her husband, their daughter with mom and I were gathered at Grammie and Pop's home for a somber blue Christmas dinner. Four years later, Billy Hayes and Jay W. Johnson wrote a country tune, "Blue Christmas," and Elvis Presley included the song in his 1957 Christmas album.

During the war, mom and I lived with her parents several times. In 1954 we were gathered at their home for Thanksgiving, but Pop was sitting quietly in his chair. "Pop, why are you so quiet?" my mother asked.

"I was thinking of Richard," he replied.

I had a close relationship with Pop. In 36 years only one time did Pop speak to me about Uncle Richard.

"When Richard came home for Christmas in 1942, he was in fantastic shape. He was rock solid from his First Special Service Force training," Pop recollected.

It was the only time I remember seeing Pop's eyes sparkle.

Grammie joined the Gold Star Mothers, a support group that met for lunch on Thursdays. For three decades she broke bread with mothers who shared a similar experience—the loss of a son.

Dec. 3, 1943, was 17 days before his 22nd birthday. Richard was KIA on Monte la Difensa south of Casino, Italy. He had a picture of me in his helmet when he died. His personal effects were returned including the picture that I found in 2011 and had framed.

Twice, I've visited Italy and climb Monte la Difensa following in my uncle's footsteps. From the top of the inactive volcano, I visualized the two-hour firefight. By Aug. 14, 1945, there were 407,300 similar stories of loss during the War.

My wish for everyone who has a loved one currently serving our county, may you **never** open your front door to see two grim-faced officers in uniform with the news that you qualify to have a gold star in your front window.

Kenneth Beaton

TRAINING WINS WARS

"One of the best ways to grasp history is to study the places where it was made." Stephen Ambrose wrote "Undaunted Courage" about Lewis and Clark's 1803 to 1805 Louisiana Purchase expedition. For a number of summer vacations, the entire Ambrose family followed in the pioneer explorers' footsteps.

In the middle of May 2014, my wife and I heeded Ambrose's advice and drove to the Nevada-Utah border, site of Wendover Airfield, a historic WW II training base at the state line. The Western Pacific Railroad established Wendover in 1907, and the community had a water tower, a round house and a train depot with a population of 200.

In the late 1930s, the U.S. Army Air Corps wanted additional bombing ranges with excellent weather, the Western Pacific Railroad to transport men and supplies, almost 2 million acres for bombing and gunnery range, water from Pilot Peak in Nevada and isolation. Wendover was selected, and the first military contingent arrived on Aug. 12, 1941, less than four months before the bombing at Pearl Harbor, Hawaii.

The Nevada Highway Department designed and paved roads, constructed and paved three 8,100-foot runways in a triangle shape. Wendover Army Air Base was activated in March 1942 and trained more than 1,000 B-17 and B-24 Bomber crews. Beginning the following month, the base began bombardment training. Phase 1 trained the crew from a heavy bomber. Phase 2 involved the training of bomber crews flying as a squadron. Phase 3 trained four squadrons to fly as a bomber group. Wendover, consequently, was the first base where all three phases occurred at the same base.

The 306th Bomb Group became the first group to train at Wendover from April to August 1942 and was assigned to the Eighth Air Force in England.

In April 1943, Gen. Hap Arnold personally selected Col. Paul Tibbets to command the 509th Composite Group, a bomb group on steroids. Tibbets was the only person who knew the entire mission. He selected Wendover because it had the largest bombing range in the world, was relatively close to Los Alamos National Laboratory, which designed the nuclear weapons, and served as an ideal location to maintain secrecy and security.

In June 1943 then Maj. Gen. Leslie R. Groves, Jr., the director of the Manhattan Project, and Arnold, Chief of United States Army Air Forces (USAAF), selected Boeing's B-29 Superfortress with substantial modifications. "Silverplate" was the codename for the modification project. Eventually, Silverplate became the codename for the training and all aspects of the mission.

Created on Dec. 17, 1944, the object of the 509th was to be self-contained. The following units were assigned to the 509th: the 390th Air Services Group; the 603d Air Engineering; the 1027th Material Squadron; the 320th Troop Carrier Squadron; the 1395th Military Police Company; the 1st Ordnance Squadron; and the 1st Technical Detachment (a Manhattan Project unit).

At his first meeting with the men of the 509th, Tibbets informed the men who didn't "wash out" would be stuck with him.

"You're training for a very special mission overseas," Tibbets said. "This training could help end the war. Don't ask what the job is. That's a sure-fire way to be transferred out. Do exactly what you are told, when you are told, and you will get along fine. Never mention this base to anybody. This means your wives, girls, sisters, family."

Tibbets informed them that their training wouldn't be easy. He encouraged them to train hard and play hard. He closed his remarks by giving them a furlough and told them, "Enjoy yourselves."

Tibbets had one standard of evaluation: He expected his men to perform the same as him, and everyone worked as a team. The best men were selected and trained for their mission.

The flight crews practiced dropping a single 10,000-pound bomb painted orange, a "pumpkin." The pumpkins had two shapes, Fat Man and Little Boy, and the iron shell was filled with concrete to weigh 10,000 pounds. Each bombardier dropped 50 pumpkins to be qualified to drop an Atomic bomb.

Four hundred FBI agents assigned to the base maintained tight security. Everyone at Wendover was instructed not to talk to anybody about their activities. The members of the 509th could not talk to each other about their job activities. If a person talked, he was immediately transferred to a distant base. Some were transferred to remote bases in Aleutian Islands where time had stood still.

Two transport ships, the SS Cape Victory and the SS Emile Berliner with support personnel sailed on May 6, 1945, for Tinian, an island that's part of the Commonwealth of the Northern Mariana Island and 100 miles north of Guam. A C-54 flew an advance party of the air echelon to Tinian. To perfect the detonation device, the flight Test Section dropped 24 test bombs in June 1945 and 30 test bombs in July. Sixteen bombs dropped in June were the Fat Man and eight were Little Boy. In July 26 of the test bombs were Little Boy and four were Fat Man.

The 509th's training paid major dividends on the Aug. 6. The "Enola Gay" dropped Little Boy weighing 9,700 pounds on Hiroshima, Japan. Capt. William Parsons, assisted by Second Lt. Morris R. Jeppson, armed the bomb while flying to Hiroshima. Little Boy fell for 44.4 seconds when the time and barometric triggers detonated the bomb at 1,968 feet above Hiroshima. There was no bomb crater. The blast and fire caused maximum destruction and killed about 60,000 civilians.

On Aug. 9, Bockscar dropped a Fat Man on Nagasaki. Hiroshima and Nagasaki were selected because they were "saved from conventional bombing to measure the total damage from each A-bomb." The Emperor announced Japan's unconditional surrender on Aug. 15, and Japan's surrender cancelled the allies' invasion of Japan. Within days of Aug. 15, the military began processing millions of men and women with honorable discharges and closing bases.

The total USAAF personnel peaked in 1944 at 2,400,000, mostly boys in their late teens or early 20s. For many it was their first time away from home. Deep inside each boy's gut, he was scared. Would he return to see his family, friends and his gal? He was being trained to perform a job as part of a flight crew to defeat Germany and Japan.

A DIVERSION FROM TRAINING

Not every minute at Wendover was consumed with training. Juke Box Cave, with petroglyphs on the wall and located several miles from the base, was discovered in 1937. It fulfilled a couple of needs. The cave is 55° Fahrenheit year-round, cooler than the salt flats. The lights didn't break the blackout rules during the war. After the concrete dance floor was poured and finished, the red-blooded officers had a socially acceptable reason to hold a young woman close.

Imagine dancing to Les Brown with Doris Day singing, "My Dreams Are Getting Better All the Time." This was the perfect time for him to whisper in his dance partner's ear, "Holding you in my arms is the fulfillment of my dreams." Dancing to Jimmy Durante singing "Besame Mucho" (Kiss me much) was the perfect time for him to make his move to taste her lips.

Each Saturday, four army buses and drivers were secured; two buses drove roundtrip to Salt Lake City and two buses drove to Ely roundtrip with every seat occupied with single women or married women who had removed their wedding rings. Remember, all the men were away from home serving their country. These women had distant memories of being held in a man's arms, smelling his Old Spice aftershave. Some of the women from Ely could have been "working girls" from the Green Lantern expanding their financial opportunities. "Carpe diem," Latin for "seize the moment."

Juke Box Cafe had wooden stairs up to the entrance and another set of wooden stairs leading down into the cave. The women's outfits complement their best features. With a final compact mirror glance at her make-up and straightening the seams of her nylons, the gals were ready to enter the Juke Box Café.

As the first 78 rpm record (think of it as a 12-inch CD) played on a windup Victrola (the first record player); several confident officers began to walk across the dance floor to the women who smiled to attract male attention. Remember, wall-flowers never get asked to dance, and the Miss Manners book was tossed out the bus window. There were no rules when it came to gaining male attention. The adventure began with, "May I have this dance?"

The Juke Box Cave morphed into a mental vacation from the crews' training. Each adventurous officer remembered what it was like to be close to a woman who had spent hours changing her mind while trying to decide which outfit to wear along with perfume, jewelry and make-up to attract a potential "dreamboat" or to earn her "Mrs." title.

The training and social fun from the 1940s is not a distant memory. In July 1975 the base was officially listed on the National Register of Historical Places. The Historic Wendover Field has a group of local volunteers led by Jim Petersen. The Enola Gay's hanger is now in the process of being restored to become a museum, and the Historic Wendover Airfield Foundation continues to fundraise and preserve the base's buildings.

Kenneth Beaton

NIGHT MISSIONS OVER
THE PO RIVER

World War II pilot John "Jack" Hill of Minden, Nev., sat in a small air-conditioned room at the Northern Nevada Veterans Memorial Cemetery waiting for the 18th mission of the Missing in Nevada ceremony.

Soon, he and a crowd of almost 200 people sat sheltered in the pavilion from the searing heat of a hot July 2019 summer afternoon. The 15 veterans being honored included 14 men who served in the Army and the 15th in the U.S. Marine Corps, all but two seeing action during World War II.

"This should've been done a long time ago," said 96-year-old Jack Hill, who flew B-25s over northern Italy during the last six months of the war. "Now, they're making it right."

For nearly two years, the Nevada Veterans Coalition, along with assistance from a bank of volunteers, the Nevada Department of Veterans Service and other private and government agencies, have been identifying forgotten veterans' remains and then a providing a military service.

"I'm glad to be here to witness this," said Hill, who moved to Minden 43 years ago after retiring from private business and the U.S. Air Force Reserves as a major. He spent 22 years in the military, the final years as an aircraft mechanic at Travis Air Force Base midway between Sacramento and Oakland. Hill also had an interested in fire science and for a time he was a battalion chief with the Contra Costa Consolidated Fire Department in Walnut Creek.

The retired aviator knows too well the horrors of wars and losing fellow airmen to enemy antiaircraft fire. Many of those bodies were never recovered.

As a guest at the Missing in Nevada ceremony, Hill also learned of another veteran's service as told by NDVS Director Kat Miller. She recalled the story of Clifford Glen—or Sandy—Prophet, who enlisted in the Army as a private after World War II broke out and served for two years. Miller noted the size of the 5-foot, 4-inch, 118-pound Oklahoman.

"He may not have been the strongest recruit they had, but after years of grueling work in the dust bowl of Oklahoma, I just bet he was one of those lanky, rugged guys that knew how to handle himself," Miller said.

Away from the war, he and his wife Vivian moved to Napa, Calif., where they raised two boys, and after his retirement, Sandy and Vivian Prophet moved to Reno. Sandy died in 1981 followed by his wife in 1994 and his two boys, Ron in 2003 and Larry in 2013.

"But because Sandy does not have family with us here today does not mean he—or the rest of our veterans—were not loved," Miller said. "I found great pictures of Sandy and his family and from their genuine smiles and body language on that family, you could tell how very close their tough childhoods had brought them."

Hill, who said he was honored to be at the Missing in Nevada ceremony to receive the flag that was placed in front of the urns, grew up in Piedmont, Calif., and attended two years of junior college. After his high-school graduation, he became an airplane mechanic at McClellan Field northeast of Sacramento, but the events of Dec. 7, 1941—the bombing of Pearl Harbor—changed his direction in life.

"Then stuff hit the fan," he recalled of Dec. 7. "I was working on a P-40 when we were surprised on that day. We had two shifts, days and nights, but afterward, we had three shifts. The boss told me to take off and be back at 1 in the morning. I was put on the third shift."

When the U.S. Department of War opened another repair station at Elmendorf Field outside of Anchorage, Alaska, Hill and a cousin left sunny California for The Last Frontier. But after a year, Hall wanted to fly and enlisted to become a pilot in the Army Air Force, the predecessor to the U.S. Air Force. After passing a battery of tests to determine if he was more qualified as a pilot, bombardier or navigator, he entered the Army Air Force aviation training at Lemoore, Calif., and received the news he wanted to hear. He qualified as a pilot.

"My pilot training took me eight to nine months total, and I wound up in advanced training. I went to La Junta, Colo., and that was a great deal. They were flying B-25s. That was a big step.

The U.S. Army Air Force had taken over the airfield and expanded it to accommodate a large number of aircraft and training flights. For Hill, flying the B-25 medium bomber was his top priority although his training also alternated between single- and twin-engine aircraft. After two more stops for training, he found himself in Italy with the 47th Bomb Group, 85th Squadron during the last year of the war. Hill was flying nighttime bombing raids of the Po River in northern Italy, trying to disrupt the Germans from crossing the river and heading toward the Father land.

"It turned out OK, but it was difficult high flying trying to find these spots where the Germans were crossing," he added.

If nighttime flying presented its challenges, so did the harsh winter of 1944-1945. Hill said icing became a problem when planes took off from their field at Grosseto and flew over a high mountain range toward the river.

Steven R. Ranson and Molly Moser

RIDIN' THE RADIO WAVES

1919 was a great year. Everette Furr was born and took his place with the Greatest Generation. At 10 years, the stock market crashed and the Great Depression began. After surviving 12 years of the Great Depression, he joined the Navy in September 1941.

Furr graduated from boot camp in San Diego and became a radio operator. His orders were to board the USS Nitro (AE-2), an ammunition ship bound for Hawaii, and he was assigned to Kaneohe on the north side of Oahu.

Established in 1919, Kaneohe became a U.S. Navy sea plane base, the U.S. Marine Corps 3rd Regiment base and the Marine Aircraft Group 24th Combat Logistics Battalion 3 base with a 7,800-foot runway. Furr was assigned to a squadron of sea planes, PBYs. Kaneohe was attacked nine minutes before Pearl Harbor on Dec. 7, 1941.

The PBY derides its name from "Patrol Bomber Yacht," nicknamed after Catalina Island. The name was shortened to "Cat." The Navy equipped Cats with radar and painted them black for night operations, "Black Cats."

A Cat could remain in the air for 10 to 12 hours to locate and attack transport ships, rescue downed aircrews, locate and destroy enemy submarines and long-range patrols to locate enemy fleets. During air patrols, one of the enlisted crew prepared meals for the entire crew of ten, pilot, co-pilot, bow turret gunner, flight engineer, radio operator, navigator, two waist gunners and the vertical gunner.

Furr was at Kaneohe a short time before his squadron was assigned to New Caledonia. The officers flew their PBY to their new assignment. In May the enlisted

95

members of the crew traveled on USS Whorton (AP-7) with the USMC's 1ˢᵗ
Division before they invaded Guadalcanal on August 7, 1942.

Lady Luck protected Furr. His PBY never landed at New Caledonia. It was
either shot down or lost at sea. Within 10 days, he was assigned to a newly arrived
PBY. His new crew flew patrols every third day and sometimes every other day.

Two sea plane tenders, USS Curtiss (AV-4) and USS Tangier (AV-8), were
stationed at Espiritu Santo maintaining and resupplying their compliment of
PBYs including his. They were part of the Guadalcanal campaign. On Feb. 1, 1943,
there was an emergency scramble of two make-shift PBY crews. Both PBYs were
airborne in minutes. Furr was the radio operator for one of the PBYs. Brig. Gen.
Nathan Farragut Twining, the 13ᵗʰ Air Force Commander with 14 of his staff, had
ditched their plane in the vicinity of the New Hebrides Islands about 600 miles
from Espiritu Santo.

The Pacific had 20-foot unfriendly swells. Furr's pilot hit the crest of a swell
with such force knocking out rivets holding the plane's aluminum skin to the frame
below the PBY's water line. One of the enlisted men, Gene Musgrave, a former life
guard, swam in those swells to a life raft with seven men and towed it to their PBY.
Quickly, the survivors boarded the plane. The engines wouldn't start!

Furr carefully made his way to both engines to hard crank start them.
Immediately, the pilot turned the PBY into the wind. Everyone breathed a sigh of
relief as the damaged plane slowly lifted above the angry Pacific waters.

After gaining altitude, the two PBYs flew in formation. The other PBY
radioed Furr, "You took on a lot of water. Your plane is leaving a trail of water from
your damage sheet metal!"

Furr's pilot knew what he had to do at Espiritu Santo. Normally, he would
land at a slow speed, a safe distance from where the plane would taxi out of the water
up the cement ramp to unload his passengers and cargo. The pilot landed the PBY
at a higher than normal speed only seconds from the cement ramp with full wing
flaps. As the PBY's wheels entered the ramp, the pilot and copilot literally stood
on their brake pedals. There are no atheists in foxholes or a plane in flight with a
serious problem.

Furr used his leave to fly to the U.S. west coast. He met and married Jeanette
in October 1943. He returned from his honeymoon to spend 1944-1945 as the
radio operator on a four engine PBY2, Coronado, assigned to Saipan, one of the
Northern Mariana Islands. Unfortunately, his paperwork was misplaced. He was

never promoted to 1ˢᵗ Class Radio Operator. At Mayport Base near Jacksonville, Fla., he was discharged as ARM2 in September 1945.

After several jobs, Furr began calibrating instruments at Barton Instrument earning $1.25 an hour. Barton Instrument was purchased by ITT a couple of years later. He retired in 1981 from ITT Barton after 27 years. He and Jeanette had three sons, and they were married for 59 years when she died in 2002. Furr died on Jan. 14, 2020, six weeks short of celebrating his 101st birthday.

Kenneth Beaton

ONCE A MARINE, ALWAYS A MARINE

The year 1942 passed in a flash for Gene Ratner. The 18-year-old received his high school diploma in January five months early. Not wanting to be drafted, he enlisted in the Marines. Who knew in 11 months he would spend his first Christmas away from his parents and friends half-way around the world on a tropical island battleground?

The Minneapolis, Minn., native began a snowy train ride to warm and sunny southern California—Camp Pendleton in San Diego. After 13 weeks of weakness leaving his body, Ratner never witnessed any evidence that his Drill Instructor (DI) had one sweat gland. The recruits never knew their DIs had six shirts starched and perfectly ironed each morning. As soon as one shirt absorbed some sweat ... grab the next starched shirt. The recruits didn't have to remember anything. Their DI told them when to write home, sleep and their next assigned task.

Being converted to the Marine way, the recruits marched for their graduation ceremony. Their adventure continued when they boarded an attack transport to a rock in the South Pacific, New Zealand. At first glance the New Zealand women looked like Americans. All the New Zealand males were serving in the British Army. Those gals were anxious for male attention, but New Zealand women didn't shave their arm pits or legs. Only "working gals" were clean shaven.

Immediately, the 2nd Marine Division began advanced infantry training. Everything the 1st Marine Division learned from fighting the Imperial Japanese Army (IJA) on Guadalcanal was drilled into the "Follow Me" division. Ratner belonged to Company E, 2nd Battalion, Sixth Regiment Second Marine Division. The Second Marines landed on Guadalcanal on Nov. 2, 1942, to relieve the First Marines.

Ratner's division eliminated pockets of IJA troops by helping them die for their Emperor. Having cleared the island, the Second Marine boarded transports on Feb. 8, 1943. After refitting and training their next objective was an atoll in the Gilbert Islands, Tarawa, defended by 4,690 Japanese and Koreans. Second Battalion was assigned to land on Red Beach 1, the west end of the landings.

Imagine traveling in a LVT-1, Land Vehicle Tracked, "Alligator" slowly heading to shore in the first wave to Red Beach-1. Each Marine had the same questions. "Am I going to make it out of here alive? Who will die on the beach today? I can't disappoint my buddies."

The Alligators were heading to their beach. Suddenly, machine gun rounds began piercing through the lightly armored vehicles. The Marines landed at 9:10 a.m. on Nov. 20, 1943, with nonstop combat continuing for 76 hours. By Nov. 23, only one Japanese officer and 17 enlisted men had surrendered. To avoid being captured, some IJA committed suicide thus saving the Marines ammo.

Most of the Second Marines began evacuating Tarawa on Nov. 24; however, Ratner's 2nd Battalion, Sixth Regiment was given the order to clear the island of Japanese. They provided security while the Seabees constructed an airfield and buried 978 Marines who were wither killed in action or died from their wounds.

The Second Marines spent the next six months in Hawaii refitting and training for their next objective, Saipan, one of the Marianna Islands. While the European Theater had about six D-Days, June 6, 1944, the most publicized, the Pacific Theater had 119 D-Days. D-Day for Saipan was June 15, 1944. Nine days into the battle Ratner was severely wounded on June 24t. A Japanese hollow point bullet entered his right arm above his elbow, fractured three ribs, punctured his right lung and did a 90-degree turn to exit his back. The most horrible sight the Marines witnessed was Japanese civilians tossing their children off the cliffs. Then the parents jumped to the rocks below. The Marines pleaded with the civilians not to jump, but the Japanese government had brainwashed the civilians.

"The American soldiers will rape and kill you. Choose an honorable death, jump off the cliffs," the Japanese Imperial Army declared.

On Sept. 6, 1990, the 41st reunion of the Second Marine Division gathered at the Red Lion. Fourteen men of Easy Company, 2nd Battalion, 6th Regiment assembled, and Ratner recorded and transcribed their conversation. The following is part of his conversation.

"The loud crack of a rifle shot sounded about three feet from my left ear. Spinning around, I saw Bob Thatcher standing over the ditch, his rifle pointed down at the Jap, who was now in a totally different position than when I first observed him. Bob's arrival was pure luck on my part. His alertness undoubtedly saved my life. Eight days later my luck ran out. An enemy bullet pierced my right lung, bringing my time in E Company to an abrupt end."

"After five months in the hospital, with a severely damaged right lug, I was declared physically unfit for military service, and discharged with a 40% disability on Nov. 24, 1944. I returned to Minneapolis where I entered the University of Minnesota for a period of two years. After a variety of jobs, I moved to California where I became employed by Heublein Inc. After 25 years I retired June 1, 1985."

Ratner died in the Veterans Affairs Hospital in Palo Alto, Calif., on Aug. 8, 2018.

Kenneth Beaton

ARMY SHIP 'NEVADA' SINKS

Just recently I learned about the wartime record of another WW II ship that bore the name "Nevada." It was the U.S. Army Transport Nevada, a 221-foot, 1,685-ton cargo ship built in 1915 (a year after the battleship USS Nevada was launched) that served two years during the war delivering tanks, trucks and other heavy military equipment from the U.S, to Canada, Greenland and Great Britain.

The dramatic story of the USAT Nevada's destiny is known by only a handful of military historians. On Dec. 15, 1943, the USAT Nevada was to meet its tragic fate in the Arctic waters of the North Atlantic about 200 miles south of Greenland.

According to records received from the Historical Section of the U.S. Coast Guard in Washington, D.C., the USAT Nevada, while en route from St. John's, Newfoundland, to Narsarssuak, Greenland, became separated from other cargo ships in Convoy 5G-36 during a heavy gale. As raging 20-foot high seas and 60-mile-per-hour winds battered the ship and snow squalls cut visibility to near zero, the Nevada's lower compartments and holds flooded and the its pumps could not keep up with the inflow of water.

Capt. George P. Turiga, the Nevada's commanding officer, realized his ship was in dire straits and radioed an urgent "Mayday" call for help, the seafarers' traditional distress call that signals a ship is in danger of sinking.

The 165-foot Coast Guard cutter Comanche was the closest ship to the Nevada, and it took seven hours to reach the Nevada, which by now was wallowing at its bow with a 30-degree list.

When the Comanche came close to the Nevada, the cutter's skipper, Lt. Langford Anderson, ordered its floodlights be turned on, and they showed that the Nevada's lifeboat davits were empty and the vessel appeared to be abandoned. After circling the Nevada twice without finding any signs of life, the Comanche discovered two red flares in the distance and raced to them to find a lifeboat bobbing in the waves with 32 men aboard, according to the official Coast Guard records in my possession.

The men in the lifeboat "could be heard praying, singing and shouting 'thank God'" as the Comanche approached to pick them up. But the lifeboat "one minute lay in a trough in the sea far below the Comanche's rail and the next minute was lifted far above the Comanche's deck on the crest of a huge comer," according to a Coast Guard after-action report dated July 15, 1945 and titled "History of the Greenland Patrol."

After many failed attempts to bring the lifeboat alongside the Comanche, its crew finally succeeded in attaching a line from the cutter to the lifeboat, hauled it to the ship's side and pulled the survivors aboard. Three men who attempted to jump from the lifeboat to the Comanche fell into the sea and were lost. The Comanche also located a life raft with a half-dozen survivors, and they also were brought aboard.

Several Comanche crewmen, attired in rubber suits, jumped into the water and rescued five others who had fallen from the raft into the surging waters. The survivors also included the ship's mascot, a dog named "Grondal," reported Comanche captain Anderson in a Jan, 1, 1944, dispatch to Coast Guard headquarters marked "Confidential."

The USAT Nevada's other lifeboats and rafts were never found despite widespread searches by the Comanche and three other cutters, the Storis, Modoc and Tampa, and the disaster's final toll was 31 missing and 26 rescued. Among the missing was Capt. Turiga, the Nevada's skipper.

As for the fate of the Nevada, which, miraculously, was still afloat three days after its foundering: The captains of the four Coast Guard cutters determined that the 28-year-old freighter was too damaged to be towed to a port and salvaged. As they were making plans to sink the ship by gunfire in order to prevent it from becoming a danger to navigation, the relentless storm had the last word.

On Dec. 18, 1943, the USAT Nevada, carrying 950 tons of military cargo, sank by its bow. The 26 survivors and mascot Grondal were transported by the Comanche to Narsarssuak, Greenland, where they were delivered after a five-day voyage to the USAT Fairfax, which was waiting for them at the pier.

As for a footnote relating to the cutter Comanche:

Ten months before it rescued crew members of the USAT Nevada, the Comanche rescued passengers and crew who had been aboard the 368-foot Army Transport Dorchester that had been torpedoed and sunk by German submarine U-223 off the coast of Newfoundland.

Only 230 of the 904 aboard the Dorchester were rescued. Among those lost were four U.S. Army chaplains: Two Protestant ministers, a Roman Catholic priest and a Jewish rabbi who had given their life vests to passengers jumping into the sea as the Dorchester was sinking.

David C. Henley

WHAT CAN THE COLOR BROWN DO TO YOU?

Since all her friends had enlisted by June 1943, Phyllis Lorraine Anker enlisted in the Women Army Corps on Sept. 20, 1943, but after WAC boot camp, she taught WACs to type. Her next assignment was the newly constructed Pentagon in Washington, D.C.

To be a successful military leader, accurate and complete information is vital to make informed decisions. Every eight hours, seven days a week, Joint Chief of Staff General George C. Marshall received a complete briefing of every American military operation around the world. Anker handled top secret folders such as "Operation Overlord, For Eyes Only," the plans for the invasion of Normandy, D-Day.

Anker had overcome many challenges in her 98 years. Weighing only 4 pounds on March 7, 1919, she wasn't expected to live. Fortunately, her family doctor was wrong. Graduating as an honor student from Pershing County High School (Lovelock, Nev.) in 1937, she became a freshman at University of Nevada. She earned money for her tuition by booking piano gigs, tutoring and having summer jobs. In fact, she tutored Marion Motley, the only University of Nevada football player and the second black to be inducted into the Pro Football Hall of Fame in Canton, Ohio.

She graduated from Nevada in 1941 and taught business subjects at Eureka County High School in 1941-1942 and Yerington High School in1942-1943.

Being fluent in French, Phyllis accompanied Marshall to the June 13, 1944, Roosevelt/Churchill Conference in Quebec. A week after D-Day, Eleanor Roosevelt and Clementine Churchill sponsored a tea for the U.S. and Canadian WACs attending the conference. A Canadian WAC was known as a CWAC, pronounced "quack" by the Canadians. Anker had a memorable conversation with both hostesses.

In Marshall's office, one of her jobs was to greet each officer who wanted to see the general. She would ask the officer for a shoulder patch, and then later she would crochet 4 ½-inch x 4 ½-inch white wool squares and sew the shoulder patch to a square. When she had completed three squares, she mailed them to her mother in Lovelock. (During the war, service personnel mailed letters for free).

Ankers' Aunt Hannah was a seamstress and suggested an afghan for the patches. Phyllis with Aunt Hannah's guidance crocheted the squares together with black wool to create a 41 ½" x 64 ½" afghan, The Pentagon Patches.

Each of the 96 patches represents an Army, Corps, Division, Service Corps, Theatre of Operations, USAAF, Parachute Infantry Regiment, Location of Headquarters, Defense Command or Veterans Administration and the 16 million men and women from the "Greatest Generation."

Staff Sgt. Anker was discharged on Feb. 18, 1946, returned to Lovelock, had a whirlwind romance, and married Ted Bendure in May of that year. They had three children—Teddy, Fred and Sue. Anker taught business subjects at Carson High School and retired in 1983 after teaching in Nevada for almost 40 years.

The native Nevadan's family always gathered to celebrate birthdays and holidays, and she treasured her life experiences and those special moments with her family. She died on Aug. 11, 2017.

Kenneth Beaton

ONE OF 16 MILLION STORIES

Within days of the attack on Pearl Harbor, President Franklin Roosevelt began pressuring his military advisors to quickly strike against Japan. Several creative naval officers in Washington proposed launching 16 U.S. Army Air Force B-25B "Mitchell" medium bombers from an aircraft carrier 450 miles east of Japan. They presented their idea to Lt. Col. James Doolittle, who accepted their plan and requested to lead the mission.

At least 10 personnel support each pilot. Enter Jack Wolfe working at North American Aviation's B-25 assembly line. In late January 1942, a supervisor informed an aircraft engine mechanic and Wolfe, "I have a Top-Secret job for you two. Install these three tanks and not a word to anyone!"

Wolfe installed two 55-gallon fuel tanks in 24 B-25. Next, he connected a fuel line to the tanks, a time-consuming process. While Jack was working on the two 55-gallon tanks, several men were installing a 550-gallon fuel tank in the bomb bay between the two bomb racks. The three tanks would extend the plane's range from 1,000 miles to 2,500.

Two B-25s were lifted by a crane onto the flight deck of the Navy's newest carrier, USS Hornet, CV-8. The planes successfully launched from the Hornet off Virginia's coast. Twenty-five B-25 crews from the 17th Bomb Group (medium) were assigned to Eglin Field in Florida's panhandle. They practiced taking off in less than 500 feet.

The Hornet arrived at Naval Air Station Alameda in San Francisco Bay on March 31, 1942. The next day 16 B-25s were loaded and secured on the flight deck of the Hornet. Under a veil of secrecy, the Hornet and escort ships departed on April 2. Two weeks later, 16 B-25s were launched, and the Doolittle raiders bombed Tokyo and other cities on the island of Honshu to surprise the Japanese. Words cannot describe the boost in every American's morale.

Born April 10, 1918, Wolfe enlisted in the United States Army on Jan. 12, 1937, to experience his first boot camp. He was assigned to a 75-mm artillery unit at Schofield Barracks on Oahu. His commanding officer wanted a championship boxing team, and as a welterweight boxer, Wolfe won his share of fights. Honorably discharged from the Army in 1939, he returned to the Los Angeles area eventually working at North American to work with the aircraft/engine mechanic assembling B-25 medium bombers.

After the top secret project was finished, so was his job at North American. Wolfe received six weeks of intense, government-paid lathe and drill press training at National Supply in Torrance, Calif. Douglas Aircraft hired him to build the SBD Dauntless dive bomber for the Navy's carriers. The Navy wanted the dive bombers built as soon as possible.

Having served in the Army, Wolfe was exempt from being drafted in 1942. Anxious to serve again, he joined the United States Coast Guard in 1943 and attended his second boot camp. After several months as a Coastie, Wolfe was given a choice: Be a coxswain on a LCVP landing Marines on Tarawa, a rock occupied by thousands of Japanese in the Pacific. Wolfe's commanding officer recommended he select discharge.

After being honorably discharged, Wolfe sold his watch to ride with a woman driving her car from Houston to Los Angeles. In L.A. he decided to join the Navy and was told he had to wait until June 1944. At the local Selective Service Office, he saw a Navy chief.

The chief asked, "Why do you want to join the Navy?"

"I like the salt," Wolfe responded.

He was ordered to his third boot camp in Farragut, Idaho. After nine weeks, he traveled by train to Treasure Island in San Francisco Bay and hitched a ride on the USS Saratoga, CV-3, to Pearl Harbor. He was assigned to the "splinter Navy," a wooden mine sweeper, YMS-386 (Yard Mine Sweeper).

When Japan surrendered on Aug. 15, 1945, YMS-386 was in an Okinawa harbor. Immediately, YMS-386 cleared mines from the Japanese harbors of Kobe, Nagoya and Yokohama. Minesweepers have an expression, "Where the fleet goes, we've been."

Gunners Mate 1st Class Clifford M. Medley served on YMS-386 from June 1945 to December 1945. In his journal he wrote about YMS-386 sailing on 10/4/1945 from Buckner Bay, Okinawa, around the south of Okinawa to the Sea of China to Unton Ko on northern Okinawa. Wolfe was at the helm heading into Typhoon Louise's mountainous waves. YMS-386 and three other ships survived Louise; nine ships were lost at sea, no survivors.

On July 13, 1947, Jack and Flora Estelle Mote drove to Yuma, Ariz., and exchanged their wedding vows. Flora gave birth to their only child, Julie, in 1953. Prior to her birth, Wolfe was called up from the Naval Reserve in 1950. He served during the Korean War on an APA, Attack Transport, as a landing craft coxswain. Flora died in 2014, but Wolfe lived with Julie and her husband, Jim, who has since died

Kenneth Beaton

REPAYING THE DEBT

After giving three years of their life to their country, their country is repaying the debt more than 60 years later.

World War II veterans John Gerard and Paul Harr left in September 2014 for Washington D.C., as part of Honor Flight Nevada. Gerard served in the U.S. Maritime Service from 1943-46 as fireman and water tender aboard the William B. Wilson.

"When I was 17, I wanted to join the Navy, but I had a ruptured ear drum and couldn't," the Gardnerville Ranchos resident said. "When I was told by the Navy I was ineligible, I cried because I thought my country didn't want me."

Instead, Gerard, who died in 2015 at the age of 89, joined the Maritime Service and attended boot camp in Sheepshead Bay, N.Y.

The USMS was established in 1938 under the provisions of the Merchant Marine Act of 1936. The mission of the organization was to train people to become officers and crew members on United States merchant ships. Since the war, the service has since been largely dissolved or absorbed into other federal departments. Its commissioned officers continue to function as administrators and instructors at the U.S. Merchant Marine Academy and the several maritime academies.

"It was something that you did," Gerard said of his service. "Nobody beat you over the head. You knew what happened in Pearl Harbor. It's what you had to do, and we did it."

Gerard served in Europe and the Mediterranean and Indian oceans.

"We took 7,500 tons of high explosives to Anzio beachhead in Italy," he said. "On the way there we hit an underwater mine, but it didn't go off. Thank God, or I wouldn't be here."

The battle at Anzio in 1944 was one of the longest protracted battles of the war with more than 25,000 battle casualties (killed, wounded, missing or taken prisoner) on each side of the conflict.

Following the war, Gerard married and had children—three sons and a daughter. His wife, Barbara, died in 2008 of leukemia.

For Harr, traveling to Washington, D.C., was a birthday present to himself.

"The day we leave for Washington, I'll be 98 and one day," he said. "If the president knows John and I are going to be there I'm sure he'll come see us."

Harr, served in the U.S. Navy from 1944-47 aboard the USS Baxter.

"I'm very proud of the fact I served," Harr said. "I had a 70,000-mile cruise in the beautiful South Pacific."

The Gardnerville resident joined the Navy when he was 28 years old, even though he worked in a defense plant and had a deferment.

"I didn't want a deferment, so I signed up for the Navy," he said. "I had a son and a daughter, and I knew that when they grew up they'd ask what I did during the war, so I felt that I should be in."

Harr worked as a radarman in the Pacific.

"Radar was a wonderful thing. We could pick up anything that was out there," he said. "We got to the point where we could tell what kind of ship was out there by the pips and how they would come in."

Three weeks after Japanese forces surrendered in Tokyo, Harr visited the city.

"The whole downtown Tokyo was leveled," he said, "but the government buildings and palaces didn't have a hit on them."

After the war, Harr opened doughnut shops in California and Las Vegas before getting his broker's license from University of Nevada, Las Vegas.

Harr died in 2019 at the age of 102 years old.

Caryn Haller

MAPS TO THE PAST

Visiting the Vietnam Wall for Randall (Randy) Wolter gave him another opportunity to pay respects to his brother, who was killed in a war 9,000 miles from home.

Wolter accompanied his 93-year-old father Roy, a World War II veteran who served in the Army Air Force, on an Honor Flight Nevada trip to Washington, D.C. in June 2019 over the D-day weekend.

"My brother never came back," Randy said, tears welling in his eyes.

Wolter, who now lives in Vallejo, said he and his father also reflected on the holocaust museum and on the second world war with a stop at the World War II memorial that was dedicated to the military men and women who fought overseas or served in the United States and well as to the millions of civilians.

"We were looking at the plaques and timeframes when things were occurring. Dad was in high school at the time," Randy pointed out.

Yet, it was the Navy Museum where Randy walked away with a better appreciation of what his father encountered in the Pacific Theater from 1943-1945.

"I started relating to and identifying with him," he said, as he meticulously perused the exhibits with his father nearby.

A map of the South Pacific islands and the significance of specific battles piqued Roy Wolter's curiosity. There he saw the map of the Pacific extending from the Philippines to smaller islands eastward. Randy said the maps touched his father—who enlisted when he was 17 years old—barely out of high school.

"Originally, when I enlisted, I wanted to be a pilot," Roy Wolter said, but noted a small stutter washed him out from pilot training. "They put me in radar, and at that time it was top secret."

The Navy assigned the Hull, Iowa, native to Palau, an archipelago of more than 500 islands 900 miles southeast of the Philippines. Bombers staged their missions from Palua to make bombing runs on the Philippines, trying to wrestle the country away from Japanese control.

"We were trying to take back the Philippines for (Gen. Douglas) MacArthur. Remember what he said? We shall return," Wolter said.

The bombers flying out of Palua also dropped bombs on other Japanese strongholds, and after U.S. soldiers and Marines secured Okinawa, the Army Air Force began flying missions including bombing runs on southern Japan. Wolter, though, quickly pointed out that the Japanese also bombed the Americans.

Wolter returned stateside after the war, wanting to become a doctor, but he didn't have the money to follow his dream. Determined but not discouraged, Wolter began his college career with baby steps.

"I went to college in Sioux Falls (South Dakota) by train," Wolter recollected, explaining his first few years of schooling. "Then I had a friend who had a car, and we roomed together at the University of Iowa and came home on holidays."

Wolter eventually earned a degree in psychology, and with the sheepskin in hand, he moved to California where he earned a master's degree in psychology from Sacramento State University and then a doctorate in the same subject. Wolter established a private practice in Sacramento, but he also worked for the county's probation department. When he retired from the county service, Wolter still maintained his private practice.

Steven R. Ranson

FEELING OF FEAR

As an 18-year-old gunner, Petty Officer First Class Robert Kizer never regretted enlisting in the Navy during World War II. The California teenager said he felt fear every time he climbed into a TBM torpedo bomber, lifting off from an aircraft carrier in search of the enemy.

Known as one of the heaviest single-engine aircraft during World War II, the General Motors-built TBM Avenger flew a crew of three: a pilot, turret gunner and a radioman/bombardier/ventral gunner. In the bomb bay the Avenger carried one large torpedo or a single 2,000-pound bomb. Sometimes, crews would swap out one large bomb for four 500-pounders.

A Los Angeles native, Kizer saw action in the South Pacific during the final two years of the war. His squadron, which was attached to the aircraft carrier USS Admiralty Islands, called Pearl Harbor home. Kizer served for two years on board the aircraft carrier before he was discharged at the end of the war at Pearl Harbor.

"It was a long time ago," Kizer said, trying to remember the specific years he served. "It's something you wipe out of your mind."

Kizer's friend and companion Dorothy "Dot" Davison, also served in the Navy but after the war. She looked at Kizer with loving eyes before he retold his years in the South Pacific.

"We truly get along well. We love each other," she said.

Built in 1943, the USS Admiralty Islands sailed from Puget Sound, Wash., and to San Diego for additional training and then headed toward Pearl Harbor for its first assignment. For the next five months, the ship transported aircraft and personnel mostly to and from New Guinea. After arriving at Pearl Harbor on Dec. 24, the ship sailed for Guam the day after Christmas and arrived in the western

Pacific two weeks later. The Admiralty Islands became involved in support carrier operations to seize Iwo Jima on Feb. 2, 1945, leaving with Task Force Group 50.8 in mid-February.

"It was a good ship, great relations among the crew," Kizer said.

The aircraft carrier was a U.S. Navy Casablanca-class escort aircraft carrier, named after the Admiralty Islands group north of New Guinea. Kizer also remembers the proficiency of the ship's officer, Capt. M. E. A. Gouin, and how the crew respected their skipper, whom Kizer called a true Navy man.

Unlike other aircraft carriers directly involved with operations directly fighting the Japanese, Kizer said the squadron saw limited action against the enemy. When the TBM was catapulted off the deck, Kizer sat in the rear of the three-man cockpit facing the opposite direction, responsible for firing a twin .30-caliber machine gun.

"We saw some but not much action," Kizer recounted. "We tangled up in a couple of skirmishes, but we did some damage to the Japanese fleet."

Although not too many crews endured injuries, Kizer was accidentally shot with a .30 caliber shell between his left shin and ankle.

More than 70 years after flying in the TBM, Kizer said he remembers how nervous he was when climbing into his seat. He never had any doubt about serving, and said he never had any doubt about enlisting to protect his country.

"Eighteen years old, I was just a punk," Kizer said with a broad grin and chuckle. "I went into the Navy when I was 16 … lied about my age."

In addition to his military career, Kizer worked in Hollywood by following his father's footsteps as a grip for a movie studio. A grip provides assistance to the camera craw whenever the camera is mounted on a dolly, crane or top of a ladder.

"I guess I was too young to know better," Kizer said of his discharge and return to Southern California.

Kizer assisted the cameraman at 20th Century Fox and was able to meet many of the stars of the day including Roy Rogers and his wife Dale Evans, John Wayne and Randolph Scott.

"I met John Wayne several times. He was a nice guy and very pleasant. He wasn't puffed up with self-importance," Kizer said. "Randolph Scott was also very nice, and he let me ride his horse."

Kizer, a member of the "Greatest Generation," died in 2020.

Steven R. Ranson

ISLAND HOPPING

As a young warrior in the 4th Marine Division, 98-year-old Bayne Stevens of Gardnerville fought in three of the bloodiest battles of World War II in the late 1944 and 1945—Saipan, Tinium and Iwo Jima—each battle a test of fortitude and heroism for the ground troops from both the Marines and U.S. Army and air cover from Navy and Army aircraft.

One of the islands, though, became invaluable during the final days of World War II when the U.S. captured Tinian and then began expanding the airfields. North Field became the departure point of the 509th Composite Group with its B-29 bombers Enola Gay and Bockscar that trained at the Wendover Army Air Base in 1944 and 1945. Each B-29 dropped an atomic bomb on Hiroshima and Nagasaki respectively, thus causing the Japanese to surrender days later.

Intense fighting occurred on Iwo Jima from Feb. 19-March 26, 1945, when soldiers and Marines captured the island in what many historians call one of the worst battles in the Pacific. More than 26,000 Marines and sailors were injured, and 6,800 died out of a ground invasion force of 70,000 men. Stevens job was to clear out the bombs, grenades and booby traps, which became the young Marine's specialty. When a grader was plowing the runaway on one of the captured islands, Stevens sat on the blade watching for any unexploded bombs

"He could see what mines would pop up," his friend Ted Henson added.

Stevens had an opportunity to remember Iwo Jima after a visit to Oahu. Veterans who served during World War II and the Korean War knew their visit to Marine Corps Base Hawaii would become solemn once they finished lunch and walked to several memorials.

Accompanied by active-duty Marines assigned to the base at Kaneohe Bay, the Honor Flight Nevada veterans walked first to a memorial honoring the sailors who died on Dec. 7, 1941, when the installation was a naval air station.

Many of the veterans also visited a memorial similar to one in Washington, D.C. The replica—albeit a slight difference than the one in the nation's capital—shows Marines raising the flag on Iwo Jima's Mount Suribachi. Thirty days later, though, the American forces successfully captured the western Pacific island that provided three airfields for the United States to launch air strikes against Japan.

For the seven Marines and one merchant mariner, the inscriptions retold the heroics of three Marine divisions battling the Imperial Army from Feb. 19, 1945, to March 26.

As he sat in his wheelchair with his guardian kneeling by his side at the Iwo Jima Memorial, Stevens called his fellow Marines heroes for raising the flag and also defeating the Japanese.

The island hopping and fierce fighting have stayed with Stevens for more than 70 years, but an Honor Flight Nevada journey to Washington, D.C., in 2018 rekindled deep memories after he saw a photograph at the Navy Museum, one of the stops for a group of 28 Northern Nevada veterans who visited the nation's monuments and memorials. Their four days in Washington, D.C. served as a lead-in into the Independence Day celebrations.

Behind Stevens on a wall hung a photograph of the Casablanca-class escort carrier Attu with Marines spelling out 4 Mar Div, which was Stevens' unit. That image from 1945 brought tears to the dedicated veteran.

"I was on that," Stevens said before leaving the Reno-Tahoe International Airport. "The war had just ended, and I was back on my way to the states. It was so neat. It was an aircraft carrier and a beautiful picture of us sailing toward the port of San Diego."

The Attu arrived in San Diego on Oct. 12, 1945, six weeks after the formal signing to end World War II in the Pacific theater, with 950 veterans including Stevens lined up on the flight deck.

After the war, Stevens met Frances Green, who was born in Roaring Springs, Texas, and as a young woman, she left the Longhorn State and headed west to Los Angeles in the early 1940s because finding work was more plentiful. She met Stevens, who was shipping off to war in the Pacific, and they waited to marry after Stevens returned home. They married in Cambria Township, Mich., in December 1945.

The Stevens later moved to the San Fernando Valley north of Los Angeles with their young family. They relocated to Garnerville to spend their retirement years. Frances died in 2018, and Bayne followed her in 2020.

Steven R. Ranson

A 9-YEAR-OLD'S STORY

In November 2016 the Nevada Appeal requested any Pearl Harbor survivors to contact the newspaper to publish a 75th anniversary edition of the attack. Ruth Werts responded.

She began to tell me her civilian experience as a 9-year old, the oldest with two younger brothers and two younger sisters living with their parents in Navy dependent housing. Her dad was an enlisted sailor.

Werts' second-story bedroom window looked across Pearl Harbor at the USS Arizona docked at Ford Island. She witnessed a fire ball engulf the ship with the bow lifting out of the water. The shock wave followed immediately.

Suddenly, a low flying fighter with a red "meatball" painted on the fuselage and wings flew close enough for her to notice the pilot's goggles, moustache and a grin. Another Japanese fighter clipped the top of a neighbor's chimney.

Military and civilian medical staff reported to their hospitals. Casualties were rushed to be triaged outside the hospitals. Several thousand volunteers rolled up their sleeves and donated blood. Of the 2,403 people who died on Dec. 7, 1941, the Navy lost 2,008, the Army 218, the Marines 109 and 68 civilians. More than half of the Navy and the Marine Corps losses are entombed in the battleship Arizona.

During the attack, a school bus stopped at their house to take the Hennessey family to a safer location. Her family noticed the bus driver looked Japanese. They were reluctant to board the bus, but after a heated verbal exchange, they boarded.

One of Werts' older brothers was traumatized from the explosions. He never recovered. Ruth received her first bicycle on her ninth birthday, two days after the Pearl Harbor attack, but it was stolen a couple of days later. Food was scarce, causing

Mrs. Hennessey and her five children shared one can of beans at meal time. All military spouses and dependents were evacuated from Hawaii on Christmas Day and sailed on a military transport "tub" eating stale bread and moldy oranges. With 30-foot waves, eating was not a consideration for seasick passengers.

When their transport arrived in San Francisco, there was no available housing. After three days living on a beach, a DUKW (pronounced duck) gave them a ride to the YMCA. After a couple of months, the family was able to occupy a house and slowly, food became available.

Many probably never thought about Hawaii's civilians and their suffering during and after Dec. 7.

Kenneth Beaton

IN SERVICE TO
THEIR COUNTRY

Robert Whalen of Gardnerville, Nev., served in the U.S. Army Air Corps Thirteenth Air Force in New Guinea and the Philippines during the latter stage of the war. As a traveler on a November 2017 Honor Flight Nevada to Washington, D.C., he assisted with the placing of a wreath honoring Scottish-American Military Society. Once the official party carried the wreath to its designated place, Whalen looked forward and saluted.

Likewise, another vet on the trip, Kenneth York of Reno, assisted with the placing of the American Veterans wreath.

Whalen spent most of his military career in the back of a B-25 bomber that carried a crew of five to six aviators, eight 250-pounds bombs and a torpedo under the fuselage. Established in 1942 on New Caledonia, the 13 AF engaged in wartime operations over a wide expanse of the Pacific Theater to include attacking enemy forces holed up on many small, remote islands in addition to waging campaign over the Philippines.

"I flew on 43 missions as a radio operator and gunner," said Whalen, describing his military service aboard an aircraft known for both its low-altitude strafing capabilities and bombing runs to sink enemy ships. "It was the same type of plane Doolittle used in its run over Japan, a two-engine bomber. I thought I was lucky to get out of it. We lost 11 men in three years."

In 1942, Gen. James Harold "Jimmy" Doolittle led a bombing raid over Tokyo, the first American aerial attack on the Japanese mainland. Because of the complexity and distance of the mission, which required the planes to carry additional fuel, the 16 B-25Bs Mitchell bombers assigned to the mission dropped their bombs on and near Tokyo and then, lacking fuel to return to their aircraft carrier, flew toward China and the Soviet Union where they crash landed. Only one B-25 landed intact, and that was in Siberia.

As a radioman and gunner, Whalen, who was born in South Dakota, occupied a perch on the right side of the aircraft in the aft between the main and tail wings and near a bomb bay. Whalen manned a M-2 Browning .50 caliber heavy machine gun.

Kenneth York graduated from Reno High School in 1944 and joined the Navy. At his high-school graduation, he said many graduates who left early for boot camp returned to receive their diplomas while in uniform.

Except for the war years, the teenage Reno sailor attended the University of Nevada, Reno and was a prominent businessman for more than 50 years with Mt. Rose Sporting Goods that began downtown on Virginia Street and eventually moved to Park Lane.

"I spent a lot of time in the Philippines and then to Okinawa," said the 91-year-old York after the ceremony. "I assumed Okinawa was the jumping off point to invade the mainland."

Those plans included a worst-case scenario whereby hundreds of thousands of military personnel from Allied forces would've lost their lives. York said he was grateful those plans never materialized because the United States dropped a pair of atomic bombs on two major Japanese cities, Emperor Hirohito surrendered. York said VJ (Victory Japan) Day occurred on Aug. 14, 1945, his birthday.

"That was quite a birthday present," he said, grinning.

During 1945 and 1944, York served on a supply ship, the USS Devosa, which carried both troops and equipment. Before the U.S. Army Air Force dropped the two atomic bombs, the USS Devosa set sail from Saipan with battle casualties and headed toward Okinawa to return the men to their units.

"The Devosa was a victory ship," York said, adding the vessel carried amphibious tanks that would have been used for the invasion. He described the Devosa as being a bigger ship than an LST (landing ship-tank) but smaller than the warships.

During the war's final months, York said ships and their crews kept a vigilant lookout for Japanese kamikaze pilots hell-bent on diving their planes into American ships and trying to cause as much damage and casualties as possible. Because of the Verdosa's size and mission, York said the larger ships—aircraft carries, battleships and cruisers—suffered more damage than supply ships. The Reno resident remembered the beating the aircraft carrier USS Enterprise took during the last five months of the war.

Supporting the Okinawa operation, the USS Enterprise was damaged on April 11, 1945, by a kamikaze pilot and returned to Ulithi. A month later off Okinawa, he said, the Enterprise encountered additional kamikaze attacks. In mid-May, she suffered more losses when a kamikaze pilot slammed into the Enterprise, destroying the forward elevator by killing 14 sailors and wounding 34. After the war York said the Devosa changed it mission and began carrying occupation troops between Okinawa and mainland China.

Steven R. Ranson

UNDER FIRE ON D-DAY

Military leaders and historians alike have hailed the D-Day invasion in 1944 as the largest seaborne invasion in history and one that turned the tide in World War II.

Early on the morning of June 6 under cloudy skies and gusty winds whipping France's Normandy coast, allies began the invasion of German-occupied Western Europe and eventually pushed through enemy lines to Paris, thus liberating France. According to accounts prior to the invasion, bombers and naval bombardments pelted German fortifications, while more than 24,000 U.S., British and Canadian troops parachuted into the wooded countryside shortly after midnight. At 6: 30 a.m., allied infantry and armored divisions began landing at one of five sectors that stretched 50-miles along the coast with U.S. forces concentrating primary on Utah and Omaha beaches.

One man who witnessed the D-Day invasion and survived the thick of the fight was Kenneth Shockley, who, as an 18-year-old mariner in the Merchant Marine, ferried troops on a small landing craft from the larger Navy LSTs (landing ship, tanks) to Omaha Beach.

Shockley would maneuver the landing craft—which he described as a pickup bed with a gate—toward the beach and then drop the front ramp in the water to allow soldiers to run under fire.

"I lost a couple of buddies on Omaha Beach," Shockley said, reflecting on a monumental day that left the young Ames, Iowa, native in awe of all the firepower but sad with the human carnage. "They were brothers... and one was killed outright."

Shockley, though, thought he could save the other brother and pull him back to safety. When Shockley tried to rescue the young man, who also came from Ames, his lieutenant "kicked him down." He ordered Shockley to leave the young soldier behind and return to the landing boat.

Even after 70 years, discussing the invasion's details does not come easy for the 88-year-old Shockley. As the pilot of a small landing boat, Shockley ferried soldiers to the beaches not once, but three times under enemy fire. German snipers halted scores of allied soldiers wading in the shallow water after they left the landing boats or as soon as they hit the beaches.

His voice then grew quieter.

"They went to shore under a hail of bullets," Shockley said. "The Germans knew we were coming, and they would just shoot everyone who tried to land."

Shockley said everyone involved with the invasion prayed for the best, yet—to this day—he doesn't consider himself a hero or a Merchant Marine having courage.

"You get there safely or you die. That was the choice."

Shockley was very direct with his response. He couldn't gloss over the landing or the human carnage.

Although military planners deceived the Germans of a supposed invasion near Calais, Shockley said the enemy was still entrenched in concrete bunkers that overlooked the Normandy coast.

"The top of the cliffs were supposed to be barren, but they were full of soldiers," he recounted. "The Germans were on top, opening up with machine gun fire. We lost half our men before they went to shore. I could've driven on the beach, but I would draw fire from the top of the cliffs."

As the fighting waged between the allies and Germans, the invasion troops received a break. Shockley said B-26 bombers and smaller fighter bombers from England flew over the English Channel and over the remaining German strongholds, dropping bombs on their heavily fortified positions.

"That ran the Germans out of there," Shockley said.

Once the U.S. soldiers secured the beachhead, Shockley and his comrades stayed one night on the beach. Each soldier or sailor staying on the beach carried weapons ... for Shockley, he had to carry a machine gun.

Prior to his arrival to England, Shockley and thousands of other Americans arrived on Liberty ships, which were designated as noncombat vessels. They remained docked in England for three weeks.

"We didn't know why we were waiting," Shockley said, puzzled about the rapidly changing events.

Shockley remembers when paratroopers jumped behind enemy lines and heard of one place where the Germans were overrun. They retreated into a tunnel system that connected the bunkers. Although thousands of lives from both sides were lost on June 6, Shockley said the invasion had to be executed.

"D-Day put the Germans on the run … they had to retreat," he said.

Shockley knew it was his duty to serve his country during World War II. His father served during World War I as a runner from camp to camp. Near the end of the war, Shockley's father was gassed and later transported back to the United States. Because Kenneth Shockley was too young at the time, he lied about his age to enlist in WWII and then completed six weeks of basic training at Sheep's Head Bay, N.Y.

"You couldn't even blink unless you were told that you could do it," Shockley remembers. "If you saw a single scrap of paper or a cigarette butt on the ground, you'd better pick it up or you'd be in trouble for that too."

After basic training ended, the command kept Shockley back for three more weeks because his commander suspected he was younger than the other recruits. During that time the Merchant Marines and Shockley's parents sent correspondence back and forth to determine if the young Iowa resident had reached the age to serve. Time ticked by slowly for the young 18-year-old who was confined to barracks until his command resolved his situation. Time in the barracks frustrated Shockley.

"One day I sneaked out of the barracks and went down to the docks where the boats were tied up," Shockley wrote. "I slipped into one of the boats and pulled the oars over me so that no one would see me there. After a while, I fell asleep."

Shockley said an officer walked by the boat and must have heard him snoring. He ordered Shockley out of the boat and to his office. For the entire day, Shockley sat in a chair despite the officer knowing the young seaman was waiting for him. Near the end of the day, Shockley said the officer told him to return to the barracks. A small library existed below the floor, and before Shockley was dismissed, the officer showed the teenager a trap door.

"The officer asked me if I like to read, I said that I did, and he showed me a trap door in the floor and told me to go down in it," Shockley said.

Shockley found the light switch and turned it on. The officer told Shockley he could "hide" in the library and read until his "go" orders came in.

"I loved to read, and so I spent a lot of time down there," Shockley said.

Eventually, his orders arrived, certifying him old enough for duty.

Besides the D-Day invasion, Shockley also saw other action. He was part of a crew that transited the Panama Canal to the Pacific, and near the end of the war in 1945, his ship sailed through the Suez Canal on its way to fight the Japanese. They never arrived in the Far East.

Shockley said they received word the Japanese had surrendered, so the ship stopped in India and unloaded most of the ship's supplies and equipment.

While Shockley's legacy included being part of the D-Day invasion force, one of the most important honors came in 1997 when all young men who left Ames High School before receiving a diploma received an honorary graduation. Also in the 1990s, Merchant Marines, many of whom died while serving their country, finally received veterans' status.

Although the Normandy countryside and beach are peaceful today compared to the bullets flying over soldiers' heads or bombs exploding on German locations, more than 2,000 men lost their lives either in the murky water or on the blood-drenched Omaha Beach.

Yet, etched in Shockley's mind was a horrifying experience for an 18-year-old Iowa boy who quickly grew up to be a man fighting in defense of his country, and despite good odds he avoided the hail of German bullets that came from the cliffs, easily targeting the intrepid landing ship pilot.

Steven R. Ranson

USS NEVADA AND D-DAY

The 75th anniversary of the June 6, 1944, marked D-Day landings on the beaches of Normandy in northern France during the last full year of World War II.

More than 156,000 American and allied troops and 283 warships, including the battleship USS Nevada, participated in the landings named "Operation Overlord," the largest amphibious invasion in history that led to the liberation of France and the defeat and surrender of Germany on May 7, 1945. Less than four months later, Japan formally surrendered, bringing WWII to a close.

The D-Day landings and earlier combat operations in German-occupied France have always brought poignant reminders to my wife, Ludie, and her family. Five weeks before D-Day, Ludie's second cousin, Pfc. Dean E. Kail, a 19-year-old Army draftee and parachutist, was shot to death in mid-air over France by German snipers during his descent from an Army Air Force C-47 transport plane. Kail, who would have been 93 years old this year, was from Yakima, Wash., and a member of the 515th Parachute Regiment, 13th Airborne Division. He had made plans to attend the University of Washington, his parents' alma mater, when released from the Army.

Kail rests under a marble cross making his name, rank and units alongside 5,255 other American dead at the Epinal American Cemetery and Memorial which lies on the banks of the Mozelle River in northern France. Not far from Epinal is the Normandy American Cemetery at Coleville-sur-Mar overlooking Omaha Beach where lie the remains under marble crosses and Stars of David of 2,400 Americans who lost their lives on D-Day as well as 9,387 other Americans who took part in the defeat of Germany.

As for the USS Nevada, it joined the other 282 allied ships that provided naval gunfire, troop and equipment transport and other support of the D-Day landings on Omaha, Utah, Gold, Juno and Sword beaches.

Launched at the Boston Navy Yard on July 11, 1914, the 583-foot Nevada had been partially sunk during the Dec. 7, 1941, during Japanese attack on Pearl Harbor that left 50 Nevada crewmen dead or missing and 109 wounded.

The battleship, however, was refloated, towed to the Puget Sound Naval Shipyard in Washington for repairs and modernization, then sent to the Aleutian Islands where its big guns supported the landings of 12,000 soldiers on Japanese-held Attu and Kiska islands, and then sailed to the coast of France to support the D-Day landings.

During the invasion, Nevada's 10 14-inch guns battered German land fortifications and emplacements as enemy shells fell harmlessly around her and mines floated nearby, none of them striking their target. The Nevada expended 876 rounds from her main batteries and 3,500 from her five-inch guns. Nine U.S. Navy warships and 11 large landing craft were sunk during the invasion. More than 30,000 Germans were killed or wounded and 15,000 taken prisoner.

Following D-Day, the Nevada's guns supported allied landing operations in the Mediterranean before the battleship returned to the Pacific where it led the last WW II battles against the Japanese. In mid-July 1948, the Nevada, which had been decommissioned following the war due to old age and obsolescence and had been heavily damaged and was still radioactive after serving as the main target ship during the post-war atomic testing on Bikini Atoll in the Marshall Islands, was purposely sunk by U.S. Air Force and Navy gunfire approximately 65 miles southwest of Hawaii.

President Donald Trump, who had been on a state visit to Great Britain, joined leaders of other allied nations whose military forces were present at the Normandy landings. Thousands of WW II veterans, Europeans and tourists attended the D-Day and week-long events which included flyovers of allied WW II and present-day military aircraft and visits to Normandy-area villages, museums, churches, WW II military airfields and fortifications, cemeteries, ports, landing beaches and battlefields.

Most of the participants and witnesses to the D-Day landings are now in their 90s or have died, and it will not be long before there will be no one left to describe in person what happened at Normandy that historic day 75 years ago.

David C. Henley

CONNECTING TO
WORLD WAR II

A single rumpled burlap sack that fell from the sky above Holland has connected two Carson Valley residents for a lifetime.

Former U.S. Army Air Force pilot Clarence Godecke, who died in 2016, dropped that sack into the backyard of Garry Den Heyer, 81, who was a small boy living in Sheveningen, a district within southern Holland's The Hague.

"I want to thank you personally for what you have done for us," Den Heyer of Gardnerville, said as he touched Godecke's arm. "I still personally feel I can never replace what the U.S. has given me."

The two Valley residents came together in 2015 in honor of the 70th anniversary of the end of the war in Europe.

From May 1-8, 1945, U.S. pilots traded in their bombs for thousands of pounds of aid bags to drop near Holland's coast in the last mission they would fly during World War II called Operation Chowhound.

Godecke, a lieutenant colonel of the 338 Squadron of the 96th Bomb Group, responded to Den Heyer's thanks by explaining his emotions taking off on that mission, the last of his career.

"I was very glad to do that after dropping nothing but bombs for years," the 95-year-old said. "It was nice to do some good. I had a little different emotion about this mercy mission than any other I'd flown, but I took it on."

Although he volunteered for a second tour of duty, Godecke was a little apprehensive about flying the mercy mission.

To ensure their safety during their mission, the U.S told the Germans, who continued to occupy Holland right up to the end, of their intentions.

"We got a message one day from the operations officer, who was actually my best friend, saying we had another mission to fly. I told him 'I thought we were done over here.' He said this was something different," Godecke recalled. "I was told we had sent word to the Germans about our food drops down to the day and the time, and were just waiting for a reply from them to get started. Next thing I heard, the mission was set for a 3 a.m. briefing. There I was told I would fly from (England) to The Hague at 500 feet. There would be markers on the landscape of where to drop. I was excited and asked 'Great, you heard from the Germans.' My friend told me, 'No.'"

Godecke leading two wingmen along the coast of The Hague became the guinea pig, checking to see if the Germans would fire on them.

Although the British Air Force had been delivering aid in a similar fashion in a mission called Operation Manna the week before, Godecke was still apprehensive of the U.S. version, which would include more than 70 planes.

"I was told to fly the course, and if I didn't get shot down, I was to go out of The Hague and follow in at the tail end of the operation," Godecke said. "I remember there was a pit right by the coast full of Germans and their guns. We were so close we could see them laugh. We were looking at the barrel-end of those things. I think I held my breath the whole time. It was a great relief when they let us go by."

Den Heyer, who was about 7 years old at the time of the food drop, remembered watching the planes fly over his home.

"They flew so low we could see their faces," Den Heyer said. "We could hear them all the time. You wouldn't believe how Holland was thankful to the U.S. We saw their planes and knew we were safe."

Like most Dutch at the time of the German invasion, Den Heyer was separated from his mother and two sisters to live with a family elsewhere in the country for his protection.

"We had a good-sized yard and grew all kinds of vegetables and potatoes," he said. "We had to share everything, though, and at that time I knew if I went down in the cellar where we kept everything, I had to whistle so I wouldn't be accused of stealing."

While only a single bag of aid containing coffee, chocolate and beans dropped near Den Heyer's home, he recalled the relief it brought his neighborhood.

"I remember the day my 'aunt' found something in the backyard," he said. "We only found one thing but we were very happy and proud to have found it. We were hungry like everyone else, but not to the point that we were going to starve like some of our neighbors…it's not every day that something falls in your backyard."

The bag that landed in Den Heyer's backyard stayed in one piece, however, not all of them did.

Godecke remembered watching the Dutch scramble to pick up the contents of the ruptured sacks.

"As we came by, we saw people grabbing the bags and scooping up all the coffee or chocolate off the ground. They didn't leave anything on the ground. It was apparent they were hungry and desperate." Godecke said. "They would always stop and wave as we went over again."

Every rank of the Air Force flew during the food drops, Godecke said.

Over a week nearly 11,000 tons of food were delivered.

"Everyone wanted to go on these missions," Godecke said. "We had all the help we needed. We had brigadier generals flying during the food drops."

In 1990, 45 years after flying his last mission, Godecke and 140 other men who dropped aid in Operation Chowhound were invited back to Holland as guests of honor.

For 10 days Godecke and his comrades were shown the countryside and fed local cuisine, but Godecke remembers the trip being an emotional one.

"People turned out to stand by the side of the road," he said. "All they wanted to do was try to touch us. I usually just kept walking, but I finally gave in and stopped and talked to a lady with a baby that kept tugging at my sleeve. She said 'This is my grandchild and without you having brought food to my daughter who was very ill, they wouldn't have survived.' She was crying great big tears. Soon I was crying great big tears."

"I hope we never forget what these men did," Den Heyer said. "Everybody should learn to have sympathy for those in need, just like the U.S. did for Holland."

Sarah Hauck

TURNING POINT

On a cloudy, windy early morning of June 6, 1944, the largest amphibious invasion in military history began its quest to recapture most of the European continent from Hitler's control in what has been called as "The Longest Day."

Operation Overlord stretched along five Normandy beaches, a massive drive to push the Germans back and put them on the defensive as allied troops planned to storm across France and eventually into Germany. The invasion, informally referred to as Operation Liberation by President Franklin D. Roosevelt, was immense with 56,115 U.S., British and Canadian troops, 6,939 ships and landing vessels, and 2,395 aircraft and 867 gliders. The invasion's success became a turning point in the war.

Both Roosevelt and British Prime Minister Winston Churchill discussed more than one year before the actual D-Day invasion that an offensive attack on the European continent must drive back Hitler's army. Operation Overlord began with paratroopers dropping behind enemy lines in the predawn hours, and warplanes and Navy ships continuously bombarding the northern French coast to take out enemy artillery positions. One such ship was a Pearl Harbor survivor, the battleship USS Nevada, which fired on the Germans by trying to take out as many fortifications as it could.

Witnesses also said a long line of LCIs (Landing Craft Infantry) and LSTs (Landing Ship Tanks), an amphibious assault craft that landed on the beaches to unload tanks, extended for miles along the horizon toward the British Isles. When the front ramps on hundreds of landing ships lowered, scores of soldiers entered the water and onto the beaches with a barrage of bullets spraying at them. Scores of young soldiers, many of them barely out of high school, died instantly after German machine gun fire mowed them down during the first wave of landings.

Army Pfc. Lynn Bradt, who grew up in upstate New York but now lives in Reno, witnessed the first-day attack from LCI-99, which landed on Omaha beach at H-Hour+1 or 7 a.m. The chaotic scene of soldiers wading to the shore in strong currents and high tide was harrowing to all including Bradt, a member of the U.S. Army's 5th Division. LCI-99, though, struck an underwater mine and became immobile after Bradt went to shore in a "Duck" or DUKW, an six-wheel drive amphibious vehicle.

During Operation Overlord, 4,126 landing ships and crafts took part in the invasion, which Bradt called the most harrowing experience in his life.

Bullets whizzed by soldiers' heads to keep the Americans pinned down on the shore until they could reorganize and begin their drive toward a long bluff dotted with German bunkers. Gunfire grew intense as one soldier described it as the rapid striking of typewriter keys on a metal surface. Of the five beaches, Omaha endured the heaviest fighting with an estimated 34,000 soldiers rushing the heavily mined beach, many of them falling in a swath of German machine-gun fire. More than 2,400 hundred soldiers and sailors died or were wounded or missing on the first day.

Bradt's youngest son, Jeffrey, transcribed his father's thoughts on D-Day and the days after until he returned home.

"When we stormed the beach at Normandy, some of the Ducks sank, and there is such a suction when they go down that the drivers could not get out and went down with them," Bradt said. "I was going back and forth from the beach to the ships with cargo. At one point, the bilge point came on, and I could see water coming into the hold fast. If it gets up the engine, I'm sunk. So I rode up on top of the cowl on the way back to the beach so I could jump off if I needed to. I made it back and drove the duck up onto the beach and pulled the plug to let the water out."

Once troops scaled the bluff and wiped out German fortifications, they began their drive to Paris by first capturing Saint-Lô, a German stronghold, over a six to eight-week span.

"Omaha was the first battle I was involved in," said Bradt, who trained at Camp Young, Calif., and Camp Bradford, Va. "After that I was dodging bullets and picking up body parts."

Meanwhile, Bradt and others ferried supplies from the ships to the shores and even inland in the DUKWS. He remained behind with other drives for eight weeks to undertake the gruesome task of recovering body parts from hundreds of corpses that were strewn along the beaches and returning them to a central point.

Bodies were identified for burial, but at the time, they were placed in a ditch but then moved later to a cemetery on the hill.

After his time in Normandy, Bradt drove a truck into Belgium but eventually became embroiled in another incident. Many American soldiers had moved inland, so Bradt and other DUKW drivers used their vehicles as convoy trucks to transport troops.

"Going alongside the hill, I could see woods at the bottom," he said, referring to the Battle of the Bulge. "I had an uneasy feeling there were Germans camped in there lying in wait for us."

Bradt, who enlisted in February 1943 and left the Army in October 1945, put in 33 months fighting the Nazis. Years later when he was working at Eastman Kodak in Rochester, N.Y., one of his fellow workers, a former German tank driver, and was, coincidentally, in the same woods. Hitler's tanks did not attack the advancing allies, a fact that puzzled Bradt.

"Why didn't you blow our heads off," Bradt asked his co-worker.

"We couldn't. We were out of gas," came the response. "We would have given away our position and the air power would have wiped us out. We didn't shoot because we were all out of gas."

Until Bradt left Europe, he drove supplies to the troops.

Bradt departed Europe on a Liberty ship from Marseille, France, in late August 1945, but at the time, their command didn't tell troops of their destination. Before the ship reached the Strait of Gibraltar, an announcement on the loudspeaker rapidly changed their moods.

"Attention … our destination is New York City," bellowed the voice.

The soldiers then rocked the ship with applause and hollering. They were sailing home.

After a long career with Kodak, Bradt and his wife Rose Marie, whom he married in 1946, moved to Nevada to be closer to family and to take Jeffrey to the University of Nevada, Reno. For seven years he lived in Hawthorne, a two-and-half hour drive southeast to Reno, because of Hawthorne's heritage with both the Navy and Army..

"He loved it there," said Chuck Bradt, a son who lives in Incline Village on the eastern shore of Lake Tahoe.

Chuck said his parents enjoyed living in a military town and became involved in Hawthorne's community activities such as the participating in the annual Armed Forces Day.

"He loved to wear his World War II cap, and everyone saluted him," Chuck said.

Six years ago, Lynn suffered a stroke, but Chuck said his father stayed in rehabilitation in Reno and his sisters looked after their mother at a nursing home in New York State. In 2018, Rose Marie, the love of Lynn's life, died. The Bradts, who had a large family with 15 children and numerous grandchildren, were married for 72 years.

Lynn Bradt, who was accompanied by Chuck on a 2015 Honor Flight Nevada to Washington, D.C. and then in February 2020 to Pearl Harbor, said he was in awe with the memorials he saw on both trips. During the trip to the nation's capital, the formal laying of the wreath at the World War II memorial impressed Lynn.

During the five-day trip to Pearl Harbor, the USS Arizona Memorial may have stood out more than the others. Looking at the names of more than 1,000 sailors and Marines killed aboard the battleship on Dec. 7, 1941, affected Lynn.

"He sat there and got quiet for a long time," Chuck said, as his father remembered comrades who died before President Roosevelt declared formal war against the Japanese.

Steven R. Ranson

DAY IS DONE, GONE THE SUN

My life changed when I interviewed a Pearl Harbor survivor Roland Peachtree. After asking Peachtree basic questions, I learned he was born 67 days after my dad. Immediately, I felt a connection to him. Both were about the same height, lived through the Great Depression, served their country at sea making their mark in U.S. History.

"I got tired of using a mule's rear-end as a compass and decided there had to be something better, so I joined the Navy (Oct. 17, 1934)," Peachtree said. "After my training in Hampton Roads, Va., I was stationed on the USS Maryland, BB 46, for six years."

He re-enlisted in 1940 and was assigned to the USS Rigel at Pearl Harbor, Hawaii. The Rigel was a repair ship with a machine shop, above and below water welding equipment with divers, and propeller repair capability. The Rigel repaired ships from battle damage to proceed to a dry-dock for the necessary repairs to fight another day at sea.

Peachtree had completed cutting the meat for the ship's crew by 7:55 a.m. on Sunday, December 7, 1941, another day in paradise. Under the grey painted canvas covering his portable butcher shop, Peachtree looked up to see a few puffs of smoke followed by several loud explosions in the harbor.

"Thinking it was the Army, I went ahead with my work, and little did I know we were being attacked," he recalled.

During the attack, Japanese pilots dropped two bombs near Peachtree. The first bomb landed near the bow of the USS Rigel passing through a motor lifeboat,

143

but it did not explode. The second bomb hit the water between the Rigel and a tanker full of high-test aviation fuel, highly explosive. The water spray and shrapnel injured two or three sailors. Both ships were lightly damaged.

The crew of the USS Rigel had the right men at the right place at the right time to rescue their fellow sailors on the capsized USS Oklahoma. The Rigel's crew used cutting torches to cut through the 1-inch armor plate on the underside of the Oklahoma near the propeller shaft to free the trapped crew. Without the Rigel's rescue efforts, the death toll at Pearl Harbor would have been several hundred more sailors.

The USS Rigel, with Roland's cooking contributed to the battle of Coral Sea and Guadalcanal campaign victories. The Rigel was involved in landings at New Britain, Cape Gloucester and New Guinea.

Peachtree's first wife died in 1980, but they never had children. He married Evelyn, a cousin of his first wife in 1983. He considered himself fortunate to be married to his second wife for 33 years. He did not have an answer as to his long life.

For his 10 years of service to his country, Peachtree was awarded the Navy Good Conduct Medal twice, American Defensive Service Medal, American Theater Campaign Medal, Asiatic/Pacific Campaign Medal, WW II Victory Medal and Pearl Harbor Survivor Medal. After personally witnessing and surviving four years of carnage, he said, "I hate war."

Peachtree was buried on Feb. 16, 2016, at the Northern Nevada Veterans Memorial Cemetery. At the close of the ceremony, Taps was played. The flag draping his casket was folded 13 times and presented to his wife, Evelyn.

"On behalf of the President of the United States and the Chief of Naval Operations please accept this flag as a symbol of our appreciation for your loved one's service to this Country and a grateful Navy."

"Day is done, gone the sun,
From the lake, from the hills, from the sky;
All is well, safely rest, God is nigh."
From the first verse of Taps

Kenneth Beaton

SAILOR'S HARROWING INCIDENTS

Navy electrician mate Jim Warren relived his front-row seat from two harrowing incidents that involved the USS Pittsburgh, a heavy cruiser with a 14,000-ton displacement, during the last year of World War II.

Warren, accompanied by his wife, Harriett, a former employee with a Nevada newspaper in the 1970s and early 1980s, reflected on the crew's heroic efforts to tow a damaged aircraft carrier out of harm's way and within striking distance of the Japanese mainland. With the help of Harriet, Warrant thumbed through several scrapbooks containing photos and news articles from World War II. He recalled when Japanese pilots flying in two waves dropped bombs on the Essex-class aircraft carrier USS Franklin, killing more than 800 sailors and severely damaging the ship nicknamed "Big Ben."

At the time, Warren, who served from 1943-46, remembers the aircraft carrier had sailed to within 54 miles of Japan to launch an attack against Honsh and later a bombing mission against shipping in Kobe Harbor.

"We were in a Carrier Task Force when two Kamikazes hit us," Warren said of the March 19 early morning attack on the Franklin. "They (Navy crewmen) were putting bombs and fuel in the planes. I saw it unfolding."

Warren, who first served in the Atlantic theater, said he and a photographer saw the attack from their perch aboard the Pittsburgh. According to additional eye-witness accounts, a dive bomber flying low appeared from within the clouds and dropped two 550-pound semi-armor-piercing bombs. Warren said it appeared one bomb hit the Franklin's hangar deck causing fire to erupt, and the second bomb ripped through two decks. The fire and billowing smoke shrouded the aircraft carrier as many sailors jumped overboard trying to escape the advancing flames spreading across the deck.

"We towed it out of the war zone even when Kamikazes were bombing it," Warren said, "and it was sinking. We were even picking up survivors."

Navy archives reveal that was the only time a U.S. warship pulled another out of a war zone. The vividness of the attacks on the towed aircraft carrier, however, still resonate for Warren, who moved to Nevada in 1959.

The smaller Pittsburgh maneuvered into position after the aircraft carrier began listing to one side and drifting toward the mainland. The cruiser hooked up an 8-inch messenger line to the aircraft carrier's inert capstan. Once crews attached a steel cable between the two ships, the Pittsburgh began towing Big Ben away from the war zone at 3 to 7 knots.

Eventually, Warren said the cruiser pulled the Franklin more than 100 knots away from Japan until the aircraft carrier mustered enough power to reverse course and return to Pearl Harbor for repairs.

The carrier group then cruised toward Okinawa.

"We were the first task force ready for Japan," Warren said.

If Japan hadn't surrendered after atomic bombs were dropped on two Japanese cities, the United States and its allies were set to invade the mainland with thousands of troops, ships and planes.

But Mother Nature wrecked the task force's plans.

Warren and his crewmates aboard the Pittsburgh encountered the strength of a powerful 130-mile per hour typhoon in early June that rocked the ship with 100-foot waves and tore off a large section of the bow.

"We had water shooting into the compartments," Warren said, trying to remember the precautions the crew took or the ship would've sunk.

After a week of battling the typhoon and high seas, he said the Pittsburgh changed course and headed to Guam, but on June 24, the cruiser then left the island and sailed to the Puget Sound Naval Yard in Washington state, arriving in mid-July.

Steven R. Ranson

BELATED FAREWELL

Life aboard an aircraft carrier in the South Pacific provided its own grueling battle of survival, especially during the last two years of World War II when Japanese pilots and soldiers ramped up their attack on the approaching Americans.

U.S. naval forces sailed from island to island, staging both ships and aircraft in bringing the continual fight to the formidable Japanese armada of ships and planes. During the latter stages of the war, Japanese pilots ramped up their kamikaze attacks, particularly against American aircraft carriers that prowled the South Pacific as allied forces drove toward Japan and an all-out attack on Tokyo.

Reno sailor Pete Parisena had a front seat to war, serving aboard an aircraft carrier as a gunner. Even after the war officially ended on Sept, 2, 1945, and until his death in 1988, Parisena never talked about the war with his family or friends, never revealing his assigned carrier's name or his overall experiences.

"He told a couple generic stories, but he said he saw some horrific things," said his son Gary Parisena, also of Reno.

Parisena, who gave his father a long, overdue goodbye in April 2019, remembers him as a valiant sailor who served in the Navy for three years. Thirty-one years after his death, Parisena, along with 14 other veterans, were eulogized for their sacrifices to a grateful nation before their remains were interred in the columbarium at the Northern Nevada Veterans Memorial Cemetery in Fernley.

Pete Parisena, who was born in 1925 in Bordeaux, France, emigrated from Europe to the United States in 1930 with his mother and brother as they looked for better opportunities during post-World War I. Eventually, they received American citizenship.

"They came here to Reno," said Gary, who graduated from Reno High School in 1970. "My grandmother ran the Star Hotel on Second Street between Lake and Center. My family is Basque, and they catered to the Basque families."

Around the corner, Gary said, was one of their favorite restaurants, the Santa Fe, which served Basque food in a family-style setting. Two years after the United States entered World War II, though, Gary's father enlisted in the Navy. Once he returned to Reno after leaving the service in December 1945, the sailor became a sheet metal worker employed by Ray's Heating and Sheet Metal, a longtime family-owned firm.

During the 1980s, though, Gary lived in the San Francisco Bay area, but the closeness with his family had grown distant. After his father died 31 years ago, his mother assured him his father would be afforded a proper funeral. Not until earlier this month did Gary realize his father's remains had not been interred. He saw a newspaper article announcing a military service for 15 veterans whose remains had remained unclaimed but were still in possession of a local mortuary. As Gary skimmed the list, he stopped, stunned. There, on line 12, was his father's name along with his years of service.

"I thought my mom took care of everything until I saw the notice," Gary said. "I was completely in shock. I called Lynda and she told me what was going on. I was overwhelmed knowing that he wasn't taken care of."

Lynda Freeman, a volunteer with the Nevada Veterans Coalition, works with local mortuaries to arrange for remains to be transported to the NNVMC for a proper military service and burial. During most Missing in Nevada ceremonies, no family members have attended.

Tom Draughon of the NVC, who presided over the ceremony, said the military service was unique because Gary Parisena received a folded U.S. flag on behalf of his father and the other 14 veterans.

"It doesn't happened very often, but it's nice when it does," Draughon said.

During the service, Draughon offered words of condolence and inspiration, while the ceremonial team fired a 3-volley salute and buglers played Taps. Draughon said five Nevada Army National Guardsmen and seven sailors from Naval Air Station Fallon, along with members of the NVC, carried urns to place at a table or the ceremony and then proceeded afterward the urns to the columbarium the final resting place.

"Today, we proudly remember and thank each of the veterans for their service to this nation," Draughon said. "They all earn the title of veteran and patriot and undying love of country."

After the interment at the columbarium, Gary Parisena, who was accompanied by his friend Pamela DuPré, placed a family portrait of his father on a shelf in front of the urn.

"I'm so happy he's here," Gary said, his eyes reddened. "It was moving and moving for all who are up on this wall."

Draughon said the service had the right amount of respect.

"I talked to Gary afterward, and he was emotional but very thankful," Draughon added.

Steven R. Ranson

MISSION AND DUTY

Mary Burks was an important veteran who flew to Washington, D.C. They are all VIPs.

Burks, whose son Bill retired in 2019 as adjutant general of the Nevada National Guard, served during World War II as did her husband.

After a reception for Honor Flight Nevada travelers, Bill pushed his mother, an Army nurse during the war, in her wheelchair to a special area where she received a patriotic hand-sewn quilt as a small token of appreciation for her service and being part of the Honor Flight Nevada family.

Overwhelmed with the attention, Mary Burks, who hails from—appropriately—Libertyville, Illinois, was at a loss for words.

"I enjoyed the people," Mary said, also beaming when asked about placing a wreath at the Tomb of the Unknown Soldier at Arlington National Cemetery.

"It was a once in a lifetime opportunity," said Bill, who accompanied his mother on the trip as her guardian. "Watching my mom lay the wreath at the Tomb of the Unknown Soldier was unbelievable, something I couldn't believe was happening. It was so surreal."

Seeing the memorial brought tears to her eyes for this nurse who arrived on the island of Tinian in 1944 until the Army reassigned her to Kyoto, Japan after September 1945 as part of the occupation force. Tinian, 1,500 miles away from Japan, became a major staging island for the B-29 Superfortress bombers Enola Gay and Bockscar, each carrying an atomic bomb that was dropped on Hiroshima and Nagasaki respectively.

"She knew who (Paul) Tibbets was," Bill Burks said of the Enola Gay pilot, adding the B-29s, a four-engine propeller-driven heavy bomber, were new to the war in 1944.

As with all personnel on the island, the days and hours were consumed with the mission and their duties.

"She was a surgical nurse, nothing on the front line. The patients were brought to them," Bill Burks added.

After the two B-29s dropped their atomic bombs in August 1945, the Japanese surrendered and officially signed the documents ending the war on Sept. 2. From there, Burks said his mother became part of the occupation under General Douglas MacArthur's command.

Bill Burks was surprised with the attention his mother was receiving.

"What stood out for me were the groups of school who would come up to her," he recalled. "It didn't make any difference which memorial or monument we were at."

During the whirlwind trip to Washington, D.C., Mary met students at the Navy Memorial who wanted to be photographed with their newest heroine. She visited the World War II memorial and saw the columns marked with the names of each state. She encountered woman runners on a Marine ruck run who stopped.

"They all wanted to get a picture with her," Bill said.

Later, when visiting the U.S. Marine Corps Iwo Jima memorial, two female Marines wanted to be photographed with the World War II veteran, and Bill had the opportunity to snap a few photos of his mother next to the Vietnam Women's Memorial, which depicted three nurses with a wounded soldier.

Bill Burks didn't know if his mother would have the opportunity to participate in an honor flight to Washington, D.C. Her husband and Bill's father died in March 2018, and he felt the timing was right for her to send an application to go on the flight.

Steven R. Ranson

WORLD-CHANGING EVENTS

It's been 66 years since then 88-year-old Minden resident Milt Croall was honorably discharged from the U.S. Coast Guard.

Reviewing an article he wrote last fall for The Quarterdeck Log, a journal for Coast Guard combat veterans, it's apparent that memories of his service in the Pacific Theater of World War II are still vivid in his mind – kamikazes screaming through the sky, beaches enveloped in mortar fire, fallen comrades and enemies floating in the tropic shallows.

"Our LCVP was one of the boats selected for the gruesome task of transporting the bodies," Croall wrote of a battle in the Marshall Islands. "Two Marines with a stretcher and a Catholic chaplain were charged with the handling of the dead, with the chaplain collecting the dog tags – truly the saddest day of the war for me."

Despite being in the middle of world-changing events, Croall counts May 8, 2012, as one of his most memorable days.

On that day he joined 62 veterans, 49 from World War II, on a prestigious honor flight that took him from central Missouri to the war memorials of Washington, D.C.

"This was one of the most memorable, thrilling and emotional days of my life," Croall said.

In a way, the event brought closure to a journey that started in October 1942, when Croall, then 17, enlisted in the Coast Guard.

Originally from Santa Clara, Calif., Croall wrote that when the recruiting officer asked him why he'd chosen the Coast Guard, he replied that he "liked the ocean better than mud."

"He then asked why not the Navy? My reply was I liked small ships better than large ones," Croall recalled.

Having worked two summers in a cannery, Croall was cited for mechanical experience and sent to Hemphill Diesel School in Queens, N.Y. He graduated as a motor machinist mate, second class, also known as a motormac, and soon returned to Alameda, Calif., where he patrolled the San Francisco Bay in a 48-cabin cruiser.

Shortly after deciding to marry his high school sweetheart, Phyllis Roll, the motormac was shipped to the East Coast to train for war. By the end of 1943, he was aboard the USS Cambria motoring through the Panama Canal, one of several ships heading to Hawaii.

"The Navy men griped that they had to go to war aboard a Coast Guard ship," Croall remembered.

He was later transferred to the USS Arthur Middleton, recently returned from Tarawa, and assigned motormac to a landing craft for vehicles and personnel, also known as a Higgins boat.

In February of 1944, Croall set course for the Marshall Islands. His first experience in combat was landing troops on Engebi Island amid mortaring and machine gun fire. It was the next landing on Parry Island, in the same atoll, where Croall was tasked with transporting fallen comrades to an adjacent island to be buried.

"On the way back to Pearl Harbor, one Japanese prisoner died as well as one Marine, and both were buried at sea," he wrote.

After brief repairs and an outbreak of dysentery, the USS Middleton joined the task force assembling for Saipan.

"The D-Day at Saipan saw two separate attack groups – ours being diversionary, however. After a smoke screen was laid down, all our boats made a right turn and joined one group hitting the beach," Croall said.

When the Middleton suddenly pulled anchor due to the quickly approaching Japanese fleet, Croall stayed behind in a 36-foot Higgins boat with three others. For nine days, the sailors lived off K rations and drinkable water from the shore.

"At night we would anchor out on the coral reef as the beach was not yet secured, as one boat crew sadly found out," Croall said. "Each evening we were visited by 'Machine Gun Charlie,' flying just too high for our 30-caliber machine guns to reach."

On July 20, 1944, Croall finally married his sweetheart during a 48-hour liberty in California. By September, however, he was heading for the Philippines under the direction of Admiral Chester Nimitz and General Douglas MacArthur.

"During the initial landings I watched a single Japanese torpedo plane make it through all the flak and hit the cruiser Honolulu," Croall wrote. "The next day, there were more air raids as we were still unloading ships. An Australian cruiser took a bomb. I witnessed General MacArthur and his staff wading ashore. There were dead Japanese floating in the water."

Croall made several trips back and forth between New Guinea and the Philippines, transferring personnel and holding practice landings. Between sudden attacks of Japanese bombers, there were moments of calm respite, surreal in contrast.

"Once, while on free time, we pulled up to this beautiful, snow-white, sandy beach thickly lined with coconut palms," Croall remembered. "We were looking for pretty shells when, upon looking up, we saw all these natives standing, holding spears, beetle nut-dyed hair and teeth filed to points. Needless to say we scrambled pretty damn quick into our boat and left."

At Lingayen, Croall guided Higgins boats through a maze of unexploded rockets.

"Resistance was light thankfully, and later in the day when all was secured, Filipino people came to us," he said. "The women wanted soap, the men cigarettes, and the children candy, paying with Japanese invasion money."

On D-Day at Okinawa, April 1, 1945, Croall remembered that, "Kamikazes filled the sky – some hitting their targets, and many crashing into the sea."

"One crashed just off our stern. The fifth day we left for Saipan, completely unloaded, passing a task force of our battleships and cruisers," he said. "The sea was rough, and being empty, the ship really tossed about."

Okinawa was the last battle Croall saw.

"Most of us had nearly two years overseas and expected to be transferred right away, but only those with over two years were listed to go stateside," he said. "My wife, Phyllis, and several other wives wrote to the Coast Guard commandant in Washington, D.C., and soon all with 18 months or more were sent ashore."

The couple finally had their honeymoon, although food and gas were still being rationed as everyone awaited the end of the war. With a wife and seven battle stars, Croall was discharged from service on Oct. 6, 1945.

"The Middleton was eventually transferred to the Navy and used to bring our troops back home," he said. "It was eventually placed in the mothball fleet and years later scuttled."

More than six decades later, Croall was called upon again to leave his home and travel across the country, this time as a decorated war hero.

His daughter Charlotte Beuselinck had filled out the necessary application and made travel arrangements, with help from son-in-law Paul Beuselinck, and son Bob Croall.

On May 8, 2012, the aged motormac joined 49 veterans of World War II, 13 of the Korean War, and 47 caregivers on the Central Missouri Honor Flight. The group had a police escort to St. Louis, where they boarded a plane for Baltimore.

"The veterans were allowed to leave their shoes on," Croall said. "We did, however, get a pat-down."

In Maryland, people were lined up inside the airport to greet the heroes, waving flags, clapping and shaking hands. The veterans then boarded two buses and were escorted by police to the World War II Memorial in Washington, D.C.

Although he saw other memorials and the Arlington National Cemetery, Croall was hit especially hard by the tribute to World War II. He stood in front of the stone pillar representing Nevada's contribution to the fight.

"It was very somber to see the wall with all the stars on it – each star's worth 100 people who passed away," he said. "They had a memorial to the landing crafts, the men who were charging the beach, and I was having those thoughts and feelings of what happened so long ago. I guess it was a reward in a way. It made me feel that those three years of my life were not wasted, but put to good use."

Flying back to St. Louis later that evening, the veterans got a surprise mail call.

"Unknown to us, our families and friends were asked to write us a note," Croall said. "Thanks to my daughter Charlotte, with help from my son Bob, I received 18 letters. I was astonished and grateful."

Back in Missouri, the group was escorted not only by police, but by 523 motorcycles.

"The bikers would pass by single file, revving engines," Croall said. "Along the way we passed two bonfires with people waving flags to us. The police had closed the on-ramps, so we did not slow or stop at intersections. More city police were there to help, all donating their time."

Arriving at their hotel at about 2 a.m., Croall said he couldn't believe the throngs of people waiting for them.

"When I got off the bus and in my wheelchair, I was pushed by one of the bikers, leathers and all," he said. "The crowd was clapping and cheering. I saw Charlotte and Phyllis in front of the crowd."

Besides thanking his family, Croall thanked Steve and Sharon Paulsell, who organize the event each year, and the schools, companies and other organizations who make donations to fund the flights.

"What do you say? I told them in a note of thanks that I had heartfelt gratitude," he said. "It was so outgoing and gracious – a wonderful thing. I never dreamed I would have the opportunity."

Croall died less than a year after this article was published.

Scott Neuffer

NUMBING COLD
AND GERMANS

The numbing winter cold. snow and wind pulsating across western Europe in late 1944 slowed troops down in Belgium as the Allies faced both the elements of weather and Germans.

Christmas Day 1944: Sgt. Luther Gordon and his fellow infantrymen hunkered down defensively along the Outhe River to prevent the German troops and their equipment from crossing a bridge as described by his granddaughter Jaymi Bryant in a narrative of Gordon's service.

The Battle of the Bulge in which Gordon fought became the last major German offensive campaign of World War II that was launched in the densely forested Ardennes region of Wallonia in Belgium, France, and Luxembourg. That two-month battle resulted in the Allies defeating the Germans, a prelude that Adolph Hitler's military ranks were thinning and that overall defeat looked inevitable.

Meanwhile, in the frosty skies above them, heavy U.S. bombers and fighter escorts exchanged fire with German fighters. As an Army soldier in the 290th Infantry, 75th Infantry fighting in Belgium, Gordon and the rest of a column moved out and headed toward a small town to wait for the chow trucks. The distant sound of shooting sounded closer for Sgt. Luther Gordon. After Gordon and his men had a cold snack—not a hot meal as promised—they moved out with the column reaching the top of a nearby hill.

"Word came back that there were dead Germans in the road ahead," he remembered in a memoir written 24 years ago and provided by his family. "This put the realization into most of us that we were about to engage the enemy."

Within the timber, soldiers established their positions with platoons aligning their mortars and machine guns. Gordon and his buddies dug into the right flank, while other soldiers scattered to other positions.

"That was the last time I saw either our second squad or the mortar squads," Gordon remembered. "I know they were somewhere in the timber but did not know where."

Away from their positions were the Germans, equally entrenched in the wooden area with tanks and artillery. Fighting had commenced between the American soldiers and Germans with casualties occurring on both sides.

The fighting became fiercer as Gordon described.

"It was while along the edge of the woods that Tommy Mathis came and told me the other ammo bearer, Tom Womble, had been bayoneted and killed. Tommy was in a state of shock and worried about his twin brother who was in the other M.G. Squad somewhere down off the hill. I told him to take off. Shortly after Tommy left Eddie Winsjansen, our second gunner, came by and said, "I am going off the hill, Eddie had a hole in his helmet with blood coming down his face and a bloody rip in his pant leg.

"1st Lt. 'Dutch' Meier came by and said he was going to scout the hill. He said if he did not come back that what NCO's remaining were to take the rest of the Co. off the hill. (Not many of us left by then.) A short time later one of 'Dutch's' messengers came back and said 'Dutch' had been captured, stood against a tree and shot in both arms. Those of us still in the area decided to go up and get "Dutch". As we started up the hill the second messenger came down and said "Dutch" had been killed."

During the battle, a German sniper shot Gordon in the left arm, but he continued to return fire until he depleted his ammunition. Undaunted by his lack of ammo, Gordon raced to a captured German machine gun position that had been captured earlier, grasped the weapon and began to return deadly fire again until reinforcements arrived.

The second time Gordon suffered a bullet wound came in May 1945, sadly on the same day his brother was killed and who is buried in the 10th Mountain Division Cemetery in Italy.

Gordon received two Purple Hearts, a Silver Star and a Bronze Star., quite the heroism from a man the Army drafted after he tried to enlist in the Marines.

As many heroes from The Greatest Generation, Gordon never talked about his gallant deeds during World War II, yet his family felt the strong need his story would not be forgotten. A retired California Fire district manager, Gordon lived in Benton and Bishop, Calif., before relocating to Fallon.

Through the Honor Flight Nevada program, Gordon and his son Jeff flew to the nation's capital for a three-day tour to see both the civilian and military monuments and to share camaraderie with other veterans.

Jeff accompanied his late father on both the flight and with our interview. At 92-years old, Luther Gordon had difficulty with his sight and hearing. Jeff said the trip left an indelible impression on both men. After boarding a flight from Reno to Baltimore with much fanfare, the veterans and their caretakers or family members saw an appreciative nation extend its arms to give each veteran the hugs and gratitude that each deserved.

After resting Friday night at a hotel in Washington, D.C., the veterans then spent Saturday, the second day, touring Washington, D.C. and visiting the sights.

"We met Bob Dole (former U.S. senator from Kansas and World War II hero) at the World War II memorial," Jeff said. "He tries to go anytime he knows there's an Honor Flight. "We went to Arlington (National Cemetery) and saw the changing of the guard and the placing of the wreaths."

For the eight hours they were touring Washington, Jeff said they saw monuments dedicated to each branch of military service. The veterans – many of whom had never visited Washington—expressed awe at the sights and with the people they met. Since the day was also the anniversary of the start of the Korean War, they also witnessed Korean soldiers at the monument reading names of people who died. After arriving back at the hotel, the veterans had mail call where they received packets and letters from school children or family members.

This led to some veterans talking about their experiences.

"It was hard to keep a dry eye hearing all the stories," Jeff said. "It was the most rewarding part (of the trip) to see the smiles on their faces."

Steven R. Ranson

NAVY'S 'GHOST' FLEET

The aging rustbuckets, proud veterans of America's past wars, come into view as the early morning fog begins to fade.

Lashed together and sitting in rows, the U.S. Navy and Maritime Administration's floating cadavers moored here in the middle of Suisun Bay are drenched in history.

At least three alumni of this "ghost" or "mothball" fleet east of San Francisco had Nevada-related names: The ocean-going tugboat USS Winnemucca, the Las Vegas Victory and the oiler USS Truckee.

Other ships have included the battleship USS Iowa, the Glomar Explorer spy ship built by Howard Hughes and hundreds of World War Two, Korean War, Vietnam War, Cold War and Gulf War Victory and Liberty ships, tankers, cargo and supply vessels, destroyers, cruisers, battleships and LSTs.

The Iowa now serves as a floating museum at the Port of Los Angeles, the rest have long since been scrapped, and the National Defense Reserve Fleet here, which had about 80 ships in its inventory just a few years ago, is now whittled down to 16.

And most of these remaining 16, like those at the nation's other reserve fleets at Beaumont Tex., and James River, Va., will soon be heading to the scrap heap as well, says Michael M. Novak, director of Congressional and Public Affairs at the U.S. Maritime Administration (MARAD) which operates the three fleets.

The decrepit ships are on their way to the scrap heap because they are obsolete, unseaworthy and thus no longer viable as backups to the Navy's active fleet. And they also are causing environmental damage by shedding paint and other toxins into the water such as asbestos, lead, zinc, copper and cadmium, said Novak, who added that the reserve fleets still will be maintained to accept further ships for eventual use or scrapping.

Some of Suisun Bay's floating fossils have been towed to Texas and Asia for scrapping.

More recently, however, several of the remaining ships are undergoing much shorter voyages en route to the guillotine: They're been dismantled just a few miles westward across the bay at the re-opened Mare Island Naval Shipyard in Vallejo which was built in 1854 and closed in 1996 following downsizing and closure of U.S. military installations.

A private firm appropriately named Mare Island Ship Yard LLC is taking apart and scrapping the obsolete ships but not before removing their historical artifacts such as deckhouse wheels that turn their rudders, compasses, port lights, cleats and interior signage that are sold to museums and antique shops.

Rust and pollution are then scrubbed off before shipyard workers, who have placed the ships in drydocks for easy accessibility, dismantle them and the scrap metal is sold to the highest bidders.

One of the warships at Mare Island awaiting the shipbreakers' acetylene torches has borne four names.

Launched in 1939, the 492-foot ship initially was a merchant vessel named the Del Orleans. In 1941, it was acquired by the Navy which renamed it the USS Crescent City and converted it into an attack transport, and later into a troop transport. During its military career, the Crescent City won 10 battle stars following combat during the invasion of Guadalcanal and other World War Two Pacific landings.

In 1971, it was renamed the Golden Bear and operated as the training ship at the California Maritime Academy. In 1999, its name was changed to Artship when acquired by an Oakland non-profit organization that tried, unsuccessfully, to turn it into a floating cultural and performing arts center.

Other ships scrapped at Mare Island have included the fleet oil tanker USS Roanoke, the MARAD bulk cargo vessels Solon Turman and President, and the cargo ship USS Ambassador that served during operations Desert Storm and Desert Shield.

These ocean-going dinosaurs will sail no more. Their fates are sealed. They soon will become salvage.

But someday they will return … as paper clips, razor blades, pots and pans, and Nissans, Toyotas and Hondas.

David C. Henley

REBUILDING KEY AIRFIELD

TINIAN, Northern Marianas Islands—The temperature and humidity are reaching 90 on this tiny island in the remote western Pacific, and I am standing on undoubtedly the most famous runway on earth.

One of four runways that comprise North Field on this U.S. Micronesian territory about 50 miles northwest of Guam, Runway Able is where World War II was won.

At 2:45 on the morning of Aug. 6, 1945, U.S. Army Air Force Col. Paul W. Tibbets Jr. flew his B-29 Superfortress "Enola Gay"—named for his mother—from Runway Able and headed toward Japan.

Six hours later, the aircraft dropped the world's first operational atomic bomb over Hiroshima. Named "Little Boy," the bomb killed an estimated 75,000.

Three days later, at 3:49 a.m., a second B-29 left the same runway, also bound for Japan.

Piloted by Maj. Charles Sweeney and named "Bockscar" after the aircraft's flight commander, Capt. Fred Bock, it dropped an A-bomb called "Fat Boy" over Nagasaki, killing approximately 50,000.

Fearing more bombs would be dropped, Emperor Hirohito told his countrymen by radio on Aug. 15 that Japan would surrender unconditionally, and it did so on Sept. 2 when Gen. Douglas MacArthur presided over Japan's formal surrender ceremony on the deck of the battleship USS Missouri moored in Tokyo Bay.

Today, 75 years after the atomic bomb drops and the end of WW II, long-abandoned Runway Able and North Field are coming back to life.

Initially named Ushi Point Airfield by the Japanese, who had owned Tinian and neighboring Saipan since 1914, the islands fell into U.S. hands in July of 1944 when U.S. Marines stormed ashore and captured them following the bloody battles of Tinian and Saipan.

Ushi Point Airfield was renamed North Field, lengthened from 4,000 feet to 8,000 feet by Navy Seebees, and served as a launching point for U.S. air attacks against the Japanese mainland, the Philippines and Okinawa.

But after the A-bomb devastations, Japan's surrender and the end of WW II, the U.S. closed North Field and its concrete and crushed limestone airstrips became overgrown by weeds and brush.

My exploration of Tinian began at the island's small local field following a 10-minute, eight-mile flight from Saipan aboard a six-passenger Piper Cherokee, the only commercial air service available.

I was met by Oregon-born Don Farrell, a local historian, former high school teacher here and current chief of staff and military advisor to Tinian Mayor Ramon De La Cruz.

We visited San Jose, the island's quaint little capital, the nearby fishing and commercial port, the Las Vegas-style 420-room Dynasty Resort and Casino that looms over the town and Taga Village, a collection of 15-foot-high limestone pillars called "latte" that were built about 1500 AD to honor native Chamorro chiefs and their families who, incredibly, lived atop the pillars in wood and thatch houses.

We then drove to North Field along Broadway Blvd., so-named because 40-square-mile Tinian resembles the shape and size of Manhattan Island.

As we neared the airfield, we came upon a rusting WW II Marine armored vehicle and the ruins of Japan's massive wartime air operations headquarters, both partially hidden in the dense jungle foliage. And I also photographed the deep pits that housed the two atomic bombs before they were hoisted aboard the B-29s for their fateful flights to Japan.

As I stood sweltering on Runway Able, Farrell, 67, who sports a long white beard, told me that it and Runway Baker have been rehabilitated because of the current "pivot," "tilt" or "rebalance" to the Pacific of the militaries of the U.S. and its regional allies to ward off possible adventures by China and North Korea.

U.S. bases, some run jointly with our allies, are being enlarged, built and re-established in Australia, South Korea, the Philippines, Guam and here at North Field, where a U.S. Navy amphibious ship recently disgorged a contingent of Marines and their heavy earthmoving equipment that included tractors, skip loaders and dump trucks which were used to clear the fields and repair its potholes.

Floodlights and a mobile radio communication van also accompanied the Marines, and in short order Navy F/A-18 Hornet fighter jets and Marine Corps KC-130J Hercules transport aircraft were making day and night landings and take-offs on the runways, the first here since the end of WW II, during training missions that involved wartime contingencies, search and rescue, and disaster relief scenarios.

Soon, military aircraft from Australia, South Korea and, ironically, Japan were joining their American counterparts on the airfield, and ground troops from the four nations also participated in artillery and ground-to-air weapons training at the field.

Although it is not known at this time if North Field will be permanently re-established and rebuilt, Runway Able once again is in use following a 69-year break. As I stand on the field, I can almost visualize B-29s Enola Gay and Bockstar leaving on their frightful missions.

David C. Henley

BLOODIEST 82 DAYS

The final push to Tokyo launched April 1, 1945, and for 82 days, thousands of Americans and allies stormed Okinawa after months of island hopping in the western Pacific. The invasion on Okinawa's southernmost island became the largest amphibious assault in the Pacific Theater that included an invasion force of more than 200,000 U.S. military personnel to include 103,000 soldiers, 88,000 Marines and 18,000 sailors and aviators.

Securing Okinawa became the bloodiest battle in the Pacific for both the Americans and Japanese.

Okinawa, which sits less than 500 miles from the southern tip of Japan, held significant importance as a final staging area for the invasion of the Japanese main island, but those plans never came to fruition after two atomic bombs destroyed Hiroshima and Nagasaki on Aug. 6 and 9, respectively. The two attacks caused Emperor Hirohito to call for a surrender and ceasefire less than one week after the B-29 Superfortress Bockscar dropped its devastating load on Nagasaki.

Argus "Gus" Harold Forbus and his son Jim wrote an account on the Marine's island hopping during World War II, for a Nevada newspaper in 2012 and 2013. The elder Forbus, who died eight years ago, was part of the invasion force that landed on Okinawa 75 years ago. He spent 20 years in the U.S. Marine Corps before working in the civilian sector and eventually moving to Fallon where many relatives still reside.

Before landing on Okinawa, the 6th Marine Division trained on Guadalcanal after securing the island in July 1944. For Forbus and the other Marines, they described the training as "fairly relaxed" since many of them had combat experience and knew the warfighting traits of the Imperial Japanese Army(IJA). Forbus used his experience to train the new troops and young officers.

169

"They (Marines) received close overhead live-fire from machine guns," Forbus recounted. "We instructors were right in there with them to give them moral support. We took them through realistic ambushes – how to set them and how to get out of them when necessary. For training purposes, we had a mock village built, complete with two-story buildings. We concentrated a lot on close-in fighting with a lot of hand-to-hand combat."

In the morning, the Marines trained in the field and then the instructors used the afternoon for small unit or individual training.

Once training ended, the Marines procured beer to celebrate their departure from Guadalcanal, knowing that many of them would not return to the United States alive. The Marines boarded troop transports for their 3,300-mile journey to Okinawa for what many described as a "pretty boring trip."

Forbus said on the morning of the invasion, the Marines heard the call for "last meal" before loading on the landing crafts, but Forbus didn't have time. Instead, his early afternoon breakfast consisted of a can of cold C rations.

"We arrived off Okinawa the night of March 31, 1945," Forbus remembered. "You cannot imagine the sight, and I hope I never see the like of it again. Ships of every description were as far as you could see. The air was full of fighter planes. All types of guns were firing from the battleships to the LSTs (landing ship tanks). It seemed that every ship was firing at the island. The planes and ships made coordinated attacks at the island landing beaches while the landing craft took the troops to the beach. The shelling of the island was unbelievable."

Forbus and the first wave first stepped on the island on Easter Sunday, which was also April Fool's Day. He described many of the young Marines as scared. Everyone's adrenaline was high. When the Marines hit the island, they encountered very little resistance and moved quickly to take out the enemy's machine guns and snipers. Forbus said he didn't lose a man on the first day until after they reached Yon Tan Air Field. The Marines crossed Yon Tan in about five hours and continued to press on until they reached man-made caves and pillboxes, which they cleared out with white phosphorous and fragmentation grenades because the Japanese soldiers refused to surrender. Once the Marines sealed the caves, they began to advance although the Japanese defense was stubborn. Unable to receive additional company support, Forbus' platoon withdrew.

The Marines headed north to Mount Yaetake, Okinawa's highest mountain which had to be taken. Once again, Japanese resistance made it difficult to secure the landmark.

"It was so steep that no wheeled or tracked vehicles could make it up the mountain to act as our support," Forbus wrote in his account. "We battled for three or four days with scattered resistance before we hit their main line of resistance. It was there that we had a minor, pathetic banzai attack on the second day of the attack, but we easily repulsed it; however, the next day was when we had our first real banzai attack on the island. This attack was terrifying."

Forbus said screaming Japanese soldiers with fixed bayonets rushed their positions. The Marines finally pushed back the retreating enemy, which Forbus said was good, because they were almost out of ammunition. When Forbus and his men neared Mount Yaetake, they encountered more opposition from Japanese infantrymen. Neither ground vehicles or tanks could maneuver on the mountain's steep foot. Flamethrowers had to accompany the squads as the Marines clawed their way up the mountain. Forbus described the Japanese as determined not to allow the Americans on the mountain.

The Marines pushed the Japanese back a short distance, but the enemy reorganized and charged the squad with bayonets, grenades and rifles firing. Fighting eventually evolved into man to man with casualties mounting on both sides and neither side willing to wave a white flag and retreat. Ammunition continued to dwindle, and resupplies weren't available. The fighting's intensity caused the Marines to think of alternatives.

"If they had come at us again, we would have had to resort to K-Bar knives, machetes and the Marine Raider stilettos since none of us had bayonets," Forbus described. "We always managed to stop the Japanese before they got to our wounded. The Japanese were brutal with wounded or prisoners, horribly torturing and killing them."

The Marines sucked it up, drove the Japanese off the mountain and secured it … so they thought. The enemy regrouped and attacked the Marines with another large force, but the Americans had replenished their grenades and ammunition. Intelligence tipped off the Maines that the Japanese were regrouping for an attack. Once again the Marines pushed back the Japanese up the hill. Because the Marines were so close to the enemy, Forbus said the Marines couldn't call for air strikes or naval gunfire. The only way to take the mountain was by direct combat—infantry against infantry.

Forbus described the combat as some of the worst fighting by dislodging the Japanese from their stronghold. Casualties soared on both sides, but the Marines eventually took Mount Yaetake; yet the Americans anticipated another enemy surge, and the Japanese didn't disappoint. They mounted a banzai attack with bayonets and rifle ammunition, but the Marines overwhelmed the Japanese with grenades and rifle fire.

The rest of the night was quiet once the Americans repelled the latest attack.

"The next morning we moved out with my platoon in the lead," Forbus recalled. "We patrolled several hundred yards and couldn't find any sign that the Japanese were still active in the area. The battalion commander held us up, and we established a temporary defensive position. We ran small patrols out in all directions as a safety measure since we never knew if the Japanese were still lurking in the area."

Forbus said the company moved out after being replaced. Army trucks stopped to give the Marines a lift to the rear echelon area where the leathernecks received replacements and grabbed necessary equipment and more ammunition.

In May, the Marines pushed north toward Naha, Okinawa's largest city and capital, and on June 4, the Americans made another full-scale landing on the peninsula. The Marines initially encountered light resistance before the enemy made a final attack to push the Marines back. The regiment made a second full-scale landing, but the Marines fought the Japanese steadily during the night.

When Forbus and the other Marines entered Naha, they discovered the bombing, artillery and naval gunfire had pounded the Okinawan city except for pockets of snipers and soldier that impeded their advancement. Once the Americans and their allies secured their area, Forbus said he avoided a close call when leaning against a Sherman tank—a sniper wounded him.

"He missed me, but the copper and lead in the bullets hit rapidly against the tank splattering me with shrapnel," Forbus said. "I was hit in my left shoulder, left hand, the left side of my face and head. I thought that I'd had it. I didn't think a person could lose so much blood from the fine punctures from the shrapnel and bullet fragments. It really scared the hell out of me, but my ace squad leader was probably more scared."

Forbus reported to an aid station, and medics removed most of the shrapnel and lead. He returned to his platoon. Another sniper, though, nailed Forbus several days later by firing a round through the Marine's right thigh missing the bone and femoral artery. After arriving at the aid station, Forbus evacuated by a hospital ship to a mobile hospital on Tinian Island.

The Americans paid a step price in securing Okinawa. More than 12,500 soldiers, Marines and sailors died, while more than 36,000 suffered wounds. On the other hand, more than 110,000 Japanese soldiers died, and another 100,000 Okinawan civilians perished.

The years of fighting in the Pacific and the final months of the war left Forbus with a profound thought on fighting against the Japanese:

"It is never good to look back as we usually don't see what we would like to see. Any adult who has lived through a war understands that war is hard to cope with and has lasting effects on everyone. Whether or not they participate in combat with the enemy or in the rear echelon supporting those actively engaged in combat, or those serving on the home front—all are affected. When in combat, we accept many things as part of the battle that we have to cope with. Afterward, we try to understand what happened and why and was there a better way to accomplish the task."

Steven R. Ranson

USS ORMSBY NAMED FOR NEVADA PIONEER

Many Nevadans are familiar with the remarkable histories of the battleship USS Nevada and the patrol frigate USS Carson City, which were among the nearly two dozen warships bearing Nevada-related names that served in combat during World War II.

The USS Nevada, for example, is memorialized in an extensive, permanent exhibit at the Nevada State Museum in Carson City. And the USS Carson City also occupies a special place of honor in the capital city, where its bell, wartime history and photos of the ship are displayed in the foyer of city hall.

But nowhere can be found recognition of the highly-decorated USS Ormsby, a WWII attack transport which was launched 75 years ago this month, bore three names during its 27 years at sea and was named for pioneer Nevadan MAJ. William Matthew Ormsby.

Of equal importance, the major's name also was given to Ormsby County, one of the first counties created by the Nevada Territorial Legislature in 1861, which had Carson City as its county seat. In 1969, however, Ormsby County and Carson City were consolidated into a single city-county government named Carson City, and the 108-year-old Ormsby County was wiped off the map forever.

William Ormsby, though, unlike the ship that was to carry his name, has not escaped the attention of historians.

Born in 1814 in Pennsylvania where he gained the title "major" that reflected his service in the state's militia, he migrated in 1857 to the tiny settlement of Genoa in then-Utah Territory, became the local agent for a stage line, built the Ormsby

House hotel in nearby Carson City in 1860 and, along with several other distinguished Northern Nevadans, pressed President James Buchanan to declare what is now Nevada a separate U.S. territory. Congress and Buchanan eventually did so, and on March 2, 1861, Buchanan's last day in office, he signed the measure into law. Three years later, Nevada became the nation's 36th state.

But 14 months before Nevada achieved territorial status, Ormsby, who many believed could have become a Nevada governor or U.S. senator, met death at the age of 46 while leading a force of Nevada volunteers who, on May 12, 1860, rode from Carson City to an area near present-day Silver Springs to avenge the killing of five settlers by Paiute warriors who had charged them with kidnapping and abusing two Indian girls. Including Ormsby, 75 of his men were killed and 46 wounded. A handful of Indians were killed and injured in that Pyramid Lake War which UNR historian James Hulse writes is "the most bloody slaughter in Nevada history."

Twelve days later, more than 200 soldiers from Fort Churchill and 500 volunteers from Carson City, Virginia City and Silver City sought out and defeated the Indians. Nearly 160 Indians and three or four white men were killed in this second confrontation.

As for the history of the USS Ormsby County:

The 493-foot ship was launched on July 21, 1942, by the Moore Dry Dock Corporation in Oakland as a civilian cargo ship named the SS Twilight. A year later, the ship was acquired by the U.S. Navy, reconfigured into an attack transport and renamed the USS Ormsby. It was the first of three ships to be built in the "Ormsby Class," and the other two were named USS Pierce and USS Sheridan.

The Ormsby carried a complement of 46 officers and 478 enlisted personnel, was capable of reaching a speed of 17 knots and was armed with two 5-inch guns, two 40-mm guns and 18 20-mm guns. And, like most of the other WWII ships with Nevada geographical names, its wartime service was confined to the Pacific, where it supported amphibious landings and invasions on Japanese-held islands. During its commissioned service, the Ormsby also transported thousands of troops and their equipment to and from front lines throughout scores of islands in the Pacific theater. The ship was in the thick of things at landings on Tarawa, Guam, Guadalcanal, Peleliu, New Guinea, Leyte and the allied landings at ports in China.

The Ormsby earned six Battle Stars and the Asiatic-Pacific Area Medal as well as the Navy Occupation Service Medal and the China Service Medal. She suffered her only casualties of war while participating in the Guam landings, where one officer and two enlisted men were killed when a Japanese shell struck it in the bow.

After three years of Navy service in the Pacific, the USS Ormsby was decommissioned in 1946 and sold by the government to the United States Line, which refigured it into a commercial cargo ship and gave the vessel its third name, the SS American Producer.

For 23 years, the SS American Producer plied the Pacific, carrying a wide assortment of civilian cargo as well as U.S. military vehicles, heavy weapons, ammunition and building materials headed to U.S. installations in South Vietnam during the Vietnam War.

But in March of 1969, when setting out from the West Coast while carrying bombs bound for Da Nang, South Vietnam, it was seriously damaged after hitting a pier in San Francisco. Because repairs were deemed too expensive for the 27-year-old ship, it was sold later that year by the United States Lines to a scrapper in Taiwan, where the ship was torn asunder and turned into scrap metal which eventually became razor blades and automobiles.

David C. Henley

FROM MECHANIC TO PILOT

Anyone who thinks the 2007 to 2014 economic downturn was a big deal, the 1929 to 1941 Great Recession was an economic TSUNAMI!

Most male high school graduates who had celebrated their 18th birthday enlisted in one of the branches of the armed forces. Why? Because there would be one less mouth to feed! It was no different in New Kensington, Pa., when Robert Lloyd celebrated his 18th birthday on Nov. 24, 1939.

The local Army recruiter was talking to Lloyd trying to make his recruit quota. He told the recruiter, "I really want to join the Navy and be stationed in Honolulu, Hawaii." The recruiter countered with, "Join the US Army Air Corps, and I'll get you assigned to Honolulu." Lloyd enlisted on Dec. 11, 1939. After boot camp, he was ordered to board an Army transport in Brooklyn, NY, cruised through the Panama Canal to San Francisco and finally docked in Pearl Harbor, Hawaii, the middle of paradise.

At the U.S. Army Air Corps' Hickam Field, Lloyd became an aircraft machinist. When 21 B-17s landed at Hickam Field on May 14, 1941, he was assigned to one of them. For every pilot there were 20 support personnel from mechanics, cooks, fire fighters, meteorologists, clerical staff and others.

Sundays were casual in 1941 until Dec. 7 of that year. That morning Lloyd and his fellow machinists were ordered to wait for the arrival of a flight of B-17s due to land after 8 a.m. They heard a couple of distant explosions at 7:55 a.m. Within seconds all hell broke loose! Japanese bombs destroyed his squadron's hanger, killing 22 of his fellow machinists. Two Japanese Zeros banked above the shocked machinists exposing the red "meatballs" on their wings. In a knee jerk reaction, Lloyd dove under a low boy trailer with three fellow machinists. Instantly, Bob was a man fighting for his country.

As the flight of B-17s flew over Hickam to land, nervous anti-aircraft gunners assumed any plane in the air was Japanese. They fired at our B-17s! An officer identified the planes and ordered, "Cease fire!"

When the first wave of Japanese planes returned to one of the six Japanese carriers 200 miles northwest of Oahu, Lloyd ran to headquarters to the 22nd Material Squadron, a reinforced concrete building. Soon, the second wave of Japanese planes began to attack. Hickam Field had lost 189 personnel with 303 wounded. Every plane was damaged or destroyed.

Most of the 2,500 American killed during the attack were enlisted men and officers, a few civilians were collateral damage. The wounded were rushed to military or civilian hospitals. Hundreds of survivors rolled up their sleeves to donate blood as the medical staffs triaged the wounded. The doctors, nurses and hospital staff worked tirelessly to save lives.

Lloyd and his fellow survivors rushed wounded to hospitals. Next, they transported the dead to the nearest morgue to be identified, matched with body parts and receive a proper burial. They cleaned the hanger floors with hoses.

Five months after the attack Lloyd entered flight school and earned his wings. He flew a dual engine fighter, the P-38. The B-25 was a two-engine medium bomber similar to flying the P-38. He flew a P-39, Aerobat. The engine was behind the pilot. If the crew crashed, a P-39 the blue star in their parents' window changed to a gold star. Later he flew an A-26 which was a two-engine plane designed for low level strafing and bombing. The letter A was for attack.

Lloyd was 21 when he flew his B-25 from Greenville, S.C., to Presque Isle, Maine, to Gander, Newfoundland and then across the Atlantic Ocean to Iceland, Scotland and Wales and finally to Casablanca on the coast of North Africa. After arriving in Casablanca, he watched the newly released film, "Casablanca" starring Humphrey Bogart and Ingrid Bergman. Casablanca, was released two days after his 21st birthday, Nov. 26, 1942, in New York City.

Lloyd flew 22 low level missions, a few over the island of Patmos where St. John wrote the Book of Revelations. He flew 40 mid-level bombing missions, totaling 62 and served as command pilot in the 379th bomb squadron, 310th Bomb Group, 12th Air Force. After 21 years, he retired as a captain in 1960. Lloyd died Nov. 19, 2019, a week before his 98th birthday.

Kenneth Beaton

BOMBING RUNS
OVER GERMANY

Thirty-two missions over hostile territory in less than six months.

Daylight bombing runs targeted Limborg, Koln, Dresden, Berlin, Leipzig—to name a few of the German cities receiving the brunt of allied bombs. Togglier Sheldon Beigel or "Shel" carried out missions over Germany as a crew member on a B-17G during the wind down of World War II against the Nazis.

One of the workhorses of the U.S. Army Air Force, the B-17G heavy bomber with its additional armament conducted scores of missions against the enemy's industrial complex and military targets to break the spirt of the German people and destroy Adolph Hitler's army. The "G" model had more features than the earlier planes. The bombers had additional firepower in addition to a remotely operated chin turret that provided the plane with 13 50-caliber machine guns. The majority of the B-17s flying in combat were either the F or G models.

Beigel's memory of his time stationed in the quaint countryside of England from 1944-1945 is sharp. The 95-year-old Massachusetts native remembers details of his military service overseas in the during World War II, explaining how his unit became the model for the 1949 movie, "Twelve O'clock High." While the movie epitomized Hollywood, the B-17s and their crews mirrored the real conflict of life and death.

"As a bombardier, I sat up front," said the tech sergeant, who flew 32 combat missions for the 369th Bombardment Squadron, which was part of the 306th Bombardment Group based at Royal Air Force (RAF) Thurleigh 45 miles north of London.

Included in the 32 bombing runs were three special missions completed in early May before Germany surrendered. After completing a five-week bombardier school, Beigel flew missions from December 1944 to May 7, 1945, one day before fighting officially ended in Europe. As a newly minted togglier who armed and dropped bombs, Shel often flew with 1st Lt. Robert H. Wood's crew before the pilot left for the 364th Fighter Group, 1st Scouting Force in Feb. 23, 1945.

During the winter months and into early spring, the crew faced frigid temperatures that plunged to minus 30, even minus 40 below zero. The freezing temperatures and the lack of oxygen at 25,000 feet required personal survival skills and support from their equipment.

In the B-17 configuration, a bombardier who sat in the front and a navigator squeezed inside a bubble under the pilot and co-pilot and served as the eyes for oncoming aircraft and for initiating crucial bomb drops over strategic targets. They both had access to mounted machine guns since they were flying in the "G" model. The space allowed little room for two grown men who would squeeze in the tiny space for hours. Bombardiers, as a whole, struggled to keep their composure even with the impending threat of German planes flying toward them with machine guns engaged. Shel said the German planes would line up straight and head toward their B-17G Flying Fortress.

"We had puny 30-caliber machine guns with very little ammunition," he said, describing what B-17s mounted to defend themselves. "The Germans came down straight to the aircraft they selected. Ammunition was very limited because of the weight."

All guns were mounted and could either be used for firing or removed for secure storage of service. The only machine gun capable of rotating 360 degree was mounted in the belly turret position and could move 360 degrees. The top turret could spin 360 degrees, but it could not fire in the direction of the bomber's tail.

Beigel admits, though, the four-engine B-17Gs with 10 airmen had limitations ... doing the most with the least assets. Because of the tight space, the normal crewman stood no taller than 5-foot-7 inches and weighed between 165 to 175 pounds. The men aboard each Flying Fortress had very little room to maneuver. The available room on the aircraft dictated the space limitation.

"We were responsible for our area," described Sheldon, who grew up on his family's dairy farm as a child. "If you needed to shoot, you shoot."

Each mission's success depended on the bombardier's ability to make good use of time, but Beigel said other factors figured into his duties aboard the B-17. As a bombardier, he took into consideration the weather, the time to drop the bombs and the positions of other U.S. planes when flying information.

Each bombing mission required meticulous planning and preparation. Before flying across over the North Sea into Germany, the crew rose in the middle of the night at 3 a.m. and once showered and dressed, they attended a briefing to review their charts and listen to intelligence reports, and once the briefing ended, the men headed toward the field to their bombers. Sometimes, Beigel said breakfast would either be chowed down before or after the briefing.

Shel said the B-17s took off from Thurleigh shortly between 8 to 9 a.m.—sometimes much earlier—and returned in early to late afternoon depending on the distance of the mission and enemy resistance. Beigel's decisions became an important part of the crew's mission: He was tasked with dropping bombs accurately on targets inside Germany. Many dangerous daylight bombing runs zeroed in on the factories and critical cities such as Limborg, Dresden and the capital Berlin twice—once on Feb. 3, 1945, and the second time more than two months later on April 23.

Beigel told students at Reno's Truckee Meadows Community College in 2019 about the perils of his two missions against the German capital as allies advanced from the west and the Soviet Red Army pushed toward Berlin from the east.

"War is work, sweat, and death—it stinks," he said.

Beigel also recounted his missions to the Mighty Eight Air Force Museum: "Bombing Dresden (Feb. 1, 1945). Couldn't see to drop bombs due to heavy rising smoke. Lost both wingmen planes to ME 109s. Cologne was difficult target as well. Best experience was bombing Berlin on two different missions. I also recall the extreme cold during the Battle of the Bulge and bringing us down 20,000 feet to get under the cloud coverage to strike as the German armor below."

Beigel said the key toward flying to a target and returning to Thurleigh—whether it was skill or luck—depended on the missions and support. He said formations protected the B-17s flying into Germany. Formations and the number of planes varied—some missions requiring as little as 200 planes, others requiring upward to 1,000.

"We had some distance between the airplanes," he recalled. "We had to have the wingtips pretty tucked to each other with very little space."

Formations improved over the months. In early 1943, the planes flew in a wedge formation with squadrons flying above the cloud layer and by the end of 1943, the B-17s relied more on fighter escort and radar. Essentially, the formations enabled the massing of aircraft for their bombing runs and provided better group defense. Twelve aircraft squadrons flew in three squadron groups, and each group spread out over 4-mile intervals. This was the formation the B-17s used from Beigel's arrival in England to war's end.

"I flew as many as 10 missions in 10 days," Beigel said. "I'm the last standing member of my crew. Nobody's left. I could tell you stories, and there's nobody to say yes or no."

The bombers also flew over the enemy territory by carpet bombing their targets. Beigel and other crewmen knew it was kill or be killed on each mission.

"The Nazis tried to kill me, and I did everything to where they couldn't," Beigel said. "I evidently succeeded killing them because I am sitting here. The plane is a war machine, and if I weren't flying, it would've been someone else."

After the war ended in Europe, Shel and other airmen received orders to return home, but before they did, they wanted to check out their work over their targets. Beigel marveled at their efficiency.

"We all piled into an airplane and flew over Germany," he recalled. "We couldn't believe our own accuracy."

On each of his 32 missions, Beigel made split-second decisions on which targets to bomb, which not to bomb.

'We droned on at 180 miles per hour and we only had one shot at it," he said. "I flew many combat missions in this airplane."

During the 29th mission, Beigel's crew faced a close call. Their B-17 crashed on a plowed field in occupied France after the Germans shot it down. In addition to Biegel, two pilots and navigator suffered injuries. He told the Reno college students he relied on his childhood tracking skills. Shel told his men not to step in the peaks of the furrowed earth.

"Instead they should step over the peaks and proceed diagonally across the rows toward the bushes. That way, the Germans couldn't track them easily," he said. "They made it to the brush and hid there waiting."

Luckily for the crew, British—not German—soldiers arrived at their site, but they had to convince the Brits they were allies. Instead of being dressed in Army Air Force uniforms, Shel's crew wore their flyer's overalls for the mission. Beigel relied on his wit by using his Massachusetts' accent to call out American terms.

"We're all yanks—we're all yanks," Sheldon hollered.

Convinced, the Brits rescued the crew, who returned to Thurleigh.

Although he earned a number of medals during his military service, the crash always triggers his thoughts on one of his most prestigious awards. Beigel received the French Legion D'Honneur in 2015 from the French Consulate General in San Francisco. Established during Napoleon's rule in 1802, the French Legion D'Honneur is the country's highest award for either military or civil conduct.

Beigel retains an immense love for the B-17. He saw "Sentimental Journey" at the Minden (Nevada) Airport in early September 2019 and reminisced of his time aboard a Flying Fortress. The "Sentimental Journey" built in 1944 is one of only 10 B-17Gs that is still flying.

In February 2020 at the Pearl Harbor Aviation Museum, Beigel sat in his wheelchair in front of the wreckage of an B-17, staring at the fuselage of the "Swamp Ghost," which crashed in 1942.

"It's a shame to see her this way. You promise me you will fix her up," he said to a member of the restoration team.

Even with the passing decades, the memories of more than 75 years ago are still fresh for Beigel who still admires the role the B-17 played in World War II.

Steven R. Ranson

FLY IN WASPS' FOOTSTEPS

Stunt pilot Frank Hawks unknowingly changed the direction of history for half of America's population on Dec. 28, 1920, yet it seemed so innocent. He took a 23-year-old former tomboy who defied normal female behavior for a 10-minute flight.

"By the time I had got 200 or 300 feet off the ground, I knew I had to fly," exclaimed Amelia Mary Earhart.

Earhart invested $1,000 in flying lessons to become America's 16th female pilot in 1922, the second person to fly across the Atlantic Ocean to Derry, Ireland and set 15 flying records. She changed attitudes.

One day during the 1934-35 school year at a junior high school in Bayonne, N.J., the students had a choice of two assemblies—Major Bowes' Amateur Hour, a radio show like American Idol or Amelia Earhart. She changed the life of at least one eighth grade attendee, Hazel Marjorie Stamper.

After the assembly, Stamper and several female classmates met and asked Amelia for her autograph. At that moment, Stamper was consumed with flying! When she graduated from Lincoln High School in June 1939, she wanted to attend an aeronautical college. Her father insisted she attend Pace Secretarial College in New York City.

"The main reason a girl should go to college is to meet a good husband," he said.

Stamper commuted from New Jersey to Pace, "as if it were a prison." She flunked out of Pace Prison. Needing a job to pay for flight lessons, she was hired her as a secretary at Prudential Insurance Company in Newark. Earning $18 a week was a challenge for Stamper because flight lessons were $8 an hour.

Stamper dated a pilot with a seaplane based in Ridgefield Park while gaining more flight hours. Her first solo was in his sea plane.

"I participated in the usual ritual of buying Cokes all around over at Gus' Restaurant. I had finally joined the ranks of all my aviation heroes, especially Amelia," she said.

Stamper joined the Civil Air Patrol in early 1942. At the same time all the military airports were moved 200 miles inland for security, another challenge. Stamper read Look magazine to discover the Piper Aircraft Corporation had converted a factory to building L-4 liaison planes for the Army Air Force. After two weeks of training, Stamper was a welder on the graveyard shift and took flying lessons during the day. She applied to Piper was because flying lessons were $1.12 an hour for employees.

After six months, Stamper celebrated her 21st birthday. She and several female Piper employees traveled to New York and enlisted in the Women's Airforce Service Pilots, WASP. At Mitchell Field she received the same physical as male pilots. She passed her physical and reported to Avenger Field in Sweetwater, Texas, on Nov. 1, 1943.

Stamper wrote in her diary, "Jacqueline Cochran, the foremost woman pilot in America, took 25 American women pilots to England to study the ATA, Air Transport Auxiliary, whose women were already ferrying British fighters and bombers."

Stamper added this about WASP training.

"We would be instantly sent home if we dated instructors. But at one point, so many good students from our class were washing out, we knew something was wrong. Something was. There were male personnel who were trying to get rid of as many of us as possible. We marched to the flight line singing the Funeral March. Every day we thought would be our last, so when a group of our instructors found out we were going to a cabin at Sweetwater Lake on weekend, they met us openly, put our luggage in the cars, and we had a party that night at the lake.

"I had a big crush on my instrument instructor, but had never dared date him. But this was not a formal date, and we 'smooched' for hours, as did everyone else. That was my one and only time with Jerry. The excessive washout rate stopped, and things got back to normal when they fired the one or ones who were responsible."

Stamper's Class 44-W4's graduated May 23, 1944, at Avenger Field. Her mother's heart was filled with pride watching her daughter as a member of the honor guard. General Hap Arnold, commanding general of the Army Air Force, "liked to pin on our wings at graduation (before Cochran stopped that)."

Flying is dangerous! Thirty-eight WASPs died serving their country. Two were Stamper's classmates: Trainee Mary Homes Howson was killed in a mid-air collision on April 16, 1944 at Avenger Field. Peggy Wilson Martin was killed test flying a BT-13 on Oct. 13, 1944, near Marianna, Fla. During the second world war, the USAAF lost 88,000 aviators; 73,000 on war missions and 15,000 in training or practice.

After the war, Hazel Stamper became a mother, raising two sons and two daughters. Her world turned 180 degrees. How ironic—she flew planes hundreds of miles an hour but **never** drove a car.

Today's women fly in the footsteps of WASPs. You may decide to read "Those Wonderful Women in their Flying Machines" by Sally Van Wagenen Keil. Sally's aunt, Mary Parker Audrain, was also a WASP.

Maj. Fred Wilson accompanied Mary Parker when she soloed in a B-17. After the flight Wilson asked Parker's flight instructor, Lt. Logue Mitchell, "I've never seen a student so proud of soloing that thing. By the way, who's Charley Parker?"

"Her father, I think. Why?" Mitchell responded

"We got out on the runway, were cleared for takeoff and just before she hit the throttle, and she said, 'I'll show you, Charlie Parker!'" Wilson said. "Those gals are something."

Every WASP had something to prove, and they loved to fly. Mary Parker's dad was wrong about her. She was one of 13 WASPs who ferried B-17s from the factories to a base in England.

After 33 years with the help of USAAF Arnold's son Col. Bruce Arnold: Congresswomen Lindy Boggs and Margaret Heckler introduced H.R.3277 and Sen. Barry Goldwater of Arizona introduced S247. The legislation passed by unanimous consent and was signed by President Jimmy Carter on Nov. 23, 1977. Besides their veterans' benefits, WASPs who had passed away, have an American flag placed next to their grave marker on Veterans Day.

Stamper was 89 when she lost her battle with cancer in 2002. Her youngest daughter, Susan, loaned me her mother's diary. Susan has proudly represented her mother at several WASP reunions at Avenger Field in Sweetwater.

Kenneth Beaton

DUTY TO COUNTRY
AND COMMUNITY

Stitched on his ballcap was his history of military service: World War II, Korea, Vietnam. Many veterans like William Curry who are now in their 90s answered their country's call to don a military uniform, complete basic train and head off to fight the enemy thousands of miles from home.

At the age of 19, the Buffalo, N.Y. native enlisted in the Army because life, he thought, was better in the military. The years after the Great Depression were still difficult for many people, black or white, but the Army pitched an offer most poor young men couldn't refuse during the war years. Curry, an African-American who grew up in a household with five siblings, said they all slept in one bed. Independence beckoned him.

"When the war started in the 40s, they offered three meals per day and a bed to sleep in by myself," he recalled. "I jumped for the opportunity to get a big salary of $30 a month. That was a lot back then."

Curry's father also served in the Army from 1917-1981 in Bordeaux, France. When his father was 101 years old, France presented him with the French Legion of Honor.

Reports of the war printed in the newspaper grabbed his attention, and he joined the Army, completed basic training and headed to Georgia for infantry training. He also learned two sets of rules existed for soldiers, one for whites and the other for blacks. This, he thought, is not right because he didn't experience segregation's harshness while living in a northern state.

The city boy from Buffalo also learned he had a special talent for firing a rifle. At rifle range, the sergeant directed him to hit a target.

"I aimed the rifle and got a bullseye," Curry said. "They couldn't believe it. They took me to the target range many times, and they couldn't believe how good I was at hitting the target. I never fired a gun in my life before."

Curry figures his good aim and eyesight led to his success on the range.

Within weeks, Curry's training lent itself to his survival in Africa. Curry and other soldiers received in training how to become more efficient with their weapons and with the usage of a bayonet. Immediately, Curry knew the bayonet was used for close contact. With success gaining under their belts, Curry's unit left for Sicily with their entire day-to-day living essentials packed on their backs.

"We were stationed in North Africa and received training with our bayonets on the rifles," Curry said.

Soon, though, Curry's unit boarded a ship and headed toward Sicily, ready to assemble and mount an attack on Italy's southern tip. From there the Allies inched their way toward Italy's border with France.

Not only was it a test of wills to be the only African American in his unit, but it also was a test to remain alive.

"I got wounded during the invasion of the northern part of Italy," explained. "I was stabbed with a bayonet and had to go to the hospital— a field hospital—for a short period of time," he said, adding he returned to his unit. "At that time, they didn't bring the bodies back to the United States. They were buried wherever they were killed. We lost so many young men."

Orders came down directing Curry and hundreds of soldiers to move toward Normandy and link up with Allies in the north commanded by Gen. Dwight D. Eisenhower. German resistance began to slow down Curry's unit, and they arrived at Normandy shortly after the invasion begun.

"We were a small group and we were already near Normandy when the invasion started, and we combined with Eisenhower's units. We just kept going," Curry said.

As the war began to wind down, Victory Europe Day declared on May 8, 1945, would lead to an eventual major change for Curry. He left the military and returned to New York City to work in a post office, lamenting the time spent in the Army and what it offered a young man. Curry, though, missed the military and when the Army and its Air Corps split into two military services in 1947, Curry opted to join the new Air Force and was assigned to civil engineering, eager to earn a new vocation and not be in a segregated unit. Curry's RED HORSE team of deployable engineers found themselves in the middle of a new war, though, in the early 1950s.

In 1974, he retired from the military after 27 years at McLellan Air Force Base northeast of Sacramento, Calif., and eventually met the woman there who would become his wife. They later relocated to Reno where they would raise a daughter, and his wife would retire as a master sergeant with the Nevada Air National Guard. His daughter Bayo, a physician with Saint Mary's Regional Medical Center, and her husband have two daughters.

Curry led by example, saying education was important.

"I went to college after the military," he pointed out. "I was persistent, and I got my degree in education from the University of Nevada."

For 26 years he worked with mentally challenged children and felt not only was he helping them but also helping himself become a better person.

Curry previously took an Honor Flight Nevada trip to Washington, D.C. several years ago before accompanying fellow World War II vets on their latest journey to Oahu. The memorials impressed him both in the nation's capital and in Hawaii.

"They're all very important to men," Curry said, pausing. "I think of the men who lost their lives."

Curry is also proud of a signed letter he received from President Barack Obama and Michelle on his 92nd birthday in 2015. The retired veteran, who will have his 97th birthday on April 1, doesn't regret where his life took him over the years.

"I want people to know that I did my best. I learned while overseas, I'm living in the best country in the world called the United States. I have no respect for anyone who disrespects the flag. This is the best country in the world for anybody. I don't care what nationality you are. You work hard, go to school and get a college degree."

Steven R. Ranson

Medal of Honor and World War II hero Audie Murphy's grave at Arlington National Cemetery.

Steven R. Ranson

HOSPITAL RECOVERY
WITH AUDIE MURPHY

"*N*<sup>ot as a soldier but as an individual, I never met a nicer person.*"

*That's how William L. (Bill) Keenan remembered the late Audie Murphy (killed in a small plane crash on May 28, 1971) when both of them were confined to the 3rd General Hospital in Marseille, France, during the late years of World War II.

Murphy eventually emerged as the most decorated soldier of World War II.

Keenan, who worked as a senior engineer for Nevada Bell in Reno, was a first lieutenant with the United States Army Air Corps when he first met Murphy on Nov. 19, 1944. Five days before, Keenan was brought into the hospital with injuries suffered in a land mine explosion at the Istres airfield, 30 miles west of Marseille on the Mediterranean coast.

While in the hospital, the two servicemen became very close through joking with each other. One of the reasons Murphy kidded Keenan, whose bed was directly across the room, was because of all the patients confined in the hospital, Keenan was the only Air Corps man. All of the other men hospitalized at that time came from the 3rd Infantry Division.

"The only way a pilot could get hurt by a land mine was that you were out rabbit hunting on the airfield," Murphy would rib Keenan. "How could an Air Corps guy get hurt?—We (the infantry) do all the work."

But to counter the jibing by Murphy, Keenan retaliated: "If it's so easy, why didn't you join the Air Corps or why didn't you ask for a transfer?"

"Fly in an airplane? Not this boy. I want my feet on the ground even if it's on the front lines," Murphy would snap back.

Looking back, Keenan said it was ironic that Murphy died in an airplane crash on May 28, when, in 1944, at the age of 19, he was afraid of flying.

"I was very shocked when they located the plane with him," Keenan said. "I did think an awful lot of him."

Most of the time, Keenan continued, Murphy wanted to make up for his small size. "He wanted to prove himself a man; he was a leader. He had visions of returning to his Texas home."

Keenan tried several times after the war to contact Murphy by letters and postcards, but all the replies he received came from the public relations people handling Murphy's mail. If Murphy had received a letter from his hospital buddy, Keenan was sure, he would have received a reply form the motion picture star. But all tempts to reach Murphy failed.

"I felt Murphy did not have any knowledge of my attempts at contact," Keenan said. "If he did, he would have been happy to hear from me."

Keenan felt the war hero reputation often bothered Murphy. He believed Murphy would rather have been known as Audie Murphy, the farm boy from Texas rather than the hero of World War II.

But returning to Murphy's humbleness during the war, Keenan concluded, "Many, many people in the service received citations, medals and on and on, and I can think back, put my tongue in my cheek and say all these people deserved these awards. This may or may not be the truth, but some people did little to receive these awards. But in Mr. Murphy's case, every award he received, he deserved.

"But then again, it was like him to give away his medals," said Keenan. "He felt the awards should have been given to his group, his squad, his company or his platoon. It was like him though—not a medal hunter, but Audie Murphy, the boy from Farmersville, Texas."

Keenan was also a hero to many. After he graduated from high school in Auburn, Calif., he worked for AT&T before enlisting in the Army Air Force after war broke out. He attended flight school, earned his wings as a pilot, and flew missions over Europe in both the B-25 Mitchell medium bomber and B-17 Flying Fortress, a heavy bomber. Keenan, who achieved the rank of captain, was awarded the Purple Heart after he was seriously injured by a land mine in France.

At the end of his service, Keenan returned to AT&T in Sacramento but later transferred to Reno where he retired after a 40-year career. In 2010 Keenan died at the age of 87.

Steven R. Ranson

SAILOR FIBBED HIS AGE AT ENLISTMENT

A trail of death and destruction swallowed the western Pacific Theater during the final year of World War II as the allies continued their march toward the Japanese mainland and the Philippines.

While the Americans troops island hopped southeast of Japan, another U.S. wave aimed its sights on retaking the Philippines by capturing Peleliu in mid-September 1944 and then working their way to Leyte and finally to Luzon, home to the capital of Manilla.

As a young teenager during the latter part of World War II, Gilbert Sanchez had a front-row seat to the intense fighting and of the troops storming the beach. Sanchez, perhaps one of the youngest sailors on the assaults, had persuaded his father to allow him to enlist in the Navy when he was 15 years old.

"I lied to get into the Navy," said Sanchez, who lives in Reno. "I had been working on the Northern Nevada Railroad, (a disbanded line that began at the copper mines at Ruth in extreme eastern Nevada and wound its way to the main railroad line east of Wells.) "It was so damn cold I can't do this."

Harsh winters blanket eastern Nevada with vicious snowstorms and below-zero temperatures. Sanchez reached a breaking point of working in blizzard-like conditions.

"I went to Ely and asked my father for permission (to enlist)," Sanchez said. "I was born in 1928 but with ink eradication, I carefully put a 6 in there and went to Salt Lake City to join the Navy."

In no time, Sanchez boarded a train to warm and sunny San Diego where he began his boot camp. Afterward, Sanchez realized he would be in much warmer, humid weather once he left southern California.

"The Navy's plan was to send most of the guys overseas," Sanchez recalled.

After several months in the South Pacific, Sanchez and his fellow sailors received their first set of orders for assignment to the USS Jupiter AK43, an Aldebaran-class cargo ship that delivered goods and equipment to the war zone and the amphibious forces. Their first stop was Peleliu, a beginning step to fulfill Gen. Douglas MacArthur's vision of returning to the Philippines and driving the Japanese out.

"Our crew consisted of the coxswain, the motor mac and the deckhand, which was me," Sanchez said. "My job was to lower the ramp and raise it once the troops were ashore."

Sanchez said the crew ferried about 30 men on each trip.

"We made numerous trips," Sanchez added, describing each trip as dangerous under enemy fire.

First, a number of battleships, cruisers and three aircraft carriers softened the island with a pre-assault barrage of bombardments. On Sept. 15, the Navy's bombardment continued along with planes strafing and bombing Peleliu. Within a three-hour span, the landing crafts plowed through the choppy water, dropping off about 6,000 Marines who stormed the shore in a morning marked by a high number of casualties.

"I would lower the ramp when we hit the beach, and raise the ramp. We had a .50-caliber machine gun on the back of the boat," Sanchez, a seaman second class, pointed out. "There were more ships doing the same thing, and after all the troops were ashore, we took in supplies."

The Japanese fought their battles in the hills, but Sanchez said any enemy shelling toward the shore came in high. The crews, though, stayed in their landing boats until the USS Jupiter was ready to depart, which was within the 7-to-10-day span.

The U.S. armada of battleships, cruisers and aircraft carriers sailed west in preparation for an assault on Leyte. Shelling from Navy ships pounded targets on Leyte, preparing the island for a massive assault conducted by the Sixth U.S. Army. On Oct. 20, MacArthur waded onto Leyte's shore and, on a radio broadcast, delivered his prophesy: "People of the Philippines, I have returned."

Near the end of December, the United States' conquest of Leyte became a decisive victory in slowly recapturing the Philippines from a Japanese force that saw its number dwindle to a quarter million soldiers. On the first day of fighting on Luzon, Sanchez and the other landing boat crews braved the heavy surf in Lingayen Gulf to drop off the troops. Up and down the beach were men and stacks of supplies needed for the final push to recapturing Manilla.

After the war, time ran out on Sanchez's enlistment: the Navy discovered Sanchez's age and gave him an honorable discharge. He then joined the U.S. Coast Guard and was assigned to the USCGC Chautauqua, an Owasco class high endurance cutter that was commissioned on Aug. 1, 1945.

He served on the ship for a year before his assignment to the Carquinez Strait Light House west of Vallejo which he manned for two years before his honorable discharge from the Coast Guard. Upon completion of his three-year tour, Sanchez's brother told him he could get a job with a contractor in Reno and become an apprentice carpenter.

In looking back at his enlistment as a teenager, Sanchez said he has no regrets in fibbing about his age to serve during World War II.

"It was one of the best things I ever did in my entire life," he said.

Steven R. Ranson

PEOPLE COME FIRST

A locomotive chugs to a stop, hissing steam, at the Reno train station. Thousands of at cars line the tracks, strapped with military equipment of all sizes—guns, jeeps, trucks, cannons, tanks. Hundreds of railcars, meanwhile, are filled with uniformed U.S. Army soldiers.

In the early 1940s, a United States Armed Forces "troop train" is making one of its many railway stops dotted across the country as it mobilizes soldiers.

Reno-area residents look on as service men and women from Northern Nevada board the train. One of those onlookers in the crowd is 14-year-old Beatrice (Coffey) Thayer, a Native American with Northern Paiute and Western Shoshone heritage.

Along with her parents, Thayer is paying special attention to her fellow Native soldiers who are stepping into the railcars—soldiers who, the young Thayer recognizes, are preparing to fight not only for their country, but also for their tribes, their people.

Nearly four years later, in early 1945 with the war still raging on, a 17-year-old Thayer joined them.

"Since I was in school, not doing too good, and we were always hungry, I decided, well, maybe I can help a little bit," Thayer, now 92, recalls. "I didn't want to be a housekeeper the rest of my life, because that's the only job I could get at that time."

Thayer pauses, considering what else compelled her to enlist in the U.S. Army during WWII.

"I mainly did it because I remember the old people (who came before me)—they had a worse time than we did," she added.

Her service as a Staff Sgt. in the U.S. Army Air Force (1945-1948) and U.S. Air Force (1948-1958)—and later the Nevada Army National Guard (1973-1982)—took her everywhere from the Deep South to the East Coast to West Germany. She saw the Berlin Wall go up; she jumped out of a malfunctioning helicopter as it was touching down; and she taught herself how to type and earned a promotion.

Above all, as Thayer puts it, she "worked, worked and worked"—for her country, for her tribes and for her family.

"I was supporting my mother and father," Thayer said. "I sent them money, whatever I could. I saved it up until I had two, three hundred (dollars) and I would send it home. I just kept what I needed."

LIVING IN POVERTY, FACING RACISM

Raised on the Reno-Sparks Indian Colony, Thayer, like many Natives, grew up in extreme poverty. Born in Camino, Calif., roughly 120 miles southwest of Reno, Thayer and her family migrated to Northern Nevada when she was about 4 years old.

"I just remember we didn't have anything," Thayer says with a shrug. "I was always hungry. I used to go to school and drink water to try to keep my stomach quiet for a few minutes."

What's more, she grew up during a time when racism toward American Indians was present everywhere she looked outside of the reservation—back when establishments in Reno hung "No Indians Allowed" signs right next to "No Dogs Allowed" signs, she recalls.

"At that time, we were not allowed in any of the restaurants or swimming pools or whatever they had in (Reno)," Thayer says. "We had to be out of town at 9 o'clock at night—otherwise they would pick you up and you'd get beat up or thrown back out to the colony."

Little changed when Thayer entered the service. She'd feel hateful glares and hear racial slurs from fellow troops. On the rare times she took leave, the bigotry of the military base was worse. Thayer recalled a time when she went on leave with a friend who was visiting a priest. The priest, Thayer found, quickly revealed his prejudice toward Native Americans.

"He was not very pleasant to me," Thayer remembers. "He called me 'Minnehaha' ... And I had to share a bed with my friend and he said to her, 'Are you going to sleep with that?'

"It was very, very hard to be a Native in the service," she continued. "It was really hard at times, and I put up with a lot. But, to me, they weren't worth talking to. They thought we were wagon burners and we took their ranches away from them. "But they didn't know—they didn't know anything."

This ignorance was widespread despite the fact Thayer was one of more than 44,000 American Indians—out of a total Native population in the U.S. of less than 350,000—who served with distinction between 1941 and 1945 in both European and Pacific theaters of WWII.

In fact, American Indians have served in the U.S. Armed Forces in greater numbers per capita than any other ethnic group, according to the U.S. Census Bureau. In all, there are more than 190,000 Native American military veterans, according to the U.S. Department of Defense.

'DUTY FIRST'

Looking back, Thayer says she didn't let the hate speech deter and distract her from her objective: She was an American Indian warrior helping defend her homeland and provide for her family.

"I didn't have time to think of that stuff because ... duty first," she said. "And I had to take care of my mother and father."

Thayer was a Medical Corpsman during her first two years in service, working at various military base hospitals. She remembers working in the 3rd Air Force Base hospital in Gulfport, Miss., on the day Japan surrendered to bring WWII to a close.

"Everybody was celebrating, but I had duty at 11 o'clock at night," she remembers. "I worked. I couldn't leave."

While in the service, showing a tireless work ethic, Thayer was motivated to learn new skills and take on more responsibility, even if she had to teach herself.

As a chaplain's assistant in South Carolina at the Greenville Air Force Base, for example, Thayer taught her-self to play the piano, organ and accordion. She sang, too. Later, at Langley Air Force Base in Virginia, she taught herself how to type.

"I was a medic and wanted to do something else," she says. "So I taught myself how to type when I was working nights. They had a typewriter in the orderly room, so when I had night duty, I just typed and typed and typed. So I got pretty good and somehow somebody found out about it."

FOUR YEARS IN GERMANY

This led to Thayer's first experience overseas. In 1952, she was promoted and transferred to the 12th Air Force Base in Wiesbaden, West Germany, to serve as a senior clerk.

She proved to be an incredibly valuable asset. In fact, documents Thayer shared with First Nation's Focus stated the following:

"SSGT Thayer had various clerical duties and delivered important war correspondence to the Supreme Headquarters of the Allied Forces in Europe."

While serving in Germany, Thayer was even selected to attend the Inter-Allied Moral Leadership Conference for Women in Uni- form hosted by the Netherlands Royal Air Force.

In her downtime, she did things like explore museums in Holland and watch professional skiing in Austria.

She also met her eventual husband, who she exchanged vows with twice in one hour—first by the Burgomaster in Wiesbaden, then by the chaplain at the base. They were married for seven years and had two sons, Daniel and David.

Thayer returned to the states in 1956. Two years later, she was honorably discharged from the U.S. Air Force in October 1958.

Thayer's time in the service, however, proved to be far from over.

BACK AFTER 15-YEAR GAP

In 1973, 15 years after leaving the Air Force, Thayer, at age 48, re-enlisted in the Nevada Army National Guard.

This came on the heels of trying to join the Air National Guard but being told she had been out too long and would have to take basic training all over again.

"So I went over to the Army (National) Guard and they were happy to get me, I couldn't believe it," Thayer says with a laugh.

Holding the rank of Specialist Five, Thayer was a state recruiter who was assigned to the Army Guard's Communication Center in Carson City.

Additionally, she joined the 20th Army Band, playing the French horn and clarinet in many formal functions, including the Nevada Day Parade held in downtown Carson City.

Nine years later, in 1982, Thayer officially finished her military career after 22 years of service.

During that span, she was awarded with the following: U.S. Army Good Conduct Medal (with 5 knots); Army National Guard Achievement Medal; Women's Army Corps Medal; American Campaign Medal; World War II Victory Medal; Germany Occupation Medal; National Defense Service Medal; and the Nevada Army National Guard Meritorious Service Ribbon.

Kaleb M. Roedel

FIGHTING FOR MY COUNTRY

Sterling Phillips' voice catches as tears well up in his eyes. The 93-year-old U.S. Navy veteran is overcome with emotion as he talks about his first day back home in El Paso, Texas, after Japan surrendered and brought the hostilities of World War II to a close on Aug. 15, 1945.

Soon after fighting for his country for two years on the aircraft carrier USS Salvo Island, where he saw brave men fall in battle, Phillips unexpectedly lost the man he looked up to more than anyone: his father.

"I got to see him alive for about 10 minutes (after the war)," said Phillips, his voice shaking, the memory still close. "He had just gotten out of the shower and walked over to me and hugged me and told me that he was happy to see me home again."

Minutes later, while visiting with a friend in the yard, Phillips heard his mother's scream pierce the air. His father, Ben Phillips, 41, had collapsed.

"I ran in the house and my dad was already on the door. I said, 'what's a matter with him? I was just talking to him!'" recalled Phillips, wiping a tear from his cheek. "And that was it ... my dad was gone."

Nearly 75 years later, Phillips is recounting that heart-wrenching moment from a recliner is his north Reno home on a sunny afternoon in early June. Phillips, who served as a reman 2nd Class on the Savo Island (CVE-78), was one of 50 Nevada veterans who took a trip to Washington D.C. in June 2019 through Honor Flight Nevada. The organization takes local veterans to Washington, D.C. to visit the memorials honoring their service and sacrifices.

ANSWERING THE CALL

Years before his father passed, Phillips begged his dad to take him to a U.S. Navy recruitment office in El Paso. His father obliged.

Like many young Americans, Phillips—who was born Dec. 18, 1926, in Oklahoma but grew up in El Paso—was motivated to enlist in the military following Japan's attack on Pearl Harbor on Dec. 7, 1941.

And also like many young Americans, Phillips lied about his age to get in. Despite having to be either 18 or 17 with parental consent, Phillips enlisted as a 16-year-old.

"I wanted to go fight for my country," Phillips shrugs. "All my buddies were going in, so I had to go in. I remember that everyone like myself was trying to get into the service. I enlisted as soon as I could get in."

Before he knew it, Phillips was 800 miles west of home, stationed at the San Diego Naval Training Center. He was given shots, a buzzcut and, eventually, a uniform.

When asked what his emotions were heading into boot camp, Phillips, without hesitation, used one word.

"Excited," he stated. "I was excited. I really didn't have time to be afraid."

Phillips noted that his platoon won first place for marching at the graduation ceremony, a fact that still gives him a boost of pride to this day.

"You should've seen it," said Phillips, grinning as the moment floods back to him. "When we were marching, it almost looked like one man. All in a straight line, a perfect line."

Days later, Phillips, officially a Navy sailor, was shipped off to war. He stepped onto the USS Savo Island—a near 10,000-ton aircraft carrier with roughly 1,000 men aboard—which set out for the North Pacific Ocean. His job was in the engine room, where he made sure all the pumps—fuel and water—were working.

Save for brief windows of time on leave, Phillips would be on the ship for the next two years.

KAMIKAZE CHAOS

It's Jan. 5, 1945, and the Savo Island is providing support to U.S. troops on the beaches of the Lingayen Gulf in the Philippines.

Gunfire and explosions and screaming planes echo across the Pacific in a cacophony of hellish sounds.

In the midst of battle, Phillips and fellow comrades were aware the Japanese, at any moment, could send a suicide bomber at their ship. After all, a day earlier, a kamikaze plane sunk their sister ship, the USS Ommaney Bay (CVE-79), which had been a part of the Lingayen Gulf mission.

Phillips was in the clipping room, loading the ammunition of the ship's artillery, when he heard a crash. Indeed, a kamikaze pilot hit their ship—but just barely. The bomber sheared off the carrier's air- search radar antenna with its wing tip and splashed into the ocean. The ship's artillery unloaded on the Japanese plane.

"I was trying to shell out as much of the shells out there ... and just trying to keep busy," Phillips says.

'EXPECTING THE SHIP TO GO DOWN'

Despite being on a ship targeted by a kamikaze pilot, Phillips said the scariest time on the Savo Island was when they traveled through the Bering Strait, the treacherous stretch of sea separating Russia and Alaska. The ship was sailing for the Aleutian Islands at the time.

"That's a bad area, it's some of the roughest weather in the ocean," recalled Phillips, noting that giant ocean waves violently rocked their giant carrier. "We were expecting the ship to go down."

After a scare in the Bering Strait, the Savo Island pushed on, heading toward Japan. Days later, in early August 1945, the U.S. swiftly put an end to the war, dropping two atomic bombs on Japanese soil—Hiroshima on Aug. 6 and Nagasaki on Aug. 9.

The surrender of Japan was announced a week later, Aug. 15, 1945. It was made official on Sept. 2, when Japanese foreign affairs minister Mamoru Shigemitsu signed the Japanese Instrument of Surrender on board the USS Missouri off the coast of Tokyo. Phillips and his comrades on the Savo Island were there to see the signing of the peace treaty.

"We were there watching, standing at attention," Phillips said. "That was something to witness."

"Everybody had a tear in their eye," Phillips added.

A POSITIVE OUTLOOK

Nearly 75 years later, that time during the war, and thinking of the time missed with his father, can bring tears to Phillips just the same. Yet, immediately following the war, and even to this day, he doesn't let those wartime experiences impact his life.

After his father passed, he moved to East Los Angeles with his mother and siblings. He opened up a record shop. He joined a rock band (The Night- dreamers) as a guitarist and toured the country. He lived life. Later, he got a blue-collar job at Mobil Oil, bought acres of land in Northern California, made a home with his wife, Amelia, and had kids.

"He's always had a really positive outlook on life, which I'm pretty impressed by," his daughter Mia said. "I think that's what keeps him going for as long as he's been going for."

It's an attitude Phillips has maintained despite losing his vision four years ago. Phillips feels the strong gunpowder getting into his eyes and the bright ashes from nighttime combat during WWII contributed to his blindness.

"I don't feel old. I feel good. Like the (James Brown) song, I feel good...," he sings, cheerily. "I've got children who I love dearly and my wife. And I've got a lot of friends."

Kaleb M. Roedel

WAITING
BEFORE ENLISTING

As soon as he could join the military, Robert "Bob" LeGoy enlisted in the U.S. Navy as a radar technician, several years after the Japanese bombed Pearl Harbor and other military targets on Oahu on Dec. 7, 1941.

LeGoy, who grew up in Bishop, Calif., a small city situated near the base of the eastern Sierra Nevada about 185 miles south of Reno, distinctly recalled the day and how he learned more about the destruction of Navy ships.

"The only radio we could get was KMJ out of Fresno (California)," LeGoy recalled. "I made an antenna, and about 100 people gathered."

What they heard was numbing. Torpedo bombs either sunk or heavily damaged ships, planes on the flight line were destroyed and many people—both civilian and military—died.

During his final years in high school, LeGoy remembers his friends who answered the call to join the military.

"All my friends were all trying to enlist," he said. "My stepbrother went anyway."

When LeGoy recently visited Pearl Harbor, he pointed to a hill that had significance. A father of one of his classmates, Judd Collins, worked on a construction crew watching the attack along Battleship Row. LeGoy said Collins had a front-row seat to history in the making.

"I heard of some of those first-hand stories," LeGoy said when Collins, a longtime rancher, returned to Bishop.

What Collins saw were waves of Japanese planes swooping over Battleship Row, dropping torpedo bombs and strafing military targets with their machine guns. Smoke billowed into the air.

"When he saw the machine guns hit the ships, he decided to get out," LeGoy said.

A little more than a year after Pearl Harbor, LeGoy had enough credits to wrap up his high-school studies. He enlisted in the Navy on Jan. 6, 1943, and served for three years and three months, leaving shortly before his 21st birthday.

For the final part of his duty, LeGoy spent time on a converted trawler and refrigeration ship that had been constructed in 1936. The YP-415 spent most of its time in the Atlantic Ocean, but the U.S. Navy converted the 132-foot ship for naval service in July 1942 and commissioned it on July 17. Two machine guns were placed at the bow and stern.

LeGoy said the ship carried 32 people, but it could only seat 10 at a time for meal time. The cooks ate in the galley.

"We left San Francisco on July 25, 1945, and passed under the Golden Gate Bridge," LeGoy said, remembering the time of the crew leaving the San Francisco Bay was at 2 p.m. "We sailed to Hawaii and reached the islands in three days."

Once the ship topped off with fuel and food, the YP-415 left Pearl Harbor. LeGoy said the YP-415 was part of an assembled armada positioning itself for an invasion of Japan, which, he later learned, was planned for Nov. 1. LeGoy said those involved with the invasion force expected a high casualty rate.

"At the time, we heard about 90%," LeGoy said.

Three days after the YP-415 left Oahu, the crew learned of a powerful bomb that caused heavy damage to a Japanese city. Several major events in August 1945 changed the YP-415's mission. Two U.S B-29 Superfortress bombers dropped atomic bombs on Hiroshima and Nagasaki on Aug. 6 and 9, respectively, causing Japanese Emperor Hirohito to surrender after the second bomb.

"I didn't think too much of the first bomb," LeGoy recalled, "but on the second bomb, everyone got pretty excited about it."

Plans changed quickly for the YP-415. LeGoy said the captain changed the ship's course, and the crew headed toward the Philippines, stopping first on the island of Samar, southeast of Luzon and the capital city of Manilla. The YP-415 used the inside waterways to reach Manilla and then continued to Subic Bay, a major naval installation.

With the YP-415 arriving in the Philippines, LeGoy and the others didn't know about a formal end of the war. On Sept. 2, 1945, aboard the battleship USS Missouri, the United States and its allies signed a formal Instrument of Surrender with Japan.

Four months after the signing, LeGoy headed home and enrolled at the University of Nevada. Once he earned his bachelor's degree in journalism, LeGoy spent most of his career with Reno Newspapers, moving up the ladder to marketing director.

When LeGoy visited the USS Missouri on an Honor Flight Nevada trip to Pearl Harbor in February 2020, LeGoy spent time on the battleship's main deck reading the documents pertaining to the formal signing and looking at the ship's symbols describing the USS Missouri's missions during the war. One thing, though, stood out for LeGoy is how two sailors operating a small passenger boat to the Arizona Memorial wore crisp, white uniforms.

"We're getting on the boat to the Arizona, and the sailors were standing there with their white uniforms on," LeGoy said. "They looked fantastic."

Steven R. Ranson

DASHED
AVIATION ASPIRATIONS

Elmer Larsen missed serving overseas during World War II by months, but as a member of the "Greatest Generation," the Carson City resident had that gut feeling that he still needed to serve his country.

"I was 18 years old, and I wanted to learn how to fly an airplane," said the Wisconsin native, who's lived in Carson City for almost two decades. "So I joined the U.S. Army Air Force. I was asked if I was willing to enlist for the next five years."

With the war effort winding down and troops returning home, Larsen, who recently celebrated his 92nd birthday, said he couldn't envision spending the next five years in the military without going to battle. He did, however, transition to the U.S. Air Force when it became its own military branch in 1947.

His dreams of flying, though, came to an end since the need for pilots dwindled.

"I stayed at Lackland Air Force Base (San Antonio, Texas) and served in a basic training command," Larsen said, adding he also spent a tour in California.

During his three years of service, Larsen worked hard, studied diligently and worked his way up the promotion ladder, eventually becoming a staff sergeant. Larsen said he kept busy with record keeping, training and picking up AWOL (Absent Without Leave) service members.

When Larsen's enlistment ended, he relocated to Sacramento, Calif., where he began work as an apprentice carpenter. He applied and was hired as a building inspector and then advanced to a chief building official before retiring after a 23-year career. With a solid background working with the city, Larsen became a self-employed building consultant who oversaw construction of the Raley's baseball field and three stages of the Cache Creek Casino Resort construction northwest of Sacramento and near Woodland. The Cache Creek project became one of Larsen's greatest joys.

"This casino consisted of a 1-million gallon water tank, a four-story hotel, a three-story parking garage, and the casino was the size of three football fields with seven restaurants," he added.

Larsen, by his own admission, kept busy as a full-time consultant.

"I solved over 200 cases for the Contractors License Board and was a full-time inspector on four large fire stations," he pointed out. "I worked for several attorneys as an expert witness."

In addition to being a building consultant, Larsen used his expertise to teach two classes of contractor license law at Heald College and taught for 10 years a two-year carpentry apprentice program for the union.

Since moving to Nevada, Larsen is active in the community as a member of the Kiwanis Club of Carson City and had a day proclaimed in his honor two years ago. In addition to his career and community involvement, Larsen is the father of six adult children, five of whom are 60 years of age and older.

"You could say I have had a pretty full life," he said with a grin.

The whirlwind five-day trip to Pearl Harbor and other military related sites on Oahu may be a distant memory now for Larsen. From the reception and send off at Honolulu's Daniel K. Inouye International Airport to the tours of the Pearl Harbor Aviation Museum, the battleship USS Missouri, the USS Arizona Memorial, Larsen had a chance to remember a dark period in the country's history.

"The movie we saw brought tears to my eyes," he said of a documentary on the bombing of Pearly Harbor on Dec. 7, 1941. "When the war started, I was a young boy. I heard the news on the radio that Japan bombed Pearl Harbor. The movie brought everything out."

Steven R. Ranson

GENERATION OF
WAR FIGHTERS

A World War II waist gunner paused during his lesson on how to clean a B-25 Mitchell turret as a C-130 took off from Minden-Tahoe Airport.

The airport was awash with both modern and historic combat aircraft for several days thanks to the Collings Foundation Wings of Freedom display and exercises conducted by U.S. Marine Corps 1st Expeditionary Operations Training Group and the 11th Marine Expeditionary Unit.

"It is so interesting," Army Air Corps veteran Desmond Machen, 92, said of seeing present day Osprey refueling a head's turn away from a WW II-era B-24. "It is fun to see what has come from technology."

A pair of Osprey helicopters were being off loaded and refueled, giving the Marines some down time to talk to the veterans, who used to maintain, fly and work in the quartet of historic aircraft on display.

While the Marines are using Minden-Tahoe as a mock forward staging base, being able to break from training was an added bonus to being away from their home base of Camp Pendleton, Calif., Capt. Scott Hambley said.

"We are very lucky that the stars aligned that these planes can be on the strip at the same time," he said. "To be able to talk to and spend time with World War II veterans, who are the greatest generation of war fighters, is very fortuitous."

For Machen being able to see the planes that he loaded bombs into is extra special because of the company he shared the experience with.

Fellow WWII veteran James Mefford, 95, was a B-24 pilot during the war, first in North Africa and then in the European Theatre in Italy, where he was shot down and rescued by partisans.

Mefford received a Purple Heart for his experience.

"We were in the same unit," Machen said. "He was a pilot of the 460 Bomb Group and I took care of the turrets and was a nose gunner. He was in 760 squadron and I was in 761. We had no idea who each other was until we moved into Brookdale. I was fortunate enough to never get a Purple Heart. He wasn't so lucky."

The pair became fast friends and enjoy swapping war stories, Machen said.

Seeing the planes that he used to fly into enemy fire for more than 12 hours a day, safe and restored on the ground, was only improved by the presence of the Marines for Mefford.

"It is so fascinating to see the Marines over there," he said. "Their planes are so different. It is neat to see the new ones."

Machen and Mefford spent time under the shade of the nose of the B-25 talking to Osprey pilots about their time in the cockpit of the older planes and asking questions about piloting the modern aircraft.

Two years later in 2016 the airport hosted a similar event.

A flight of World War II aircraft that visited the airport brought back memories of World War II on the 70th anniversary of D-Day.

The B-17 Flying Fortress, B-24 Liberator, B-25 Mitchell and P-51 Mustang operated by the nonprofit Collings Foundation took off Wednesday for Stead Airport.

Johnson Lane resident Pamela Rogers said her recently deceased brother, John Hayward, would have loved to see the World War II aircraft.

"They came over so low when they flew in, but I didn't have a camera," she said. "Then I was in Carson for an appointment and I saw them fly out, and the camera was in the car."

Rogers said her brother was a flier during World War II and had a map that showed all the airports in Germany they bombed.

The brother and sister came to America in the late 1950s, settling in California. Rogers moved to Carson Valley in 1992, and her brother joined her in 2007 after his wife died.

While her brother was serving in the war for the D-Day invasion, Rogers was in Kent when the planes and gliders took off over the English Channel.

"I was also up in London with mother and grandmother at the time of the Blitz," Rogers said of the German bombing of London. "We were told to leave the coast in case of invasion, so we went to the outskirts of London right in the middle of the Blitz. That was not the right place. I even slept on the platforms on the London Underground."

Kurt Hildebrand and Sarah Hauck

VETERAN WAITED
TO JOIN THE WAR

The surprise attack on Pearl Harbor early on the morning of Dec. 7, 1941, prompted a call for volunteers to enlist in the military and fight for their country.

One such young man was Jimmie Monsoor, a La Crosse, Wisc., native who now lives in Reno, but his age at the time prevented him from serving.

"When Pearl Harbor was bombed, everybody was ready to join," he said. "I was too young. Later on, I wanted to join the Marines, but my mother wouldn't sign. She said I was too young."

Monsoor was 15 years old when the United States declared war on Japan. As the years slowly pressed on, Monsoor waited before he could join the military, but instead of volunteering at a younger age like he wanted, he received a draft notice when he was 18 years old. Within two weeks, he left for basic training. Monsoor entered the Army Air Force and spent 1945-1946 in a crucial position.

"Praise the Lord, so to speak," he said. "I was very fortunate to get in at the end of the war."

As a chemical technician, he was in charge of a bombs dump chemical storage on Guam, a small island in the Marianas that was recaptured by American forces in 1944.

"One of my jobs was to protect those bombs, and if they had a leak, I'd go in and decontaminate it," he said.

Monsoor said it was dangerous work by tending to an arsenal of mustard, napalm and chemical bombs. Each projectile was filled with liquefied noxious gas that was released when the bomb exploded. If a leak developed, Monsoor said a crew donned their decontamination equipment and fixed the leak.

To this day, Monsoor also remembers Guam's hot, humid weather, and the jungle and other vegetation that covered half the island.

"There were lots of insects," Monsoor said. "We were fortunate the island was sprayed every two weeks."

Monsoor attended basic training Sheppard Field and Wichita Falls, Texas, and completed his advanced training for chemical technician at Buckley Field, Colo. After World War II ended, Monsoor, who was a corporal, slipped into the inactive reserves, but with the breakout of war on the Korean peninsula, he was recalled. Monsoor, who spent total of 12 years in the military, remained stateside.

When World War II ended, though, Monsoor settled in California rather than returning home to Wisconsin. He attended a junior college and then California State University Sacramento where he majored in chemistry and minored in math, yet he felt his purpose in life was unfilled.

"I didn't like being a chemist," he said. "I applied to a pharmaceutical company in sales and management, and spent 40 years in pharmaceuticals."

Monsoor also had another trick up his sleeve, that of a magician. He opened a magic store to promote his hobby and was a magician who belonged to different organizations. After he retired, he and his late wife, Marilyn, had planned to stay in California, but they decided to move in Reno in 2001 where housing costs were more reasonable, and the area wasn't as crowded.

Since he can remember, Monsoor has respect for those who don the uniform to serve their country. He and Marilyn flew to Washington, D.C. in 2012 on the first Honor Flight Nevada to see the nation's memorials built in honor of the nation's fighting men and women. Marilyn, a registered nurse, served in Vietnam on aerovac (aeromedical evacuation) missions, and also in Japan and England before retiring as a lieutenant colonel. She died in 2017.

The trip to Pearl Harbor in February 2020 came as many nations remember the 75th anniversary of World War II's end. Monsoor had been to Pearl Harbor before as a young soldier and then with Marilyn after they married, but he said it was nice to be reminded of the price of freedom.

The five days on Oahu in February rekindled those cherished memories for the 93-year-old Monsoor.

"I think of my wife," he said when they saw some of the memorials at Pearl Harbor. "I wish she was here to see them again."

Not only does Monsoor reflect on his current journey to Pearl Harbor but also the need for younger generations to learn about the second world war in their classes.

"I don't want people to forget," he said. "I want them to remember."

Steven R. Ranson

DESTROYING THE
NAZI REGIME

A small piece of living history gathered at the Minden-Tahoe Airport in July 2006.

The "Yoxford Boys" are some of the remaining members of the 357th Fighter Group. They came together on July 8 for their annual reunion and a tour of Carson Valley's airport.

These men were just a handful of pilots and crew who flew the P51 Mustangs that eventually brought the German Luftwaffa to its knees during World War II.

"We owe these men a debt of gratitude," said TV personality John Tyson, who talked to the reunion group, which included seven members of the West Coast contingent of the 357th Fighter Group. "If it weren't for these men and so many others like them, we would all probably be speaking German today. They were instrumental in destroying the Nazi regime."

For area resident Michael Wyatt, the reunion was particularly meaningful. His father, Harold Andrew Wyatt, had been a member of this elite group of fighter pilots during World War II. The senior Wyatt died in 1982, but now his son attends the reunions in his place.

That morning in early July, Wyatt met with Ted Contri, the owner of a World War II survivor, a P51-D Mustang called "Sizzlin' Liz" at the Carson City Airport. Together, they climbed aboard the Mustang, painted in Nevada Air National Guard colors, for the short hop to the Minden-Tahoe Airport to join the other reunion members. As they made their approach to the runway they did a fly-by to honor the group of onlookers before landing.

Seven members of the 357th were in attendance that day which included retired Air Force Col. Henry Pfeiffer, pilot of "Tangerine and Pappy's Answer"; Harvey Mace, pilot of "Sweet Helen"; Merle Olmsted, part of the maintenance crew and 357th group historian; John Warner, maintenance; Ted Conlin, pilot of "Olivia DeH"; James Sehl, pilot of "Naughty Auty"; and retired Air Force Col. Robie Roberson, pilot of "Passion Wagon."

Among the many famous survivors of the 357th are retired Air Force Brig. Gen. Charles E. "Chuck" Yeager, who went on to write his name in history books as being the first test pilot to break the sound barrier and that of Clarence E. "Bud" Anderson, who, flying "Old Crow," distinguished himself as a triple ace. Anderson, who never missed a reunion, was unable to attend because his wife, Ellie, was ill.

Michael Wyatt became involved with the group when he read about the 357th and realized that his father was among the names not mentioned. He contacted historian Merle Olmsted who was excited to find out what had happened to Wyatt's father after the war. Harold Andrew Wyatt, part of the 362nd Squadron, had been credited with one kill, a Me109 destroyed over Germany on Jan. 14, 1945. Wyatt was the pilot of "Man O' War" named for the famous race horse so popular at the time. After the war, Wyatt had gone on to civilian life and it wasn't until after his death that the reunion group heard about his life through his son Michael who gave historian Olmsted another piece of the historical puzzle he was constructing for his book, "To War With The Yoxford Boys." Now a son could see his father get the recognition he deserved with the only regret -it happened after he died.

The 357th Fighter Group once trained at a base in Tonopah before going to Santa Rosa, Calif., and then split into smaller groups going to Oroville, Hayward and Marysville, all in California. In the fall of 1943 they were again moved to Casper, Wyo., Ainsworth, Neb., and Pocatello, Idaho, before reaching their final destination of Leiston on the eastern coast of England. On their arrival at Leiston, German propaganda radio's Lord Haw Haw (William Joyce) welcomed the 357th Fighter Group to their new location and nicknamed them "Yoxford Boys," derived from the fact that due to German intelligence mistakenly thinking the base was in the neighboring town of Yoxford, the Germans concentrated their bombing on the town, sparing Leiston and damage to the 357th.

For more information on the history of these remaining World War II heroes, log on to http://www.357thfightergroup.com or obtain a copy of "To War With The Yoxford Boys" by Merle Olmsted.

Jonni Hill

LAST OF THE 'MIGHTY MIDGET'

The ships were called the "Mighty Midgets," and their official U.S. Navy classification was Landing Craft Support or "LCS."

They were used for close gunfire and anti-aircraft support during amphibious landings, intercepting enemy suicide aircraft and boats, mine sweeping, fire-fighting, search and rescue, picket duty, to make smoke for covering larger ships from air and surface attack and as convoy escorts.

The Midgets had no names … only numbers.

There were 130 of them, built in the early 1940s at shipyards in Oregon and Massachusetts.

They were 160 feet in length, 23 feet wide, their draft was six feet fully loaded, they had flat bottoms which enabled them to be beached, and their twin screws and diesel engines could push them to a maximum speed of 15 miles per hour.

They had crews of 65 enlisted men and six officers, their multiple guns and rocket launchers provided more firepower per ton than any ship in the Navy, and they served valiantly in the Pacific island campaigns against the Japanese during World War II.

Only one of the 130 LCSs is still in existence, and it is alive, well, afloat, bears a new paint job, seaworthy and its engines are in good condition.

That ship is the LCS-102, and today it is a floating maritime museum tied up to a pier at the former Mare Island Navy Shipyard here across the bay in Vallejo from San Francisco, less than a five-hour drive from Nevada.

"Our ship is in perfect operating condition … it could get up steam and get underway today if need be," said Gordon Stutrud, who, along with fellow volunteer and Navy veteran Jason Leger, welcomes visitors, shows them around the 69-year-old, 387-ton vessel and keeps it in pristine condition with the assistance of a score of other volunteers.

"The other 129 Midgets are long gone … some were sunk or heavily damaged during World War II and most of the others were declared obsolete and scrapped at war's end. A few were acquired from the Navy and used as fishing boats. Several were loaned to foreign navies," added Stutrud as he escorted this writer to the enlisted men's quarters below the main deck and pointed out the tiny bunk rooms where sailors slept packed like sardines on narrow cots stacked four high.

The officers' quarters were equally cramped: The officers lived two men to a miniscule cabin and even the captain had a roommate, his executive officer or second in command.

Then I got a look at the closet-like kitchen or "galley" and the enlisted men's bathroom or "head" which consists of a wooden plank containing three side-by-side holes that serve as toilets, a metal urinal bolted to the wall, two showers and three sinks. The officers shared a separate head, and it, too, was terribly small.

"It was a tight fit for the men living on the LCS-102, but I hear the food on the ship was great," said Stutrud, a former Navy Petty Officer 2 who served as an electrical technician aboard the USS Hunley, a Polaris submarine tender, during the 1962 Cuban missile crisis.

LCS-102, bristling with 10 rocket launchers and 13 guns that included twin 40mm guns, 50-caliber machine guns and 20mm cannons, saw combat at Iowa Jima, Okinawa, the Philippines and Borneo, and was one of the first USN ships to sail into Tokyo Bay for the Japanese surrender in August, 1945, said Leger.

One of the LCS skippers won the Congressional Medal of Honor, three LCSs were awarded Presidential Unit Citations and six won Navy Unit Citations. The father of former Navy Secretary John Lehman served on an LCS, and Lehman and his son, Joe, are frequent visitors to LCS-102 here.

How LCS-102 ended up as a Mare Island museum ship is itself an interesting story.

Following World War II, the ship was transferred on loan by the U.S. Navy, ironically, to the Japanese Navy, and in 1966 it found another new home as a gunboat in the Royal Thailand Navy.

By the early 2000s, the ship had become too old and obsolete for the Thais, and in 2007 it was purchased by the National Assn. of LCS Veterans, loaded aboard a commercial heavy-lift cargo vessel and shipped to its berth here at Mare Island.

Today, it is maintained by the non-profit Mare Island Historic Park Foundation headed by 86-year-old Dr. Bill Mason, a World War II Navy enlisted man who had served aboard another LCS.

Known as "admiral" Mason by his fellow LCS-102 volunteers and a professor emeritus of economics at San Francisco State University, Mason was a 19-year-old sailor assigned to an LCS anti-craft gun and fired at Japanese kamikaze or suicide planes during Pacific island combat against the Japanese.

"Our Mighty Midgets may have been small, but their brave crews helped contribute to the winning of World War II. The men put their lives on the line, and they and their Midgets deserve an important place in American naval history," Mason said.

David C. Henley

DARKEST DAYS
OF THE WAR

The 20-year-old Army sergeant and his company moved swiftly over the western part of Europe in the waning weeks of World War II. As the American Army moved east across Nazi Germany in a race against time, the Russians marched to the west, first liberating Poland and then Germany's eastern border.

"It was a very forested area. We were moving along quietly with ammunition falling on us," said infantryman Robert McHaney of Reno, Nev., as he described the dense Bavarian woods. "We were told there was a prisoner of war camp in front of us and told not to call in artillery. Very carefully we started to move forward, and then we started to smell death."

About a half-kilometer away, said McHaney, soldiers arrived at the gate of the Dachau concentration camp in southern Germany northeast of Munich, the first one built by the Nazis for political prisoners. When his unit arrived, McHaney, who had also stormed Omaha Beach at Normandy during the June 1944 D-Day invasion and weathered the winter during the Battle of the Bulge in Belgium, said a company arrived before them, trying to snap open the gate's lock.

McHaney scanned the holocaust-remembrance crowd of over 800 people from one side to another, dressed in his olive-drab World War II uniform with a medal hanging from his neck and his garrison cap tilted to one side.

For the survivors, four stories of heroism and survival ... four people eventually coming to the United States to restart their lives ... four speakers keeping the audience focused on their riveting stories ... they all were eye witnesses to the atrocities and the darker side of mankind.

McHaney said he was astounded by man's inhumanity toward other each other with their stories.

"All the bravery weren't wearing uniforms. I thought how brave they were in the camp," McHaney said.

On that late April day in 1945, American soldiers and the remaining men and women who had been held at Dauchu stared at each other through the wire fence.

"The prisoners were standing there with very hollow eyes," the 93-year-old McHaney remembered with remarkable detail. "They wouldn't come out and take a step toward freedom. Anyone wearing a uniform, they were terrified of us and wouldn't come out."

What McHaney, who spent 25 years in law enforcement with the Los Angeles Sheriff's Department, and his comrades didn't know was the horror many prisoners faced daily over the months, perhaps years. Many prisoners before their arrival were put to death, while others had witnessed their loved ones being killed at the hands of SS guards or Nazi soldiers.

Another man from the audience said his father, who was in the U.S. Army's 45th Infantry Division, also liberated Dachau.

"He told me a few things, but did not say a lot," said the middle-aged son.

After his father's death, he discovered his father had won the Bronze and Silver stars and the Purple Heart.

"I am very proud of my dad," he said.

Not all the help for the concentration camp survivors came from boots on the ground. One lady said her father flew B-17 bombers and was a captain ... at the age of 19.

"He was on three bombing missions and after that, they were doing food drops," she said.

McHaney and four holocaust survivors recalled the horrors of incarceration and the struggles the Jewish people encountered during World War II in a presentation of Holocaust Remembrance: Survivors & Liberators.

A GERMAN ROUNDUP

Born in the former country of Czechoslovakia in 1928, Esther Basch was the only child of Rabbi Moises and Fanny Roth. In 1944, the Germans entered their town and within several months, Basch said the Germans forced her family, along with others in the town, to move into a four-block section of the village, a restricted area to segregate the Jews. They stayed in the ghetto for more than a month.

"I was rounded up in my hometown and they took all the Jewish people to the ghetto. We had no idea where we were going," she said. "After six weeks, they (German soldiers) put us in boxcars, and we wound up at Auschwitz."

Separated by guards, Basch headed toward the barracks with her mother, while her father went into a different direction, a fact she remembers vividly. The guard forcibly separated her 50-year-old mother from her. Basch never saw her parents again.

"My mom and dad went straight to the crematorium," she said, her voice strong but then slightly faltering.

Basch paused in the large conference room, silenced by her testimony from more than 70 years ago. Basch worked in one ammunition factory for more than nine months, but as the allies moved closer in April 1945, the guards took the prisoners and transferred them to another ammunition factory, Salzwedel, located deep in Germany.

"The Americans were nearing the first ammunition factory, and we were taken on a death march," she said, adding the prisoners walked about 100 miles in four or five days.

At their "new" factory, the Germans locked the prisoners in for two weeks, but the temporary tranquility of war shattered when the Basch and the other workers heard in the distance the noise of an advancing army, the 84th Infantry Division. After three days, allies liberated them.

"The German locked us in ... until the Americans came and soldiers slammed open the door and said 'you're free,'" Basch said.

Once liberated near the end of the war, Basch met a man at the Displaced Person camp, and they later married, coming to the United States via Israel. In 2007, her daughter contacted one of the soldiers who liberated their camp. Max Lieber, an 89-year-old New Mexican, traveled to Phoenix to see Basch and her husband. As Basch explained it to the audience, her daughter told Lieber if it weren't for the American soldiers, her family would not be here today. Sadly, Lieber died five years ago.

"I will never forget the Americans as long as I live," she said.

ROUGH LIFE IN THE CAMPS

While the Americans liberated Basch, the Russian army freed Shirley Weiss, a 14-year-old Czechoslovakian girl who was taken to Auschwitz in 1944 and later transferred to a labor camp near Terezin. She also lost her mother and four siblings to the hands of the Germans.

"My first work was at a bomb factory, but we kept moving because the Russians were coming from the east and the Americans from the west," she said.

Weiss said since she was a young teenager, the Russians left her along, but she was horrified the soldiers raped some of the older girls.

"It was very rough. Finally the Czech army came and told the Russians not to get near us because of typhus," Weiss said.

When liberated, many prisoners were very ill. By her own accounts, Weiss said she was also sick and weighed between 50-60 pounds. Weiss, though, considered herself very lucky. She said a Czech soldier asked the people if they were Czech citizens, and if so, raise their hands.

"An ambulance with two nuns picked me up and took me to the hospital," Weiss said, recalling she had broken out in hives. "When I woke up in the hospital, I said there is a God, still good people who cared."

After she left the hospital, the nuns protected Weiss and moved her to an orphanage. Weiss discovered one of her sisters was still living and they began to write to each other. The nuns paid for Weiss to travel to Canada when she was older, and after a four-week wait, she was able to enter the United States in 1948.

"I married an American soldier, and he told me I wouldn't have to suffer again," she said, adding her husband died in 2000. "I miss him so much. He was my life."

KEEPS HOLOCAUST ALIVE

Albert Garih (pronounced Gary), a young Jewish boy from Paris during the war, keeps his holocaust memory alive each and every day. Not only did he survive World War II but he also volunteers at the U.S. Holocaust Museum in Washington, D.C. to help visitors understand one of the most tragic events that murdered millions of people.

Three years to the day of Reno's remembrance, Garih approached an Honor Flight Nevada group of World War II veterans who had assembled for a group photo at the United States Naval Academy. Garih ran across the street, shouting his thanks to the veterans for saving his life when he was a young boy. He spent time talking with the veterans before they continued with their tour.

"I was in hiding most of the time starting in 1943 in Paris after my father had been sent to a camp in the Channel Islands," he said. "I was 5 years old at this time, and we (his mother Claire and his siblings) were hiding in different places."

Garih said his mother met a lady in a street market, and she was terrified knowing soldiers could take them away. A family housed the Garihs for six months until the patriarch of the family told the Garihs they needed to return to their home to be safer.

"Weeks later, we were visited by two French police inspectors, and they talked to my mother. They told my mother she needed to go in hiding again. Social workers found a place for every one of us."

Garih was placed in a Catholic boys boarding school, while his sisters went to a Catholic girls boarding school. Not too long afterward, the advancing American Army loosened the Germans' grasp on France and particularly Paris during late June 1944.

"I was in the boarding school when the allies were coming … the jeeps … the tanks … the Americans," said Garih, who was 6 years old. "They (the soldiers) gave us chocolate and chewing gum. I will remember the day for the rest of my life. It was a wonderful experience."

In 1967 Garih married Marcelle Ohayon with whom he has three daughters and 10 grandchildren.

GRATEFUL TO BE ALIVE

Hungarian Stephen Nasser moved to the United States in 1958 and eventually relocated to Las Vegas, where he lives today with his wife.

Nasser, though, gave a terrifying account of his liberation, which he called a false alarm when he was aboard a train.

"We stopped at a small station, and the station master said everyone is free. The people near the door opened the jammed boxcar and got out," Nasser remembered. "I was left alone in the boxcar … and said to myself, 'We're free.' We did not realize the Nazis still occupied that small village. They came out shooting. The people who left the boxcar tried to get back to the boxcar. They trampled over my body. "

The Germans killed 64 people who were fleeing bullets and returning to the boxcar, said Nasser; meanwhile, German planes strafed both the train and depot. Six days later Nasser woke up in a German-American hospital.

"I couldn't believe I was alive," he said, still showing disbelief with his luck. "I never thought I would survive. I was 72 pounds."

McHaney would have considered Nasser among the lucky ones based on his account of survival.

"We came to a boxcar with bloated bodies on top of each other. Their fingernails had been ripped off," McHaney recalled when his company was on patrol. "Inside we could see where they (the prisoners) had scratched and scratched and scratched inside to get out. They were trying to get the door open. Once again, we got the smell of death."

Nasser, though, strongly remembers Gen. George S. Patton's Third Army liberated him along with scores of other prisoners, a day in his life for which he is continually grateful, yet sad considering his family's fate Nasser said he was the only person in his family of 21 who survived. His brother died in his arms, and he was an eyewitness to the death of his uncle's wife and son. Three years after the war Nasser moved to Canada as an orphan—sponsored by the Canadian Jewish Congress—and then he relocated to the United States in 1958.

Nasser co-wrote a play about his experiences, "Not Yet, Pista" that had a recent three-day run in Las Vegas. He said one critic called it one of the most powerful plays he experienced. Nasser also keeps the holocaust alive with his numerous speeches to schools both in the United States and abroad.

In looking back at her experiences and looking ahead, Weiss said she is proud of her Jewish faith, a common sentiment expressed by the other three survivors.

"I was born a Jew, and I will die a Jew," Nasser asserted. "I am just as good as any other human being. We should be respectful of each other."

MY NAME IS MITKA

The heart-piercing tone rippled throughout the room, reflective of a man who spent his youth in Nazi concentration camps and as a household slave on a German's officer's farm.

From despair to his desire to be free, the composition "My Name is Mitka" reveals the hardship of survival in 1940s Germany.

"I find it more poignant than sad," said Reno violinist Van Vinikow, who performed the song along with composer Jordan Roper before an audience numbering in the hundreds at the Atlantis Casino Resort in Reno. "There's definitely sadness in the Jewish history, yet there is also hope, which I think Jordan reflected in the piece he wrote."

The two musicians, along with Mitka Kalinski and University of Nevada, Reno history professor Dr. Dennis Dworkin, revealed through music and words the hardships a young orphaned Jewish boy faced more than 70 years ago and the anti-Semitism and prejudice Jews have faced and are continuing to face.

"He (Roper) told the story of Mitka, which was really one of despair and sadness, but there is that bright part in D major," Vinikow pointed out.

Vinikow said the piece shows a hopeful side and then reverts to a reflective or forgiving side.

"There's so much in that piece Jordan captured that very well," Vinikow added.

The despair shrouding Mitka's life began when he was a young 7-year-old Ukrainian, and Nazis had invaded his homeland in the early 1940s. In one roundup that included Mitka, the Nazis killed hundreds of Ukrainians in a ravine, but Mitka, though, survived by hiding under the bodies and later crawling out. The Germans later picked up Mitka when they saw him walking along a road and put him on a cattle car destined for the Auschwitz-Birkenau concentration camp.

Mitka, who has lived in Sparks since 1959, moved frequently from Auschwitz to Buchenwald and then Dachau, the first Nazi concentration camp, in southern Bavaria near Munich. His final camp was Pfaffenwald before a German officer, Gustav Dörr, and his sister Anna, took him to their farm at Rotenburg an der Fulda in 1942 and forced the youngster to be a household slave until American soldiers freed him seven years later.

"Anna horsewhipped me, and she never like me from day one," Mitka recalled.

The Dörrs made Mitka sleep on straw in the barn during all seasons. Mitka said he will never forget the hunger and cold and the overall cruelty of the couple. He told of one story that silenced his audience, some shaking their heads in disbelief. Mitka said the Dörrs had two guard dogs, and one of the dogs, Molly, befriended him. Gustav Dörr became angry and frustrated because one of his dogs liked a Jew better than her master.

"He sent me to the field and then told me to come back," Mitka recounted. "He then showed me Molly, who had been skinned."

Mitka felt both the mental anguish and physical pain of living like an animal. The temperatures during the winter grew so cold that he would purposely step in cow manure to keep warm. His hunger gnawed at him, and when he milked a cow, he would pick up the container and drink some of the milk. When Anna discovered what he had done, she horsewhipped him.

"The news came back to the Nazi family. The milk was watered down," Mitka said.

In the late 1940s, Mitka said American soldiers discovered him on the farm and freed him, yet he never knew what happened to the Dörrs. In fact, he never knew the war's outcome until the Americans told him.

"The most difficult part of life was being free," Mitka said. "I didn't know how to handle people. I was with the animals on a Nazi farm, and I didn't know who to believe. I was free, but I didn't know how to play with the other kids."

The United Nations Relief and Rehabilitation Administration became responsible for his welfare, and he was sent to a synagogue community in the United States in 1951. According to his biography, "Mitka did not know English, could not read or write, and had little idea of how to navigate his new world. He learned rudimentary English and how to make his way in America by watching movies.

"A move to North Tonawanda (New York state) followed, which began the courtship of Adrienne. Life was good. The post-war years proceeded with the common struggles and joys of an all-American blue-collar family."

Their journey eventually brought them to Nevada where he found year-round work in construction.

The years during and after the war affected Mitka immensely. He bottled his fears and horrific childhood memories, something he never revealed to his wife or children until the early 1980s. In 1984 while searching for records, he contacted a man who said he was Gustav Dörr, and he had records in his basement.

Mitka and Adrienne traveled to Germany to look at the records and undertake more research, but Gustav Dörr had died three months before they arrived. Anne was still alive, but she didn't offer any assistance.

"If you search the way I did, you don't give up," Mitka interjected.

During his research, Mitka also discovered additional information on his mother and father, who are both buried in London. His father, a Polish officer, died in 1952.

"It's universal," Vinikow said of the music piece about Mitka. "There are so many situations in life—Jewish and non-Jewish. There's sadness, yet there's hope and happiness."

Roper, who lives in Idaho Falls, Idaho, said Mitka's story of survival is one of inspiration.

"When I heard the story, there was something about the Jewish culture," Roper explained. "The music represents the Jewish ghetto sound he was going through but still retains that hope, the light at the end of the tunnel. The main melody—an 8-bar melody—just alone took one month to get it just where I wanted it.

"I needed to develop the melody ... it is very simple, but it had to serve such a specific purpose to represent Mitka as a boy and go throughout for his homecoming to America."

For Mitka, Roper said he feels the piece ends on a sad note because Mitka must deal with all his memories.

"He lives back in some of those cells, that barn, so it was a challenge," Roper said of the composition.

Judith Schumer, chairperson of the Nevada Governor's Advisory Council on Education Relating to the Holocaust, said the Jewish people continue to grapple why the Holocaust happened and how it happened. She said the number of Holocaust survivors grows smaller with each passing day and why an annual Day of Remembrance becomes one of reflection.

Roper added there's one race—the human race, and people have hearts, lungs and eyes. "The plight of anti-Semitism is a plight against all humanity."

Steven R. Ranson

A MARINE'S
CHANCE MEETING

Raymond Stefanko wanted to serve his country during World War II, but by the time he enlisted after high school, Japan had surrendered, and an international force occupied Japan in its postwar rebuilding.

The Illinois native of Ukrainian descent, who later moved to California and then to Reno, Nev., years after he retired, became a Marine on Aug. 28, 1946, four months before the eligibility period ended for classifying servicemen and women as World War II vets. He also had a brother who served in the Navy.

The 90-year-old Stefanko and his nephew Stephen Stefanko of Napa, California, rode on a June 2019 Honor Flight Nevada, but it may be a chance meeting between Stefanko and Polish author Sonia Kaplan that he will remember most. She was signing copies of her book, "My Endless War" at the U. S. Holocaust Memorial Museum. Her story recounts her life of a Jewish woman living under the Nazis and the murder of her family. Kaplan eventually began a new life by immigrating to the United States. When Kaplan heard World War II vets were visiting the museum as part of honor-flight activities, she wanted to meet them. She wanted to thank them for liberating Europe.

"I found out she was Polish, and I greeted her in Ukrainian. They're similar languages, and she understood," Stefanko said, with a wide grin. "I thanked her for being kind to me."

Kaplan and the veterans gathered near the museum's bookstore and posed for both group and individual photographs.

Although Stefanko was born in the United States, his parents immigrated to this country when they were in their late teens, and they spoke their Ukrainian language until they acclimated to the new country.

Stefanko didn't serve overseas; instead, he was assigned to the 22nd Marine Regiment based at Quantico, Virginia. Stefanko, though still has distinct memories of the time he served in the Marines. Despite the end of World War II in 1945, Stefanko said the Marines still trained as if they were still going to war, but one of his duties at the time was serving on the honor guard.

"Our honor guard appeared before President (Harry) Truman and (Admiral Chester) Nimitz," Stefanko said. "Nimitz was very impressive. He was tall, good looking and brown-faced for being out on the bridge."

Stefanko, who had met retired U.S. Sen. Bob Dole at the World War II memorial, said the Kansas senator told him he loved Nimitz as a leader. Even Nimitz had joked about Stefanko, the Marine, being on the honor guard.

"You're not bad looking Marine," Stefanko remembers the commander in chief, U.S. Pacific Fleet and commander in chief, Pacific Ocean Areas.

Stefanko said he had pondered staying in the Marines after his enlistment ended. Because of his test scores (he was second on the list), his commanders wanted him to apply and attend Officer Candidate School. Instead, Stefanko finished his enlistment, moved back to Illinois and earned a degree in civil engineering, the profession that took him to the Golden State. Among his many projects, Stefanko was an engineer on the San Francisco-Oakland Bay Bridge when improvements to the structure were made, and was with the firm that built the Antioch Bridge that crosses the San Joaquin River. He credits his success as an engineer to his military service.

"The military gave me the ability to work with others and helped me with my civilian employment," he said.

Stefanko also met the love of his life and they married in Gardnerville, Nev. Their love of skiing brought them to Truckee, Calif., often, but they decided to move to Reno's Caughlin Ranch community and bought a house that overlooks the city.

Stefanko came away with opinions on the state of the military. After visits to Marine Barracks Washington and the Tomb of the Unknown Soldier at Arlington National Cemetery, he noted the dedication of both the Marines and soldiers.

Stefanko's eyes began to water … then he spoke.

"I'd serve with any one of them with pride."

Steven R. Ranson

VISIONS OF NUREMBERG

The former Army solider slowly walked past the exhibits, stopping at several that grabbed his attention and reminiscing of a journey he witnessed more than seven decades ago.

For 93-year-old Frank Pinkerton, he focused on the visual displays at the United States Holocaust Memorial Museum in Washington, D.C.—the train car, discarded shoes, a miniature display of a concentration camp and photos of American troops liberating the victims shown behind wire.

The final floor, though, resonated with the Elko County rancher, who was with the 53rd Reinforcement Battalion after World War II ended in May 1945. What he saw at the museum were deeply embedded memories of soldiers mingling with freed Holocaust survivors and postwar photos of German military leaders on trial at Nuremberg for their atrocities committed against humanity.

An International Military Tribunal conducted at Nuremberg, Germany, between Nov. 20, 1945 to Oct. 11, 1946, tried almost two dozen of the most influential, ruthless leaders of the Third Reich. Other courts tried additional Nazis who faced serious charges for their part during the war.

"The trials were held in the Palace of Justice," Pinkerton said, noting the building was large enough to accompany all those involved with the numerous trials and also housed a large prison.

Nuremberg, located 273 miles southwest of the capital Berlin, also held a special meaning for the Allies holding the trial there: The city was known for the rise of Nazism and the Nazi party, and the symbolism provided a somber backdrop to the trials and crimes committed by the defendants. During the war trials, Pinkerton's command assigned him to transport soldiers from Bamberg to a field hospital in Nuremberg for outpatient services.

"I had to wait for them," Pinkerton said. "I got there about 9:30 (a.m.) and picked them up around 3 (p.m.). My doctor told me since I was there, I should go to the war crime trials."

While the soldiers received their treatments, Pinkerton drove to the Palace of Justice to attend the trials from April 1946 to September of the same year.

"Seeing the trials was history," Pinkerton recalled of the International Military Tribunal. "I always remembered the Palace of Justice heavily guarded. When you went in, two MPs (military police) were behind sandbags and barbed wire. There was a long hallway, and at the end were two more MPs behind sandbags with machine guns. They were playing for keeps."

Pinkerton sat near a side gallery facing the main floor. He grabbed his headphones and dialed into the English language option so he could follow the proceedings.

"I can almost see these guys sitting there," Pinkerton recalled, his thoughts racing to 1946 when he was only 19 years old. "There were two MPs standing behind each prisoner."

The 22 prisoners sat in the last two rows of the courtroom. The one Nazi that stood out for Pinkerton was the second most powerful Nazi, Hermann Göring, commander of the German air force charged with war crimes and crimes against humanity. Others who Pinkerton recognized included Rudolf Hess and Alfred Jodl, one of the highest-ranking military offices who signed the German Instrument of Surrender on May 7, 1945.

"The only people allowed to take photos were the press," Pinkerton recalled, his thoughts shifting toward the defendants. "They looked pretty grim. They weren't smiling. They were told to speak when spoken to."

After the prosecution laid out its case, Göring's defense presented its information in March 1946. Pinkerton said Göring was full of himself when he appeared in court.

"He was the guy who had the world by the tail and nothing could go wrong," Pinkerton said.

Although his memory isn't as sharp as it was 75 years ago, Pinkerton said, from what he understood, the German people loved Göring. Furthermore, he said Hess, Hitler's deputy führer, never said anything and kept quiet.

"I'm glad I went," Pinkerton said. "It was the experience of a lifetime."

The tribunal judges handed down their verdicts in late September. Göring received death by hanging, but he never kept his date at the gallows.

"Göring escaped the hangman's noose," Pinkerton recalled. "He had a secret cyanide pill."

Pinkerton said the trials revealed the dark secrets of the Third Reich and those who committed indescribable crimes, especially against the Jews. Half the defendants received the death penalty and hanged including Jodl. The Allies then cremated the bodies and either released them to the families or scattered the ashes

"A lot of people don't have an idea," he said of the atrocities the Germans committed during the war.

After his short stay in Bamberg, Pinkerton transferred to Stuttgart where he met the master sergeant who was the hangman. Pinkerton said Master Sgt. John Woods executed a number of war criminals . During the second month of the Korean War, though, Pinkerton said Woods was in the South Pacific where he was electrocuted working on a lighting set.

Pinkerton also met a doctor assigned to the 45th Infantry Division's field hospital. The doctor told Pinkerton the advancing American soldiers could smell the Dachau Concentration Camp before they arrived because of the stench emitting from the piled bodies and the coal-fired crematorium ovens.

"The doctor said the commandant of the 45th gathered the people in town and marched them out," Pinkerton said. "They helped bury the dead prisoners. They had to dig four trenches because there were so many bodies."

By accounts, the townspeople buried more than 9,000 men, women and children.

"He told me he had dreams ... the worst he ever had," Pinkerton said, describing one conversation with the doctor.

Once Pinkerton settled into his quarters at Stuttgart, he was asked to join a horse platoon to patrol the Russian zoned boundary (Soviet Occupation Zone of occupied eastern Germany) to the east. Pinkerton said the winter of 1946 was one of the snowiest locals had seen in years. PInkerton's section became responsible for manning three outposts, 24 hours a day.

"If there were enough people, two of us would ride 15 miles out to the end of the border and back," he described. "The snow drifts were huge."

Because of Pinkerton's love for horses and riding experience, he finished his time at Stuttgart as a veterinarian technician with the 14th Constabulary Regiment and then transferred to Frankfurt near the end of his tour in Germany in 1948. His time with Uncle Sam, though, continued. After arriving in New Jersey, Pinkerton extended his enlistment in the U.S. Army Reserve, and when he was recalled for the Korean War, he served at a military hospital in Battle Creek, Mich.

Pinkerton, though, feels luck was on his side in the 1950s. He qualified to attend helicopter flight school where he could also be promoted to a warrant officer. He wrestled with the idea of extending his military obligation and flying helicopters. Pinkerton told his future wife what the Army offered, but she replied "it's either the Army or me."

He didn't hesitate with his reply.

"I chose marriage," Pinkerton said.

Steven R. Ranson

FRANCE'S LEGION
OF HONOR

It's June 6, 1944, and U.S. Army soldier Joseph Petrucci is standing shoulder-to-shoulder with 30-some fellow comrades in a landing craft hurtling through the English Channel toward Omaha Beach.

Bullets rattle the exterior of the boat. Farther ahead, men from accompanying crafts, their ramps down, spill out into the surf. Some are instantly shot and killed; others are wounded and drown in the rising tide.

Few find their way onto land.

Gunfire and explosions and crashing waves and cries for help echo in a cacophony of hellish sounds.

It's chaos; it's war.

Petrucci, machine gun at the ready, seconds away from stepping onto enemy soil, is fighting alongside roughly 34,000 men on the northern coast of German-occupied France in the Invasion of Normandy—D-Day.

Nearly 72 years later, the Massachusetts-born Petrucci is recounting that very moment—the ramp dropping; the bullets rattling; the nearby soldiers falling—from a recliner in his Truckee home on a snowy afternoon in early March 2016.

"Just before our ramp dropped, it stopped," Petrucci said of the bullets spraying the boat. "In retrospect, what happened was the boat next to us dropped their ramp before we did, and the machine gun shifted over. So, we lucked out."

Petrucci, 22 years old at the time, served as a wire chief for telephone and telegraph with the 294th JASCO (Joint Assault Signal Company) unit, which was among the second wave to hit Omaha Beach early D-Day morning. His unit was one of roughly 7,000 Allied vessels in the channel that day, as around 156,000 Allied troops (American, Canadian and British) were a part of the Normandy Invasion, which included four more beaches—codenamed as Juno, Gold, Utah and Sword.

At Omaha Beach, Petrucci's JASCO unit's job was to establish communications between the various landing parties in Normandy.

"Our function was to come ashore in the early waves of the landing and direct the Navy guns to targets," Petrucci said. "We acted as the eyes on the Germans."

However, "It was not a good landing—a lot of mistakes were made," said Petrucci.

'EVERYTHING WENT WRONG'

The strong currents forced many landing crafts east of their intended position or caused them to be severely delayed. Consequently, the landings were so chaotic that much of the equipment was lost in the early hours.

Playing a factor, Petrucci said, were the runnels, deep sand pits formed by the currents that forced soldiers to shed their equipment, which weighed up to 100 pounds. And those who weren't able to quickly enough, drowned.

"If you came off the boat and fell into one of those, you had to take off all your equipment because it was too heavy—it would sink you," Petrucci said.

What's more, after exiting the craft into the surf, the soldiers were in direct line with extremely potent German artillery. Namely, the MG 42 machine gun, which fired at a rate of roughly 1,200 rounds per minute, twice the rate of the Browning machine guns used by the U.S. troops.

On top of that, American bombers dropped their shells too far inland, missing their marks, due to orders from the Navy to delay their drops. Since low, thick clouds blanketed the sky that morning, bombers had to rely on radar, a relatively recent invention. Simply put, the Navy did not trust the radars, fearing their bombs would be dropped on their own ships.

Up to 13,000 bombs were dropped, but not a single shell hit Omaha Beach or the German guns overlooking it. In other words, no real damage was done on the Nazi's coastal defenses. More of the Allies' assault tactics failed. The fleet of amphibious tanks known as Duplex Drive tanks—a regular tank wrapped in a canvas flotation screen, typically launched from the landing craft two miles from shore—had a disastrous showing at Omaha Beach. In all, the rough sea swamped 27 of the initial 29 DD tanks.

"They let them out of the boat too far away—the water was rough." Petrucci said. "Everything went wrong ... we had no help on shore at all."

Further illustrating that point, Petrucci said the life belts they wore as flotation devices—during the landings many men had to wade 50 to 100 yards through water, sometimes neck deep—also caused unforeseen trouble.

"The life belts, when you needed it, you would squeeze it and air would fill up," he said. "It sounded wonderful, but the problem was if you had a lot of equipment on and if you put the belt on too low, it would tip you upside down—you drowned, it's very simple.

"We lost two (in our boat) from drowning."

THE ASSAULT ON SHORE

Trudging onto the beach without most of their equipment, Petrucci's JASCO unit—those who made it ashore, that is—grabbed guns and acted as infantry during penetration inland of the Nazi defenses. Within 24 hours of the D-Day assault, more than 4,000 men had lost their lives.

"It was such a terrible beach," said Petrucci, shaking his head. "That was a beach of body parts."

In the assault, Petrucci suffered shrapnel wounds on his left leg and right elbow. Petrucci doctored the leg wound himself. His elbow, which he couldn't get to effectively, was stitched by a Navy corpsman.

When the dust settled on D-Day, one of the bloodiest days in modern warfare, Petrucci and a fellow soldier, a friend, spent the night in a trench, where a dead German soldier lay.

"We slept around him," said Petrucci, adding, "They (the Nazis) used to booby trap their dead."

The following morning, they returned to the beach to obtain specialized equipment from the reserve troops to perform their duties as radiomen.

"There is a certain procedure you follow when you're directing gunfire," Petrucci explained. "You let them know 'my position is this, the front line is here, the enemy is here or the target is there.'"

Less than a week later, on June 11, 1944, the beaches were fully secured and over 326,000 Allied troops, more than 50,000 vehicles and some 100,000 tons of equipment had landed in France.

Playing a key role were the Allied air support, which took out many key bridges and forced the Germans to take long detours, as well as efficient Allied naval support, which helped protect advancing Allied troops. By the end of August 1944, the Allies had fought their way across the Normandy countryside, seizing the vital port of Cherbourg, and prepared to enter Germany.

The following spring, on May 8, 1945, the Allies formally accepted the unconditional surrender of Nazi Germany. Months earlier, in December 1944, Petrucci and his JASCO unit—because they were a specialized group for beachhead landings—were sent to the Asiatic-Pacific Theater to prepare for the amphibious assault of Japan.

"We came back to the states and then went to the Pacific," said Petrucci, whose unit was the first company to return from Europe and be deployed to the Pacific. "When the war in Europe ended, I was on an island practicing a landing."

'FRANCE WILL NEVER FORGET'

Joe Petrucci served in the Army during the Second World War for three years and three months.

A husband to Alice Petrucci for 64 years, a father of four and grandfather to 11, he is one of many soldiers who played a decisive role in the liberation of France—and Europe—from Nazi Germany.

Joe and Alice Petrucci have lived in Truckee for three years, moving to the mountain town in 2013 to live next door to their daughter, Lisa, and her family.

"I think it's incredible how selfless his generation was," Lisa Petrucci said. "To leave their families and go across the ocean and fight for people they didn't know, it's really striking of that generation that they really rose to the challenge. I am very proud of him."

For his service, Petrucci has been awarded a bevy of medals, including the European African Middle Eastern Campaign medal with two Bronze Service stars, the American campaign medal, the Good conduct medal, and the World War II Victory medal, among others.

While he was wounded during combat on D-Day, Petrucci said he did not feel his injuries made him worthy of being a Purple Heart recipient.

"I think it should only be given to people who are wounded, lose their limbs or die from wounds," said Petrucci, who felt his injuries were only minor.

Most recently, Petrucci was granted the medal of the Legion of Honor, the highest honor given by France, while surrounded by family and friends at the French consulate in San Francisco on Feb. 9, 2016.

Petrucci said the medal—all of his medals, in fact—are for his grandchildren.

"Alice said, 'you got to leave them to the grandchildren'," Petrucci said. "It was very special to have family members there, because that's why we were there."

At the Feb. 9 ceremony, Consul General of France, Pauline Carmona, presented Petrucci with the Legion of Honor.

"I am here, today, to tell you that the people of France have not forgotten," Carmona said in her speech. "Their children and grandchildren have not forgotten. France will never forget."

Petrucci hasn't, either.

"I think it's a very nice honor to have," Petrucci said. "But, I don't care if I ever had a medal. If all my medals would bring back one guy to life that we lost, it would be worth it.

"I had a full life," he continued, "four children, 11 grandchildren, good health … and all these young guys (in the war), they died."

(Petrucci died on Feb. 10, 2018, at the age of 95.)

Kaleb M. Roedel

DOWN WITH THE SHIP

Within the first 14 months of World War II in the frigid North Atlantic Ocean, a German submarine stalked a convoy steaming from Newfoundland to a base in Greenland.

Escorted by U.S. Coast Guard cutters, the convoy consisted of three ships including a passenger liner that was converted as an Army transport ship carrying no more than 900 servicemen, merchant mariners and civilians.

In the early morning hours of Feb. 3, 1943, the German U-boat identified its target and fired three torpedoes, striking the USAT Dorchester on its starboard side and below the water line. The series of explosions killed scores of passengers, while others jumped into the icy waters or crowded lifeboats in an desperation attempt to escape the carnage.

In less than 20 minutes, the ship slowly sunk to its Atlantic Ocean grave, killing 672 men including four chaplains who stayed behind to calm passengers and guide them to safety. The four chaplains, though, surrendered their life vets to help others escape the sinking ship, knowing their sacrifice would lead to their own deaths.

American Legion Post 16 in Fallon, Nev., and its Auxiliary honored the four chaplains during a ceremony in which many veterans, first-term Gov. Brian Sandoval and Mayor Ken Tedford honored the heroism of Lt. George Fox, Methodist; Lt. Anthony Goode, Jewish; Lt. John P. Washington, Roman Catholic; and Lt. Clark V. Poling, Dutch Reform.

Although the men represented different faiths, their bonds with God brought their time together during this transport to Greenland.

Legion member Lance McNeil said this is a function performed by American Legion posts to remember the four chaplains for their unselfish duty and heroism. The American Legion adopted this event to tell of the men's duty to country.

"It's also to honor the chaplains and the sacrifices they make to our troops overseas," he said.

The standing-room crowd including the governor, mayor and veterans from all branches of the military overwhelmed McNeil. During the local ceremony, representatives of each man's faith read a short biographical sketch. Near the end of each recital, a student from either the Girls Scouts, Sea Cadets or the local high school's Navy Junior ROTC placed a wreath on a stand to commemorate the fallen chaplains.

Blanche Nonkin spoke first about Goode, a Brooklyn, N.Y., native who was born in 1911 and followed his father's footsteps to become a rabbi. He received an appointment to become an Army chaplain in 1942 and was reassigned to Camp Myles Standish, Mass., in October. He previously received a bachelor's degree from the University of Cincinnati, a B.H. degree from Hebrew Union College and a Ph.D. from John Hopkins University in 1940.

Pastor Gary Pope-Sears from Epworth United Methodist Church told of Fox's service in the ambulance corps during World War I. When Fox joined the Army Chaplain Corps in July 1942 and went active duty the following month, he was then assigned to the divinity school at Harvard.

Minister James B. Sims from the Fallon Church of Christ said Poling was born in Ohio in 1910 but attended school in Massachusetts and New York where he matriculated from a Quaker high school. Poling graduated from both Rutgers University and Yale University's Divinity School. After his appointment as chaplain for the 131st Quartermaster Trucking Regiment in June 1942, he was later assigned to Harvard Divinity School.

Father Antonio Quijano Jr., from St. Patrick's Catholic Church said Washington, a New Jersey native, was born in 1908 and attended Seton Hall University where he earned an A.B. degree. He then entered the Immaculate Conception Seminary. Washington became an ordained priest in 1935 and served in several parishes unit the Japanese bombed Pearl Harbor. After the Dec. 7, 1941, attack, he received an appointment as a chaplain in the U.S. Army and first served at Fort Benjamin Harrison, Ind. He later transferred to an infantry division at Fort George Meade, Md., before reporting to Camp Myles Standish in November 1942.

Two years later after the Germans sunk the Dorchester, each man was awarded the Distinguished Service Cross and Purple Heart. Congress authorized a posthumous Special Meal for Heroism for the chaplains on Jan 18, 1961.

Kenneth Clasen, a member of Post 16, offered remarks about the chaplains. When he was 10 years old, Clasen said his mother told him about the chaplains and their ultimate sacrifice. During his military career, Clasen said talking to a chaplain made him feel better, and he also talked to chaplains on behalf of the men who worked for him; yet, the heroism of the four men of God aboard the Dorchester weighed heavily on Clasen.

"All four of them took off their life vests and gave them to the person next in line. They locked their arms and went down with the ship. Now I know why."

Steven R. Ranson

MARINES IN LOVE

Peggy (Palomino) Cavin doesn't consider herself an inspiration for young women although many would disagree with the Marine Corps vet who enlisted during the second world war.

As a young woman, she served for 22 months in the U.S. Marine Corps from 1943 to when World War II began to wind down, sealed with the surrender between the Allies and Japan on Sept. 2, 1945. On an Honor Flight Nevada trip in 2020 to Pearl Harbor and Marine Corps Base Hawaii at Kaneohe Bay, young female Marines surrounded Cavin, extending their hands in friendship and asking for photos to be taken with her. Sailors at Pearl Harbor also talked to Cavin about her service as did other veterans.

During her enlistment in the 1940s, Cavin confided other Marines said she had the best females in the Corps under her leadership. A diminutive woman, she didn't let her 5-foot frame interfere with the way she managed the Marines assigned to her. She had prior practice in developing her leadership skills with her siblings.

Cavin came from a family of five girls and one boy. She said her big brother signed up for the U.S. Army Air Force, but recruiters informed him he couldn't serve because he had four children at home.

"He was very patriotic," she said. "That left only one of us able to serve so I joined the Marine Corps."

After enlisting in 1943, she completed her basic training before attending the cooks and bakers school at the U.S. Marine Corps Air Station Cherry Point, N.C. Although the United States and its allies were slowly pushing back Japan and

Germany, she didn't know how long she would serve until mid-to-late 1944 when key battles inflicted significant damage on the enemy.

"We signed up for the duration of the war," she said, which seemed like an open contract to the thousands of Marines who enlisted.

From North Carolina, she headed west to Miramar, 14 miles north of San Diego, where the Navy trained on one side of the base, and the Marines on the other with artillery and armor. Both Navy and Marine pilots, though, trained on the same side. Cavin, who was classified as a messman or mess sergeant, served with about 200 other female Marines, and they ran the mess hall. At any given time, they served the 50 Marines.

"All my duty was stateside," she said. "I never went overseas because the war was almost over. So, I stayed at my duty station."

And Cavin's glad she remained at Miramar.

Cavin met a fellow Marine who took a liking to her. On a hiking trip with friends, she encountered a group of male Marines, but one of the men asked for her name and phone number. Donald Cavin, a decorated veteran who would later marry her after the war, produced strong ties to Nevada having grown up in the mining camps of Rosebud, Leonard Creek, Rose Creek, Gold Point, Goldfield and Tonopah before enlisting in October 1942.

The final 18 months of the war tested their love and commitment. Donald, an aviation ordnance specialist, deployed to the western Pacific with Marine Fighting Squadron 322. VMF-322 was involved with the amphibious landing on Okinawa in April 1945, one of the final major offensive attacks against the Japanese Imperial Army.

Two weeks after the war ended, Peggy left the service, and with Don later returning to the mainland, they decided to marry in Boston in October. One month later, the Marines honorably discharged Donald, who held the rank of technical sergeant.

"We got married right after," she said, smiling, and proudly reminding those standing next to her Donald was also a fellow Marine.

Because of Donald's training in ordnance, the Hawthorne Naval Ammunition Depot (later becoming an Army depot in 1977) hired him as a journeyman. During the early 1950 when the Korean War was raging, he completed two civilian tours to Japan and Korea to support the war effort. Donald rose up through the ranks at the ammunition depot before retiring in 1979 as the production chief and civilian manager for the depot.

The Cavins lived in Hawthorne for 57 years before relocating to Reno about 135 miles northwest. They had five children, three who served in the military: two in the U.S. Air Force and the other one in the Army. When Donald died in 2013 at the age of 89, the Cavins had been married for more than 67 years and were pillars in the small Nevada town where their children attended school in Mineral County. They supported community events such as the annual Armed Forces Day Parade in May and veterans organizations. The Cavins became benefactors of the Hawthorne Ordnance Museum.

For 40 years, Donald, a Distinguished Nevadan, served both elected and appointed positions on the Nevada Wildlife Commission.

Looking back at her life, Peggy expresses no regrets. She credits her son William, her guardian on the Honor Flight trip, for helping her enjoy the five days in Hawaii. The visit still gave her an opportunity to reflect on her family, her service and especially the time with fellow veterans including those young female Marines at Kaneohe Bay.

"We signed up … we were all willing to serve," she said. "The trip meant a lot to me and to the people there. I've never seen such happiness and cooperation."

Steven R. Ranson

ABOARD THE USS NEVADA

The tropical breeze snapped the flags behind him before he boarded a small boat to take him to the USS Arizona Memorial.

A 64-year resident of Lovelock, Nev., a small agriculture town 90 miles east of Reno, Robert "Pat" Patterson has a relationship with one of the battleships remembered at the Pearl Harbor naval base. During the last year of World War II, Patterson served aboard the USS Nevada, which steamed out of the harbor on Dec. 7, 1941, while Japanese planes bombed Battleship Row.

On an Honor Flight Nevada trip to Oahu, the 96-year-old Patterson stared at the memorial commemorating the USS Nevada, which served in the Pacific theater and also had a major role with the D-Day landing in June 1944.

The year 1941, though, began a time of frustration for Patterson, who grew up in Seattle. During the early years of the 40s, Patterson worked in a shipyard as a painter in his hometown. Patterson received notification of being drafted into the military in 1941, and as any young man of the time, he wanted to served his country.

"I waited and waited, and a man at the draft board said I'd be called in a week," Patterson said. "Then a week went by, and then almost six months. I tried to find out why I wasn't called when I was supposed to."

Patterson's persistence kept dogging the local board. When he sat down and talked to a person at the board, Patterson received some surprising news.

"The notice said deferred," Patterson remembers the man telling him. "I didn't ask for deferred."

The man told Patterson his employer requested him to be placed on a deferred status because there was no one who could take his place.

"We can't get anybody. They're all being drafted," Patterson recollected the man telling him.

"Yes, but I was also drafted," replied an incredulous Patterson, trying to understand the logic behind the decision.

A dejected Patterson returned to the shipyard, faced with the possibility he would be working there until the end of the war. He kept telling himself he needed to "get the heck out of the shipyard" because he was drafted. Patterson, though, learned his boss was trying to find a replacement for him so he could answer the draft notice and ship off to fight for his nation. Eventually, his supervisor found a woman to take his job.

"There were some doubts, but I didn't have any doubts," an eager Patterson said at the time, expressing confidence a woman could do his job.

Patterson headed east for his basic training at Farragut Naval Training Station, a U.S. Navy training center located in Northern Idaho between Coeur d'Alene and Sandpoint. During its 30-month existence, almost 300,000 sailors received their training there.

"All I can remember is it got to 32 degrees below zero there," Patterson said.

After his training that ended in early 1944, Patterson said he traveled to Virginia to pick up a ship, an LST (landing ship tank) that eventually found itself at the receiving end of a Japanese torpedo in the Philippines.

"That hole was big enough to drive a Jeep through," Patterson said.

With the LST beached, the crew patched the hole and began a long, return journey back to the Pacific Northwest via Pearl Harbor in 1945 where the ship sat in drydock for 31 days.

"The government inspector went down into the engine room and said he never saw anything like that," Patterson said.

As the war neared to an end, the Navy was looking for sailors to man the USS Nevada, which was at the Bremerton (Wash.) shipyard for repairs. Patterson and other sailors, once they learned of the need for a crew, jumped on a bus for the short journey to the Nevada where it sat in drydock. Once repairs were completed, the battleship took its new crew to San Diego and then to Pearl Harbor in September to shuttle other crews from Hawaii back to the mainland, a mission that extended into late October when the ship's mission changed again.

"We made four trips picking up crews and bringing them back to the states," Patterson said.

For the most part the shuttle between Hawaii and the mainland was uneventful, although Patterson recalled a powerful storm sweeping over the Nevada three days out of Seattle.

"We had waves over the stern of the ship," he said.

Steven R. Ranson

REFLECTIONS OF SERVICE

George Oliver of Sparks, Nev., came from a family of seven brothers who served in the military—mostly the Army and Navy—during World War II. The seven boys were born to a father who was also the seventh son. Oliver, the youngest, said one brother served in the Pacific Theater, another brother served on the battleship USS North Carolina, and another brother served in Gen. George Patton's Third Army.

One of Oliver's brothers, however, didn't return. He was shot down by German anti-aircraft fire and killed, and his remains were interred at the Netherlands American Cemetery and Memorial. Oliver, a Navy veteran, visited his brother's grave several years ago for the first time.

During the final months war, Oliver was preparing to sail to Japan, but he didn't go because of the emperor's surrender on Aug. 15, 1945.

"I just did my duty," he replied, not offering additional explanation.

Oliver said he enjoyed a visit to Washington, D.C. when he was on an Honor Flight Nevada trip with other veterans.

"I spent time in the holocaust museum," Oliver said of the honor flight. "We had a lot of things to do. I spent some time in the cemetery (Arlington National Cemetery) and reflected."

Reidar Lindgard of Reno, who served in the 130th Infantry Regiment, visited the U.S. Holocaust Museum in Washington, D.C. as well as other sites on the same Honor Flight Nevada trip.

"The holocaust museum really got to me," he said, "and after that, the memorials were all good."

Lindgard, now 94 years old, entered the military at Ft. Snelling, Minn. He served six years in the active Army and six more in the U.S. Army Reserve. During the latter stages of World War II in a firefight, Germans surrounded a house in which Lindgard and other soldiers were inside and captured them.

James Climo, who has called Truckee, Calif., and Sparks, Nev., both his homes, served in the U.S. Marine Corps from 1946-1952. When he enlisted in the Marine Corps, he was considered a World War II veteran because of the Allies post-war occupation of Japan and Germany and the demobilization of troops back to the United States.

"I first went into the Marines and I ended up at Seal Beach," said Climo, adding he spent all seven years of his enlistment in the United States.

Now known as the Naval Weapons Station Seal Beach, the ammunition and net depot was built in 1944 next to Seal Beach, Calif., in the northwest corner of Orange County. During the height of World War II, the Navy said the depot had two functions: "Storage and loading of ammunition onto Pacific Fleet ships bound for the war, and servicing the anti-submarine nets used to protect fleet bases and anchorages around the world."

The closest Climo came to a war zone was during the Korean War, but the Marine Corps had different plans. He traveled to Camp Pendleton Marine headquarters, instead, to be on the staff as a guard, but he declined the position. He packed his bags again and headed closer toward the Pacific Ocean.

"I was sent to Camp Del Mar in Oceanside, Calif., to become a sergeant in the motor pool with Duck Battalion, Third Marine Division," he said.

In less than two months, though, he left the motor pool to became a drill instructor in San Diego until he left the military. The Marines sought sergeants who could work with the raw recruits.

In civilian life, Climo started his career as a diesel mechanic and eventually became a refrigeration specialist to work on aircraft air conditioning for cooling the planes, not the passengers. In the 1960s, he went into the trade as a journeyman refrigeration repairman. At the time, he was living entirely in California, but since 1976, he has lived in the both Truckee and Sparks.

Climo said a recent trip to Oahu as part of an Honor Flight Nevada had more meaning considering 2020 is the 75th anniversary of World War II's end.

"Every time I go on the USS Arizona, it's heartbreaking," he said, pausing to reflect on the number of men who perished during the Japanese attack on Dec. 7, 1941.

He also visited the USS Missouri, the battleship where the Instrument of Surrender was signed on Sept. 2, 1945. He said the ship is marvelous because of its military hardware and engineering. Climo said the trip to Pearl Harbor is also meaningful in developing camaraderie among fellow veterans.

"I wouldn't trade this for anything," he said.

Climo also flew on an Honor Flight to Washington, D.C. in 2015, leaving on the anniversary of the D-Day invasion, another meaningful day that marked an important milestone in Europe.

The late Robert Kent of Fallon, Nev., served as a gunner on the USS Monterey, an Independence-light aircraft carrier that had been retrofitted from a cruiser and recommissioned in June 1943.

The USS Monterey sailed in the western Pacific Theater, and its crew reached the Gilbert Islands, combat operations with Task Force 58 including campaigns in the Carolines, Marianas and New Guinea as well as the decisive Battle of the Philippine Sea, which was the virtual end of the Japanese Navy.

The USS Monterey was one of the first ships to participate in the occupation of Japan after August 1945. Cindy Dillon-Kent said her father rarely talked about his war service.

"His ship experienced a typhoon and then a fire. I know he had to wrap some of the bodies," Kent-Dillon said. "He was a gunner, which was difficult for him."

Typhoon Cobra struck the Pacific fleet in December 1944, and at the height of the storm, several planes on the deck of the USS Monterey tore loose from their cables. That led to fires on the hangar deck.

Coincidently, Gerald Ford, who later became a member of the House of Representatives and then president from 1974-76, had served as General Quarters Officer of the Deck during the storm and subsequent fire. In January 1945, the aircraft carrier returned to Bremerton, Wash., for a major overall before returning to the Western Pacific to support Okinawa operations.

City Councilman Bob Erickson, who formerly owned Fallon Theatres and served as Fallon mayor, said his association with Kent went back to the mid-1970s when the Ericksons moved to Fallon. Erickson remembers Kent as a hard worker who spent six to seven days a week, 12-14 hours a day working in the store. He said Kent was part of "The Greatest Generation," a term coined by newscaster Tom Brokaw.

"It was a tough period of time for about 15-20 years," Erickson said of the Great Depression and war. "Bob's philosophy was shaped by that."

After graduating in 1943 from Battle Mountain High School, Ed "Señor" Arciniega enlisted in the U.S. Marines during World War II. He spent most of his tour aboard the aircraft carrier USS Essex, which was commissioned in December 1942.

The Essex, which stretched the length of a football field, served in several campaigns in the Pacific Theater of Operations, earning the Presidential Unit Citation and 13 battle stars. When fighter planes returned to the Essex, an elevator lowered the aircraft to another deck where mechanics such as Señor would work on the planes and then return the planes to combat. Sometimes, the crew wouldn't see land for months.

Once World War II ended, Señor returned to Los Angeles and planned to become an apprentice painter. It didn't take long for Señor to decide that he wanted to do something else with his life.

Señor decided to use the GI Bill and traveled 440 miles north to Reno where he enrolled at the University of Nevada, a campus of about 1,000 students but beginning to grow with the additional number of servicemen enrolling at the state's only four-year campus.

Señor received his bachelor's degree in history and Spanish in 1951, and his first teaching job took him to Fallon, a small agricultural community of 2,734 residents that is still considered the Oasis of Nevada for its warm weather and thousands of acres of land used for growing crops and raising livestock. The school district hired Señor to teach for Jack Davis, who had been called up to serve during the Korean War.

Steven R. Ranson

WELCOME HOME, DAD

Passengers on a late July afternoon Southwest Airlines Flight from Las Vegas watched intently as a casket smartly draped with the Stars & Stripes slowly rolled down a conveyor belt to a waiting honor guard.

As a courtesy to a deceased war hero returning home, passengers remained on the plane, some with their faces pressed against the starboard windows, others using their hands to wipe away a tear. The plane's captain left the cockpit to join the family and military personnel on the ramp at the Reno-Tahoe International Airport before an honor guard from the Nevada Army National Guard carried the casket with snap precision from flight 1782 to a waiting hearse.

A private service was conducted later in the week at Reno's Mountain View Cemetery for the family followed by a full military service the following day at the Northern Nevada Veterans Memorial Cemetery in Fernley.

William Twedt said having his father return home has a special meaning for the Twedt family and others whose relatives fought in World War II. The young lieutenant's arrival and military service come weeks before the nation remembers the 75th anniversary of the end of World War II on Aug. 14, 1945. The emperor surrendered after U.S. B-29 Superfortress bombers dropped atomic bombs on two Japanese cities, and the formal Instrument of Surrender occurred on Sept. 2 aboard the USS Missouri.

Second Lt. Lowell S. Twedt, who was shot down over northern Italy on Oct. 20 1944, arrived in Reno shortly before 7 p.m. on a flight that originated earlier in the day from Omaha, Neb. An Army lieutenant accompanied his casket to Reno.

William Lowell Twedt was only 5 years old when enemy anti-aircraft fire near Lozano, Italy, shot down his father's P-38J Lightning and two others. They were providing an escort for B-17 bombers on a mission to bomb oil storage tanks in the Bavarian city of Regensberg, northeast of Munich on the banks of the Danube River. Twedt said the three pilots, members of the 71st Fighter Squadron, 1st Fighter Group, crashed in the snowy, rugged Italian Alps north of Lozano, and an eyewitness failed to see any ejections. He expressed mixed thoughts about waiting for his father after so many years of him missing in action.

"I knew that he couldn't possibly be alive after so many years," Twedt said, who was accompanied at the airport by his wife and his younger son's family. "I'm not despondent over that. I'm just glad he's here and that we can give him a resting place. It's really neat that I can have him here somewhere near."

Twedt said he also has a daughter and son-in-law who live in Iowa and two other sons who reside in the Reno area.

After decades of the unknown, a break occurred more than two years ago. A retired Austrian physics instructor, who found the wreckage of a P-38 on the north face of Kirchnock near the Italian resort town of Aberstuckl, had a gut feeling it was Twedt's plane. The Austrian professor contacted the Defense POW/MIA Accounting Agency (DPAA) at Offutt Air Force Base south of Omaha to alert the DPAA of his discovery. The agency sent a team to the Alps to excavate the site, and in September 2019, they recovered the aviators.

"They also found the other pilots' buried remains," Twedt said. "They went into the village and received some information. It's quite something—you don't leave anyone behind."

In addition to finding the remains, the DPAA researchers also discovered some material evidence such as pieces from the uniform, survival gear, boots and laces, watch component and band, buttons and fragments of a holster and pistol belt. Twedt said it appears his father crashed in about 10 feet of snow at a higher elevation, and the DPAA research crew found a full skeleton. Twedt thinks the locals found the body and buried it before the Germans discovered the bodies.

"Seventy-five years .. it's amazing they found him," Twedt remarked.

DPAA requested DNA samples from Twedt, and the agency used dental records in its quest to identify the pilot. On Dec. 11, 2019, the DPAA identified the remains as those of Lt. Twedt's. Contrary to government records, Twedt said his father was born in 1917 and was only 27 years old when he was shot down

Since he finished flight school for the Army Air Force in the early 1940s, Lowell Twedt gained a reputation for being a skilled pilot. Army brass wanted to keep him as an instructor, but the lieutenant had other plans—he wanted to join the war effort and fly overseas. Born in Le Grand, Iowa, he enlisted in the military in 1942 in San Diego, Calif. According to Twedt, his father attended training in Alabama, Washington State, Texas and San Diego.

Although many years have passed since Twedt was only a toddler, he distinctly remembers his dad always wearing brown shoes. He also has memories of their home in Alabama, where his father completed his Army officer training. When his father left for Europe, Twedt said the family remained in San Diego, where his grandfather had a big orange orchard. The family relocated to Reno in 1945.

The Twedt family moved from their Iowa farm to Southern California in the 1920s. It was in high school where Lowell met his future wife, and they only had one child.

Bill Twedt attended schools in Reno and the University of Washington. He joined the Marine Corps in 1957 for almost seven months but afterward enlisted in the Oregon Army National Guard. When he returned to Reno, he transferred to the Nevada Army National Guard, serving a total of seven-and-a-half years in the military. Over the years, Twedt worked in the gaming industry in Reno and Las Vegas before retiring.

Brig. Gen. Zachary Doser, the Nevada Guard's Land Component commander, said by recognizing this aviator, he said it's a fitting way to remember the country's Greatest Generation as coined by author and newscaster Tom Brokaw.

`"We are celebrating the return of Lowell Twedt's remains from a distant battlefield," Doser said. "It's just a remarkable story of how they recovered his body and ultimately returned it home."

William Twedt said many people had high regards for his father.

"They found a good pilot, but they wanted to make him an instructor for a while, but he finally got to go overseas," Twedt said, thanking those who arranged the welcome home despite the coronavirus pandemic.

When asked what it meant to have his father in Reno, Twedt thought for a minute, trying to come up with the right words.

"Welcome home," he said glancing upward. "Now he's in the wild, blue yonder."

Steven R. Ranson

NOTES

USS Arizona's fateful morning

Fallon Eagle, Fallon Standard, Reno Gazette, 1940 Naval Academy yearbook.

Sailing Past Battleship Row

History.navy.mil

Delivering cargo in perilous seas

http://www.usmm.org/ww2.html

Nevada's only Medal of Honor Recipient

Churchill County Museum, Naval Air Station Fallon, Fallon Standard,

Fallon Eagle, U.S. Naval Academy, Nevada Aerospace Hall of Fame

'Doo' a lot with little

https://www.history.navy.mil

Launching of USS Carson City

https://www.history.navy.mil/danfs/c4/carson_city.htm

Underneath the Seven Seas

http://www.oneternalpatrol.com/uss-corvina-226.htm

A teen tracking enemy aircraft

"The London Blitz, 1940," EyeWitness to History,

www.eyewitnesstohistory.com (2001)

Honored Navajo 'code talker'

Navajotimes.com

Training wins wars

http://www.wendoverairbase.com

Ridin' the radio waves

navalhistory.org

Army ship 'Nevada' sinks

U.S. Coast Guard action report

Repaying the debt

https://www.history.com/topics/world-war-ii/battle-of-anzio

Feeling of fear

www.history.navy.mil/research/histories/ship-histories/danfs/a/admiralty-islands.html

Under fire on D-Day and Turning point

Multiple references for Normandy Landings

Narrative provided by Jeffrey Bradt

Sailor's harrowing incidents

https://www.history.navy.mil

Numbing cold and Germans

Narrative written by Jaymi Bryant

Navy's 'ghost' fleet

Michael M. Novak, director of Congressional and Public Affairs at the

U.S. Maritime Administration (MARAD)

Bloodiest 82 days

Narrative written by Argus "Gus" Harold Forbus and Jim Forbus

USS Ormsby named for Nevada pioneer

https://www.navsource.org/archives/10/03/03049.htm

Bombing runs over Germany

Truckee Meadows Community College, American Air Museum,

Reno Veterans Affairs Living History, Mighty Eight Air Force Museum,

Commemorative Air Force Museum in Mesa, Arizona

Visions of Nuremberg

https://www.history.com/topics/world-war-ii/nuremberg-trials

France's Legion of Honor

This article is published with the following permission. © 2016 Sierra Sun

newspaper, April 4, 2016. All rights reserved.

Down with the Ship

armyhistory.org

Marines in love

Mineral County Independent News, Truckee Meadows

Community College

Aboard the USS Nevada

www.history.navy.mil, Battleship Nevada: The epic story of the ship that

wouldn't sink

Welcome home, dad

Defense POW/MIA Accounting Agency (DPAA)

AUTHORS

STEVEN R. RANSON

Steven R. Ranson, the coordinator of this project, is past president of both the International Society of Weekly Newspaper Editors and Nevada Press Association's board of directors. He retired as editor/general manager of the Lahontan Valley News in Fallon, Nev., on Aug. 1, 2017, but he still writes articles as military editor for the Nevada News Group and a consortium of Nevada newspapers on military events and veteran affairs.

The NPA named Steve co-Journalist of the Year in 2012 and for having the state's Editorial of the Year for all newspaper circulation divisions in 2014. As a civilian journalist, Steve also traveled to the Arabian Sea in November 2011 to document the training done at Naval Air Station Fallon and how it relates to the operations with a carrier air wing aboard an aircraft carrier. He covers both Naval Air Station Fallon and the National Guard.

Steve embedded with Nevada Army National Guard units in Afghanistan twice—in November 2011 and November 2012. In 2011, he embedded with Nevada National Guard soldiers at Kandahar and then used Bagram Air Field as a central location. The following year, he travelled to Forward Operating Base Shank and then to Camp Phoenix near Kabul. He received two Military Reporters and Editors awards in 2011 and 2012 for his reporting from Afghanistan in addition to numerous awards from the National News Association and Nevada Press Association.

Steve spent the majority of his 28 years in the Nevada Army National Guard and U.S. Army Reserve-Panama in public affairs, command information, visual information, commander of state headquarters and battalion adjutant.

He earned a Bachelor of Journalism and Masters of Education degrees from the University of Nevada, Reno, in 1974 and 1980, respectively.

KENNETH BEATON

K enneth Beaton was eight months old when the United States declared war against Japan on Dec. 8, 1941. During World War II, his dad was ordered to U.S. Coast Guard ships on both coasts. For his first 15 years, Ken was a Coast Guard brat.

After graduating from Lynn English High School in 1958, the Massachusetts native earned an AA degree from Boston University, married, became a parent, graduated from Salem State University with a Bachelor of Science in Business Education, moved to Logan, Utah, in 1971 and graduated from Utah State University with a Masters of Education in Business Education in 1978.

After teaching from 1972-1994 in Nevada, Ken retired. He sold advertising, wrote 30-second radio spots, served as an attaché for three Nevada Legislative sessions and studied Conversational Italian for six semesters and four semesters of Creative Memoir Writing.

Ken's mom took a picture of him in December 1942 and sent it to her brother, Richard, a member of the First Special Service Force, "The Devil's Brigade." Pvt. Daigle placed Ken's picture in his helmet. On Dec. 3, 1943 Richard was killed in action on Monte la Difensa, Italy. After Ken's parents passed away, he discovered the picture from Richard's helmet with his mom's writing on the back. After 16 years of research and two trips to climb Monte la Difensa, Ken published "A TODDLER'S PICTURE: In His Uncle's Helmet" a month before the 75th anniversary, Dec. 3, 2018.

As a resident of Carson City, Nevada for over 45 years, Ken wrote an article for Nevada Magazine and seven articles for Nevada in the West magazine. He's a frequent contributor to the Nevada Appeal newspaper, and for many years he has been a voice for veterans by telling their stories during wartime, especially during World War II.

DAVID C. HENLEY

David C. Henley has been a distinguished journalist since the 1960s. He is a foreign correspondent, the former owner of the Lahontan Valley News in Fallon, Nev., a retired Brigadier General in the Army National Guard, a former university administrator and journalism professor, and Honorary Consul of Uruguay since 1999.

David is also a past president of the Nevada Press Association and has been state chairman of the National Newspaper Association. He has been involved with the General George Patton Memorial Association, the Council on America's Military Past and the National Trust for Historic Preservation. He was city editor of the Daily Trojan student newspaper at USC, from which he earned a B.A. in journalism and an M.A. in political science. He also has a PhD in communications and journalism and was awarded a postdoctoral fellowship at UCLA.

The author of "From Moscow to Beirut, The Adventures of a Foreign Correspondent" published in 2013 by the Chapman University Press, Henley has reported from overseas for the Los Angeles Examiner, the Hearst, Ridder, Swift and News Group newspaper chains, and served as Washington, D.C. correspondent for the Los Angeles Examiner and the Hearst newspapers.

He was the journalism department chairman at the University of Wyoming and taught five years at the USC School of Journalism, where he headed the school's news-editorial department. At Chapman University, David is a member of several committees and councils..

David is the recipient of many state, national and international writing awards. His column, My Turn, has been published in the Lahontan Valley News and other newspapers for more than 40 years.

Additionally, David has specialized in western military and naval historical subjects, and his book "Battleship Nevada, The Epic Story of the Shop that Wouldn't Sink" gives a comprehensive look of the battleship's history, especially during World War II.

Wendover Air Field

Steven R. Ranson